sonic experience

sonic experience

A GUIDE TO EVERYDAY SOUNDS

Edited by Jean-François Augoyard and Henry Torgue
Translated by Andra McCartney and David Paquette

McGill-Queen's University Press | Montreal & Kingston | London | Ithaca

ISBN 13: 978-0-7735-2548-1
ISBN 10: 0-7735-2548-3 (cloth)
ISBN-13: 978-0-7735-2942-7
ISBN-10: 0-7735-2942-x (paper)

Legal deposit first quarter 2006
Bibliothèque nationale du Québec

This book was originally published in
French in 1995 under the title *À l'écoute
de l'environnement. Répertoire des effets
sonores* by Editions Parenthèses

Printed in Canada on acid free paper
that is 100% ancient forest free (100%
post-consumer recycled), processed
chlorine free

This book has been published with
the help of a grant from the Centre
de recherche sur l'espace sonore et
l'environnement urbain (CRESSON)
and le Service de la recherche architecturale du Ministère de la Culture.

This book has been made possible
by a grant in aid of publication from
the Direction de l'Architecture et du
Patrimoine and by a promotional grant
from CNRS (Centre National de la
Recherche Scientifique)

CRESSON is part of the interdisciplinary research group on Architectural
and Urban Atmosphere (CNRS-
Ministère de la Culture) UMR 1563

McGill-Queen's University Press
acknowledges the support of the
Canada Council for the Arts for
our publishing program. We also
acknowledge the financial support of the Government of Canada
through the Book Publishing Industry
Development Program (BPIDP) for our
publishing activities.

Figures designed by Bruno de Lescure

Thanks to Claire Bécaud and Jean-
Claude Foulon of the Conservatoire
National de Région de Grenoble

LIBRARY AND ARCHIVES CANADA
CATALOGUING IN PUBLICATION

Sonic experience : a guide to everyday
sounds / edited by Jean-François Augoyard and Henry Torgue ; translated
by Andrea McCartney and David
Paquette.

Translation of: A l'écoute de
l'environnement.
Includes bibliographical references and
index.
ISBN-13: 978-0-7735-2548-1   ISBN-10:
0-7735-2548-3 (bnd)
ISBN-13: 978-0-7735-2942-7   ISBN-10:
0-7735-2942-X (pbk)

1. Sound – Psychological
aspects. 2. Sound.   I. Augoyard,
Jean François, 1941–   II. Torgue,
Henry   III. McCartney, Andra,
1955–   IV. Paquette, David

BF353.5.N65S6513
2006   155.9'115   C2005-907487-6

Set in 10.6/12.8 Minion Pro with Meta+
Book design & typesetting by
zijn digital

CONTENTS

Sonic Effects

SONIC EFFECTS: THEMATIC LIST

Major effects appear in bold type

ELEMENTARY EFFECTS

Colouring
Delay
Distortion
Dullness
Echo
Filtration
Flutter Echo
Haas
Resonance
Reverberation

COMPOSITIONAL EFFECTS

Accelerando
Blurring
Coupling
Crescendo
Crossfade
Cut Out
Decrescendo
Doppler
Drone
Emergence
Mask
Mixing
Rallentendo
Release
Reprise
Tartini
Telephone
Wave

MNEMO-PERCEPTIVE EFFECTS

Anamnesis
Anticipation
Asyndeton
Cocktail
Delocalization
Erasure
Hyperlocalization
Immersion
Metamorphosis
Phonomnesis
Remanence
Synecdoche
Ubiquity
Wall

PSYCHOMOTOR EFFECTS

Attraction
Deburau
Desynchronization
Chain
Intrusion
Incursion
Lombard
Niche
Phonotonie
Repulsion
Synchronization

SEMANTIC EFFECTS

Delocalization
Dilation
Envelopment
Imitation
Narrowing
Perdition
Quotation
Repetition
Sharawadji
Suspension

ELECTROACOUSTIC EFFECTS

Chorus
Compression
Print-through
Expansion
Fade
Feedback
Flange
Fuzz
Harmonization
Larsen
Limitation
Noise-Gate
Phase
Rumble
Tremolo
Vibrato
Wha-Wha
Wobble
Wow

SONIC EFFECTS: ALPHABETICAL LIST

Major effects appear in bold type

Accelerando
Anamnesis
Anticipation
Asyndeton
Attraction
Blurring
Chain
Chorus
Cocktail
Colouring
Compression
Coupling
Crescendo
Crossfade
Cut Out
Deburau
Decontextualization
Decrescendo
Delay

Delocalization
Desynchronization
Dilation
Distortion
Doppler
Drone
Dullness
Echo
Emergence
Envelopment
Erasure
Expansion
Fade
Feedback
Filtration
Flange
Flutter Echo
Fuzz
Haas

Harmonization
Hyperlocalization
Imitation
Immersion
Incursion
Intrusion
Larsen
Limitation
Lombard
Mask
Metamorphosis
Mixing
Narrowing
Niche
Noise-Gate
Perdition
Phase
Phonomnesis
Phonotonie
Print-Through
Quotation
Rallentendo

Release
Remanence
Repetition
Reprise
Repulsion
Resonance
Reverberation
Rumble
Sharawadji
Suspension
Synchronization
Synecdoche
Tartini
Telephone
Tremolo
Ubiquity
Vibrato
Wave
Wall
Wha-Wha
Wobble
Wow

FOREWORD

Sonic Experience is a stimulating and wide-ranging work by one of the most significant teams of soundscape researchers in the world today – one that has gathered around French social philosopher and phenomenologist Jean-François Augoyard at the Centre de recherche sur l'espace sonore et l'environment urbain (CRESSON) at the National School of Architecture of Grenoble. Published in French in 1995, with an Italian edition appearing in 2004, this first English edition will fortunately make CRESSON's innovative approach available to a larger readership.

"Man lives in an uneasy ocean of air continually agitated by the disturbances called sound waves." That statement, written by the acoustician Frederick Vinton Hunt around 1959, could be the epigraph for the explosion of sonic research that was then beginning. During the 1960s Marshall McLuhan began to argue that the aural had displaced the visual as a result of new communication technologies and media shifts. In 1963 American psychiatrist Peter Ostwald published *Sound-making*, the first real study of the importance of sound in psychiatric analysis – an area ignored by Freud and Jung. In 1966 Pierre Schaeffer's massive study, *Traité des objets musicaux*, appeared, introducing a new vocabulary for the discussion of sound. And in 1968 I published a little book called *The New Soundscape*, drawing attention to the importance of the acoustic environment in everyday life.

Two postwar developments, both related to technology, propelled this seemingly sudden obsession for sound research. One the one hand, the world was becoming more urban and more noisy – European cities were being reconstructed and North American cities were rapidly expanding; traffic was multiplying exponentially, forcing the construction of ever-wider roads; jet aircraft had been introduced into commercial aviation, resulting in an enormous expansion of the noise profile around airports. One the other hand, during the same period new and more accessible technologies of recording and sound analysis made it easier to "freeze" sound, to listen to it repeatedly and analyze its components the way photography and the microscope had sharpened the observation of visual phenomena.

In the 1960s many of us felt that the whole sensorium of the Western world was in upheaval. By 1970, having joined the communication department at Simon Fraser University, I had announced the World Soundscape Project – an eloquent title for a research topic that didn't yet exist and one that even my colleagues had difficulty in understanding. Our purpose was to study the effects of the changing soundscape on human behaviour and with this information begin to develop the new discipline of soundscape design. The World Soundscape Project really lasted only five or six years, but through the recordings, articles, and books that resulted, including my 1977 book *The Tuning of the World*, the word "soundscape" achieved currency in the English language.

Research was also going on in other countries and other languages. Despite the grandiloquent name we had given our project, we were conscious of how important it was that the soundscape be studied from different cultural perspectives. We all have ears, but we listen differently as a result of our culture, professions, education – and our language, since not all words dealing with sound are even translatable. We looked forward to the input from research teams in different countries studying the evolution of their own environments and how they might be enhanced through soundscape design. Then we could exchange ideas, research techniques, and creative solutions to environmental problems.

In 1979, Jean-François Augoyard published his book *Pas à pas. Essai sur le cheminement quotidien en milieu urbain** and founded CRESSON at the National School of Architecture of Grenoble. The latter development was particularly fortunate as affiliation with a school of architecture guarantees that acoustical engineers will be available to contribute their expertise. When the architect Walter Gropius was appointed director of the Bauhaus in Germany, he brought together artists from a variety of disciplines beyond architecture and out of this nexus new concepts of industrial design emerged that influenced the whole Western world. Since its inception, CRESSON has also attracted an interdisciplinary team of researchers and its publications have benefited from their interaction. It is characteristic of CRESSON's approach, for instance, to compare the physical characteristics of urban settings with the perceptual awareness of its inhabitants and users. This attention to earwitness accounts in concrete contexts has given their work a phenomenological cast and led to an emphasis on exploring the dynamic interaction between the physical environment, the socio-cultural milieu, and the individual listener.

Sonic Experience provides an accessible and usefully organized introduction to and synthesis of this innovative approach. Drawing on the resources of the entire CRESSON team, it makes a significant contribution to our understanding of the soundscape, comparable to but distinct from that of the *Handbook of Acoustic Ecology* prepared by Barry Truax for the World Soundscape Project in 1978. Whereas Truax aimed to provide definitions of acoustical terms that could describe all aspects of sound, including several new terms we invented for soundscape description, the intention of Augoyard, Henry Torgue, and their CRESSON associates is different. Although the work includes numerous descriptive terms, those of music for instance, and discusses the physical properties of acoustic phenomena, it focuses on the *effects* of sound on listeners. Over the past twenty years, the CRESSON researchers have developed the useful concept of the "sonic effect," designed to analyze the experience of everyday sounds in the contexts of architectural and urban spaces. This guide defines and analyses sixty-six of these effects. Sixteen major effects are accompanied by extended and often brilliant essays elucidating their relationship to disciplines such as psychology, physiology, sociology, architecture, urban studies, com-

---

* An English translation of this work, under the title *Step by Step: An Essay on Everyday Walks in an Urban Setting*, is forthcoming from University of Minnesota Press.

munication, cultural studies, music, and aesthetics. These essays, by no less than eleven contributors, indicate the variety of talents engaged in soundscape research at CRESSON. Many of the approaches differ strikingly from what we are used to in the Anglo-Saxon world and confirm the expectations voiced earlier – that the perspectives and results of soundscape researchers from other cultures would be richly stimulating.

For instance, *Sonic Experience* draws on terms from classical rhetoric and exploits the relationships of complementarity, synonymy, and opposition between these. Asyndeton, which means a phrase that omits a conjunction, is used to refer to the common habit of ignoring sounds in order to preserve our equilibrium. In everyday speech we might call it "screening out." Synecdoche, a figure of speech in which a part stands for the whole, is presented as the complementary faculty of distinguishing what one wishes to hear out of the general flux of acoustic events – "selective listening." The substantial discussions that explain terms such as these contain valuable information and sometimes provocative opinions.

The extended essay on synecdoche/asyndeton shows how this pair of effects forms the basis of the notion of sonic effect itself: hearing implies a state of preparedness to both ignore and listen to sounds. Synecdoche forms part of what relates the individual to his or her environment and the article refers us to Pierre Schaeffer's "*oreille primitive*," the ear of the first humans, constantly on the alert in a potentially dangerous natural environment of storms and wild animals. Birds and animals still live in a perpetual state of terror but civilized humans will sense it only in an alien environment, while traveling in a strange land or alone in a country house at night where every squeak is heard. It is in circumstances such as these that the synecdoche effect emerges prominently and one longs for the reassurance of known sounds, acoustic anchors.

The oscillation between apprehensive and relaxed listening is discussed under the entry of another related effect, metamorphosis, where the instability of the soundscape is dramatized by an apt quote from Merleau-Ponty: "The perceptual 'something' is always in the middle of something else." This is a welcome discussion because of the tendency of researchers to think of the soundscape as static data, like a photograph or a diagram; I have attended conferences of acoustical engineers where not a single sound was played, though many slides and diagrams were shown.

The longest entry in *Sonic Experience* is that under ubiquity, attesting to the importance of "presence" in the modern soundscape, which is now exclusively urban for an increasing number of people. In fact, everything in the urban environment is present and seems to be happening everywhere at once. There are fewer distant sounds in the city, just as there is less distant viewing. The loss of distant hearing is one of the most significant changes in aural perception in history. The urban environment has compressed acoustic space and confused directionality, making it often difficult or impossible to locate sources. This applies just as much indoors as outdoors, as when the proprietors of shopping malls, hotels, and department stores play music from 200 or 400 identical speakers, providing a ubiquitous presence whose centre is everywhere and whose circumference is nowhere. That, the article notes, is how the medieval theologians defined God. There you have it: the schizophonic voice, invisible but authoritative and omnipresent. In *The Tuning of the World* I called this "sacred noise" and showed how it could be applied to any loud or oppressive sound that is exempt from social proscription. In medieval society, church bells were never proscribed though they were the loudest and most persistent sounds in the city. Today it is traffic noise and amplified pop music. Although reportedly at the top of the list of noise complaints in every modern city, the power and influence of the industries behind these noises is such that they continually escape repression. *Sonic Experience* provides an insightful and wide-ranging analysis of the ubiquity effect's fundamental relations of sound, space, and power; how these manifest themselves in the built environment, the body, media systems, religion, performance and cinema; and what the effect's implications are for social interaction and control, psychology, and daily life.

One of the most exotic and intriguing terms in the guide is sharawadji. The entry tells us that the expression was brought back to Europe by seventeenth-century travelers to China and that it denoted an unexpected perception of beauty in the absence of any discernable order or arrangement. Here the concept is transferred to the realm of the urban sound environment with its multiple and cacophonous sounds that defy classification – "the din or racket of carnivals, demonstrations, or children's games." The sharawadji effect arises in a situation of rupture, where perceptive confusion gives way to an inexplicable aesthetic pleasure. This element of rupture and the dynamic tension involved in the pleasure makes sharawadji closer to the sublime than the beautiful. But the guide carefully distinguishes sharawadji from Kant's sublime, noting that sounds become sharawadji less by their excessiveness than by their implausibility. Sharawadji is the sublime of the everyday – a subtle sublime, without splendour or theatricality, arising from a brouhaha, sonic muddle, or other strangely discordant sound "that magically and suddenly transports us elsewhere."

This leaves us with the observation that in order to communicate a sensation you must have a word to describe it. *Sonic Experience* provides a rich lexicon of such words and so will do much to relieve the frustration of incommunicable listening experiences.

R. Murray Schafer
Indian River, Ontario
January 2006

TRANSLATORS' NOTE

The original version of *À l'écoute de l'environnement: Repertoire des effets sonores* was developed by researchers at the Centre de recherche sur l'espace sonore et l'environnement urbain (CRESSON), in France, to summarize and thematize practical and theoretical work conducted in the field of sound and other perceptions in the built environment. The *Guide* therefore includes a significant number of concepts originating at CRESSON, for which no direct translation is possible. The final selection of English sonic effect terms was therefore based on available publications and common vocabulary used by sound practitioners and thinkers. Two particular publications are worthy of mention in reference to the translation of headings: Björn Hellström's doctoral dissertation[1] and R. Murray Schafer's review of the French edition of the repertoire.[2] French quotations for which no English translation existed (as is the case for many research reports published by CRESSON) were freely translated with the original reference information retained. In all other cases, English publications were used and the references updated.

This English edition – *Sonic Experience: A Guide to Everyday Sounds* – has also been updated in collaboration with the authors. A minor sonic effect – Tartini – was added by Augoyard and a number of recent publications of interest have also been added to the bibliography. We would like to thank Lisa Gasior for her assistance with the translation, and we commend editor Ruth Pincoe for her excellent work.

Andra McCartney and David Paquette

ABOUT THE AUTHORS

Jean-François Augoyard, a philosopher, urban planner, and musicologist, is a research director of the Centre Nationale de la Recherche Scientific (CNRS) and the founder of the Centre de recherche sur l'espace sonore et l'environnement urbain (CRESSON Ambiances architecturales et urbaines) at the National Scientific Research Centre and École Nationale Supérieure d'Architecture de Grenoble (ENSAG). He is primary instigator of research on sonic effects and supervised the original edition of this repertoire, for which he wrote the introduction. Augoyard collaborated with Henri Torgue, Collette Augoyard, and Jean-Jacques Delétré on this updated translation.

Henri Torgue, a sociologist, urban planner and composer, was responsible for the revision of the original work, and is also the author of the entries on anamnesis, repetition, and wave. Pascal Amphoux, a geographer, architect, and professor of architecture, wrote the entry on ubiquity. Olivier Balaÿ, an architect, urban planner, and professor at ENSAG, wrote the entry on filtering. Grégoire Chelkoff, an architect, urban planner, and professor at ENSAG, wrote the entries on cut out and metamorphosis. Jean-Jacques Delétré, an engineer and professor of acoustics and lighting at ENSAG, was responsible for the entries on niche and masking. Jean Dalmais, architect, wrote the entry on resonance. Martine Leroux, a philosopher and sociologist, wrote the entries on remanence and sharawadji. Jean-Pierre Odion, an acoustician, wrote the entries on drone and reverberation. Jean-Paul Thibaud (CNRS), a sociologist, urban planner, and research director at CNRS, wrote the entries on imitation and synecdoche.

sonic experience

An Instrumentation of the Sound Environment

THE BROKEN SOUND

Over the centuries, Western culture has relentlessly attempted to classify noise, music, and everyday sounds. Philosophers, authors, scholars, and musicians have worked to abstract and assess sounds on a scale of purity, musicality, and intelligibility. In contemporary opinion, cacophonous, thundering noise is taken to signify the malaise of an anti-human reliance on technology. Ordinary noises and mundane sounds that are not perceived as either annoying or musical are of no interest. Listening to other cultures will, however, reveal that the term "noise" does not automatically involve disturbance, and also that the term "music" does not possess a single universal meaning, nor does it necessarily refer to a common perception of the way sounds are composed.[1] Within hunter-gatherer societies, the primary attention given to ordinary sounds, and their functional as well as symbolic value, is both shared and shaped by the whole community.

So let us not be limited by cultural or stereotyped assumptions. We may discover that sonic marks unconsciously guide our behaviour. Even though they are not included in the linguistic abstraction of scholarly discourse about music, phonology, or acoustic engineering, ordinary sounds nevertheless operate through everyday actions and dialogue, shaping our professional practices as well as our everyday life. As often happens, art already grasps what knowledge does not yet perceive. Contemporary musical practices cheerfully mix all sounds. Inspired by the Futurist movement, *bruitism* has influenced composers since the beginning of the twentieth century.[2] Today, the production of non-heard unclassifiable synthesized sound signals disturbs traditional academic distinctions. What else can we say about media soundtracks in which music, dialogue, and noises merge in the temporal flow of narrativity, if not that they mimic this "never really silent" stream of sonic experience that we might call the "everyday soundtrack"?[3]

Let us listen to our cities. Is it not the very nature of the urban environment to make us hear, whether we like it or not, this mixing of sounds? Dull murmurs, machine noise, the shifting and familiar acoustic racket created by people – every urban moment has a sound signature, usually composed of many sounds together. Beyond classification, "the city rings" (or as Schopenhauer said, "Die Welt klingt").

This instrumental dimension of urban space requires examination and reflection. Firstly, no sound event, musical or otherwise, can be isolated from the spatial and temporal conditions of its physical signal propagation. Secondly, sound is also shaped subjectively, depending on the auditory capacity, the attitude, and the psychology and culture of the listener. There is no universal approach to listening: every individual, every group, every culture listens in its own way.

The city has sometimes been described as a real musical instrument; the material and spatial characteristics of urban morphology can in fact be compared with similar aspects of acoustic instrumentation.[4] The analogy, which calls for measurement and examination,[5] only considers passive acoustic properties, and therefore does not deserve deeper interest. The metaphor really inspires analysis in relation to performance, the ways to play and conduct sounds, the design and use of effects. What instruments are available to technicians and researchers, administrators and users, designers and inhabitants? What is the sonic *instrumentarium* of urban environments?

ORIGINS OF THE CONCEPT OF THE SONIC EFFECT

An Unobtainable Tool

Like any other environment, the urban sound environment can be subjected to two types of operations: it can be considered as an object of description, or as an object of transformation. The quantitative tools required for this work are numerous and the possibilities of acoustic measurement, including recording techniques and information analysis, are constantly progressing. Different types of built spaces nevertheless do not benefit equally from research and technology. While some listening spaces (such as auditoriums and halls) seem to receive extensive modelization and simulation, other sites do not. In fact, neither open spaces nor small enclosed ones can yet be measured with sufficient precision. For this practical reason, and also because in inhabited space quantitative valuation cannot take into account the whole human dimension of acoustic phenomena, the use of qualitative tools is necessary.

Two questions must be raised. Are there qualitative tools specifically adapted to the analysis of a sonic environment, and what is their operational value? Can we define qualitative tools that could be used in conjunction with quantitative ones?

At the beginning of the 1980s, a number of different approaches to the description of sonic space were developed in France, inspired by the morpho-typological method of classification frequently used in architecture. But can the visual bias of architectural typo-morphology be adapted to the sound domain? Except for basic measurements – for example, the transmission loss coefficient between outside and inside – measurements and scales dictated by visual architectural typology cannot coincide with sonic space properties.

Another difficulty is the particular physical and perceptive structure of sound phenomena including space, time, and ecological relationships that are specific to each context. Thorough and lasting observations can be undertaken in a single public space.[6] Such attention to time may uncover subtle and interesting information about architecture and people. This work is nevertheless so complex that its overall typology remains cursory. The researcher can only describe, for instance, the seasonal rotation of a place based on four general types of sounds: natural, animal, technical, and human.

A third approach involves the sound phenomena *in situ* analysis, which involves an attempt to harmonize the use of quantitative and qualitative tools. Many models of integration have been proposed or are under development. Many interdisciplinary methods of observation using acoustical measurement, spatial descriptions, and psychological surveys have been designed.[7] However, the descriptive concepts involved generally cannot be used easily and equally by all of the concerned disciplines.

The Sound Object and the Soundscape: Two Enticing Tools

During the 1960s and 1970s, two fundamental interdisciplinary tools for sound analysis were invented: the "sound object" (*l'objet sonore*) and the "soundscape." Both have three functions: description, explanation, and interdisciplinarity. But are they really fulfilling our expectations?

In his famous *Traité des objets musicaux* (1966), Pierre Schaeffer disrupted academic classifications of noise, sound, and music, and created a new musicology. This work presents a general phenomenology of the audible. The key concept is defined not as a musical object but more precisely as a *sound* object that can represent any sound of the environment. The notion is quite complex and its richness cannot easily be demonstrated in a few words.[8] The concept of the sound object can be used in three different ways. From a practical and empirical point of view, it describes the interaction of the physical signal and the perceptive intentionality, without which there would be no perception. From the theoretical point of view, it is a phenomenological quest for the essence of sound. Finally, from the point of view of instrumentation, the sound object is intended to be the elementary unit of a general and multidisciplinary solfège of sounds.

While the precise and complex method proposed by Pierre Schaeffer can sometimes be criticized, the outstanding concept of the sound object has become the basic material manipulated by an increasing number of sound designers. The concept of the sound object can be fruitfully used not only for sound by sound composition but also for every sound analysis.[9] However, even with the ever-increasing possibilities offered by real-time analysis, if the sound sequence is slightly complex or is spread over time, or if conditions of production are taken into consideration *in situ* and not simply simulated, then sound by sound analysis becomes extremely ponderous. In consequence, although the sound object is an essential tool in education or sound design, it can hardly be used as a fundamental concept for the description and analysis of urban sounds.

Another attempt to understand the sound environment in a qualitative way emerged in the 1970s. Its main field of application is the sonic dimension of different ecosystems (rural and urban) that surround humans in their everyday existence. In 1980 in France, the story of the invention of "soundscape" was related and analyzed by architect and sound designer Bernard Delage. Poetic, naïve, and holistic in intention, many urban environmentalists claimed that the sound environment could not be limited to acoustical evaluation (in its strict sense) or to the battle against noise. There was one key concept missing.

At the end of the 1960s R. Murray Schafer introduced the term "soundscape."[10] Through his books and some of his compositions, Schafer constructs a sound environment as one would a musical composition – a masterpiece of nature. In this sense, the term soundscape does not simply refer to a "sound environment"; more specifically, it refers to what is perceptible as an aesthetic unit in a sound milieu. Shapes that are thus perceived can be analyzed because they seem to be integrated into a composition with very selective criteria. One of these criteria – the selection of *hi-fi* soundscapes – is justified from both an aesthetic and an educational perspective. "We need to clear our ears" wrote Schafer. This didactic approach concerned with quality of listening across civilizations was largely restated under the theme of acoustic communication by Barry Truax in 1984. However, the application of the criteria of clarity and precision discredits a number of everyday urban situations impregnated with blurred and hazy (not to say uproarious) sound environments, which would then belong to the "lo-fi" category. We must therefore question whether, other than for the fields of aesthetic analysis, creation, and conservation, the use of the term soundscape remains useful and pertinent.

We lack the generic concepts to describe and design all perceptible sound forms of the environment, be they noisy *stimuli*, musical sounds, or any other sounds. The concept of the soundscape seems too broad and blurred, while the sound object seems too elementary (in terms of levels of organization), to allow us to work comfortably both at the scale of everyday behaviour and at the scale of architectural and urban spaces. To use a linguistic analogy, the soundscape corresponds to the whole structure of a text, while the sound object corresponds to the first level of composition: words and syntagmas. We are short of descriptive tools to work at an intermediary level, that of sentence grammar or – to leave the linguistic comparison – the level of a code defining possible configurations between the three terms to consider in our observation: acoustical sources, inhabited space, and the linked pair of sound perception and sound action.

Three Fields for a New Notion
Since the beginning of the 1980s, researchers at the Centre de recherche sur l'espace sonore et l'environnement urbain (CRESSON)[11] have wondered about this deficiency in tools to fulfill three criteria: interdisciplinarity; suitability to the scale of the urban situations to be observed; and capacity to integrate dimensions beyond aesthetic design. The notion that has finally been adopted and placed at the heart of our process is that of the "sonic effect," which is becoming more and more necessary in the three fields in which it is particularly effective: social sciences, urban studies, and applied acoustics.

The sonic effect was first used in the social sciences. Our work on perceptions and everyday sound behaviours[12] indicated four important psycho-sociological processes: sound marking of inhabited or frequented space; sound encoding of interpersonal relations; symbolic meaning and value linked to everyday sound perceptions and actions; and interaction between heard sounds and produced sounds. These four processes are common not only to everyday, non-specialized sound experiences but also to those that take place in a space filled with disturbing noise or music. We were thus dealing with phenomena that could not be described either as basic reactions to a *stimulus* or as simple subjective impressions, but that in fact seemed like aesthetic operations including active shaping with particular local configurations of the physical sound element. The information collected through various surveys was analyzed as *effects* relative to a context and a local organization. Surveyed inhabitants spoke directly of effects such as cut out, niche, masking, and reverberation (often called echo).

From this psycho-sociological point of view, the environment can be considered as a reservoir of sound possibilities, an *instrumentarium* used to give substance and shape to human relations and the everyday management of urban space. There is an effect to any sonic operation. The physical signal is under a perceptive distortion, a selection of information and an attribution of significance that depends on the abilities, psychology, culture, and social background of the listener.

The second field of application of the sonic effect is constituted by urban planning and the forms of this sound *instrumentarium*, the city. Architectural and urban knowledge are considered necessary in our process since constructed space itself shapes many sonic effects. Our psycho-sociological surveys called for direct observations and statements to confirm or contextualize the information given by inhabitants. Could we observe a sonic effect directly? Could we measure it and analyze its spatial context?

Some effects, such as those related to memory (remanence, phonomnesis) and semantic effects (imitation), are totally independent from conditions of production, but most of the major effects depend directly on spatial context. Without a particular organization and morphology of a space, there can be no reverberation, resonance, cut out, ubiquity, or natural filtration. Applied acoustics shows how space, volume, shape, and materials all determine the propagation of sounds. But urban zoning, the layout of road systems, traffic maps, and the distribution of socioeconomic activities can also offer other efficient possibilities for sound information or interpretation to citizens. It is the combination of passive acoustic capacities and particular sound sources or actions that produces some effects – such as resonance, cut out, and ubiquity – as characteristics of urban space.[13]

The third field – applied acoustics – cannot be limited to the description of sound signals, as if the initial physical state of the sound phenomena remained the only reference, outside of which any distortion related to space considered a simple accident. Sound is a propagation and is therefore directly connected to circumstances. It is linked to the characteristics of the constructed environment and the physical conditions of hearing and listening (including filtration, anamorphosis, and listener's location).[14] Also, measurements, projects, and constructions in built space inevitably produce quantifiable characteristics. Inversely, knowledge and experience of architectural and urban configurations allows us to predict certain acoustic behaviours. Space and sound are integrally linked. Moreover, modern physics provides an opening for circumstantial and modal phenomena; some effects, including the Doppler effect, masking, the cocktail effect, and the Lombard effect, have been defined and described in acoustics for a long time.

To sum up, the sonic effect, sometimes measurable and generally linked to the physical characteristics of a specific context, was not reducible either objectively or subjectively. The concept of the sonic effect seemed to describe this interaction between the physical sound environment, the sound milieu of a socio-cultural community, and the "internal soundscape" of every individual.[15] What is the nature of this operative concept?

DEFINITION OF THE SONIC EFFECT

The Sonic Effect: A Paradigm

The sonic effect should not be understood as a full "concept" in its strict sense. The example of the "soundscape," prematurely presented in the 1980s as a miraculous, qualitative, and hedonistic concept by urban planners, architects, and landscape designers, is an important warning. This eagerness to approach sound like any other object and to use a key word, which in fact masks a deficiency in our knowledge about sound, is largely responsible for the loss of focus and unlikely relevance of a term endowed with a particular and precise meaning.

The effect may not be a concept. The survey of objects it refers to remains open. The notion is only partly understood; the sonic effect is paradigmatic. Halfway between the universal and the singular, simultaneously model and guide, it allows a general discourse about sounds, but cannot dispense with examples. Rather than defining things in a closed way, it opens the field to a new class of phenomena by giving some indication of their nature and their status. Finally, it characterizes the modal or instrumental dimensions of sound. Because of these properties, the sonic effect traverses and is enriched by different fields of knowledge and experience.

The Effect: Between the Cause and the Event

The specific meaning of the term "effect" that we can easily use is found in physics, in multi-media art, and in the electronic and numerical instrument industry. Moreover, it bears a semiotic, philosophical meaning.

Physicists of the last two centuries turned their attention toward "effects" as facts whose appearance did not refer directly to a cause. In this sense, the effect is not an object itself. Noise or sound, for instance, do not physically "change" in the Doppler effect; it is the relation between the observer and the emitting object that is modified, when the former or the latter is moving at sufficient speed. The physics of "effects" is not only born of relativity; it also opens the way to a phenomenal thinking banned from the exact sciences for many centuries. The effect not only indicates a necessary cause; it is also the mark of an event. The "Doppler effect," the "Kelvin effect," and the "Compton effect," all refer, in this second meaning of the term, to the context surrounding the object and its appearance. From this point of view, the perceptible "effect" is directly linked to a circumstantial cause.

The physics of natural events is thus renewed with thinking that has existed for more than two thousand years. Outside of the logic of objects and attribution that became familiar to us in the West, stoics were developing another logic dealing with events and actions in progress. This logic of the sense implies a theory of effects in the meaning that we use it here.[16]

Astonishment and the Sonic Effect

The sound-effects editor focuses attention and tricks on the sound event itself. "Simple means for maximum effect" is probably the first rule of well-mastered sonic effects, as illustrated by professional practices in cinema and television, at least when they are not subjugated to sound effects from CDs and other archives.

The second rule would correspond to the Platonic theory of the simulacrum: one must produce enough falsehood to appear to be true. The gap between the model object and its representation, where all the subtlety of sonic effects production takes place, is guided by the effectiveness of the feeling caused in the listener. This knowledge of sound reconstitution provides essential indications of the nature of the sound experience.

"Sonic effects" as heard in modern technological instrumentation (reverberation, delay, flange, fuzz, phase, etc.) probably favour a riot of useless effects. But sound has always been a privileged tool to "create an effect," to astonish (*étonner*, in its etymological sense). Sound undeniably has an immediate emotional power that has been used by every culture. This surplus of feeling that exists in the perception of sounds in a spectacular context (such as the soundtrack of a movie) or during an exceptional situation (such as historical or collectively memorable events) does not disappear in the everyday sound environment. As soon as it is perceived contextually, sound is inseparable from an effect, as subtle as it can be, a particular colouration due to collective attitudes and representations or to individual traits. In this way, there exists, between the sound and the sonic effect, not a relation of similarity but rather a set of mutual references between the sound, physically measurable although always abstract, and its interpretation, the particular fashioning by which it enters into perceptive development.

In fact, any perception implies some effect, that is to say a minimal work of interpretation. This is the case for any propagation that happens outside of the laboratory, as we have already seen. As soon as a sound physically exists, it sets into vibration a defined space, weather, vegetation, etc. Sonic effects provide a context and common sense for physical and human dimensions of sound.

THE COMMON SENSE OF SONIC EFFECTS

What Is the Use of the Sonic Effect?

Here, we have a tool suitable for the concrete sound environment that allows us to integrate the domains of perception and action, observation and conception, and analysis and creation.[17] The sonic effect produces a common sense because it gathers together into unified and harmonious listening what other disciplinary knowledge divides. It also gives everyday listening pragmatic value.

Over the years, we have had several experimental objectives. The following examples, provided abundantly in the body of the repertoire, are here reduced to a minimum.

1 *Assisting acoustical measurement*
   Measurements at a micro level are too variable and it seems to be extremely difficult to observe repetition of the phenomenon *in situ*. The analysis of a situation using sonic effects offers a range of

validated models uniting the quantifiable and the qualifiable. Our descriptors can better orient the choice and use of measurements.

2 *A multidisciplinary instrumentation for the analysis of complex sound situations*

Complex contexts, such as neighbourhood noise situations, cannot easily be analyzed by a single battery of measurements, a knowledge of laws, and an examination of facts. Analysis using sonic effects offers a solution that respects the complexity of phenomena *in situ*, while promoting interactivity. With this tool we can analyze situations as varied as building sites, noise complaints, interpersonal communication in the new media, the acoustic organization of a downtown crossroads, the sound comfort of a nineteenth-century city, the soundscape of train stations and harbours, or the cultural identity of cities.[18]

3 *Assisting tools of representation*

To be more effective, the cartography of noise must evolve toward a more general representation of the sound environment. It must include qualitative data such as type of source, occurrence, periodicity, or type of reception. The sonic effect allows us to synthesize the main characteristics of a chosen site, but we must also develop appropriate graphical expressions. This type of research does not simply refer to the development of computer-aided design; it is also important to analyze cultural sound codes[19] either by signs or through procedures of metonymy. Several examples can be found in the repertoire.

4 *A tool for architectural and urban intervention*

The precise and multidisciplinary description of spatialized sonic effects is predictable in an interesting way. Our observations show, for instance, that the predictability of the ubiquity effect depends on the urban landscape (with its acoustical characteristics) and the specific use of a space (that is, the type of sources). The "Beaubourg"[20] sonic effect is also predictable through all of its cycles, depending on the morphology of a public space and its social use. This knowledge helps to define aspects of the sound identity of an urban project, and also assists in urban planning and decision-making. At the level of architectural conception and urban design some effects participate fully in the conception of the space and contribute to shaping its identity.[21] Examples include the clear reverberation of tiled Mediterranean houses, the cut out effect in artistic or cultural exhibitions, sound masks in industrial installations or open-plan offices, and the confused sound metabolism of new shopping centres. The sonic effect is probably one of the most subtle tools of architectural and design projects. The lack of awareness of designers concerning this notion is probably due to a mental block caused by visual culture and education.

5 *An educational tool serving the general experience of listening*

There is a real fascination on the part of both children and adults with well-known (although quite complex) sonic effects such as echo, ubiquity, telephone, and wave. Any program of listening pedagogy should use this primary individual sonic competence. Everyday perception is never simple. Complexity must be one of the prerequisites on which the teacher will rely to promote a comparison between a naive experience of everyday listening and specialized or expert practice.[22] The exploration of musical domains could, for instance, rely on everyday listening experiences, since the musical experience of creators is likely influenced by the environment. How could we otherwise explain the astonishing Doppler effects found in the compositions of Gustav Malher or the obvious mark of reverberation and release effects in a passage of *The Miraculous Mandarin* by Béla Bartók, not to mention the striking contrast between closeness and distance in many of Claudio Monteverdi's madrigals?[23]

An integrative process that would bring together distinct cultural sound experiences is possible, as we will prove in the multidisciplinary exploration of the proposed effects. Such a process relies on two assumptions. The first assumption is generic: perceptive organization is fundamentally the same in everyday and specialized listening. The second assumption is anagogical: the unification of sound phenomena must happen through a rediscovery of the pre-categorical approach to listening. A listening practice that starts with a return to the consciousness of early listening (as Merleau-Ponty would say) concerns sound specialists as much as urban environment planners and educators.[24] Listening to sonic effects and developing the capacity to identify them are part of a rehabilitation of general auditory sensitivity.

READING AND LISTENING TO THE GUIDE TO SONIC EFFECTS

An Interdisciplinary Journey in Two Readings

The guide to sonic effects is the fruit of an interdisciplinary collaboration that lasted for about ten years. The researchers of CRESSON – as engineers, architects, town planners, sociologists, philosophers, geographers, and musicologists – patiently collected sonic effects by searching through the substantial archive of interviews gathered through the years; by searching through numerous spatial observations and architectural descriptions; and by consulting acoustic descriptions of the constructed environment. For each specific effect that was noticeable in a given set of data, we searched for echoes and correspondences in other corpora. For example, the reverberation effect, while perfectly described by acoustics, can also be applied to the domains of social communication or to rituals and mythologies. We can also evaluate both the physical model of the cut out effect perceived in an observation of a constructed space and its ethological value. The domains of literature, musical creation and the audiovisual arts also offer many correspondences, illustrations, and inspirations.[25]

Reading is also an incitement to interdisciplinary analysis. The text is intended for readers who are not necessarily experts but who are nevertheless curious about sound, urbanism and architecture, anthropology and contemporary culture, or elementary pedagogy – in short, readers interested in the physical and human environment of this century. The original French text was designed to include what amounted to a secondary text, composed of numerous cross-references, specialized examples and illustrations, notes, and bibliographical and archival references. In the present English version, most of this material has been integrated into the main text.

The resulting text is neither an encyclopedia that gathers the totality of known elementary effects (the list of minor effects effectively remains open) nor a dictionary that presents a glossary of the basic elements of the contemporary soundscape (an improbable enterprise, as mentioned above). This work is a repertoire of effects in several different ways. It records sonic effects that are sufficiently known to be clearly described and identified on site or during listening. It also records the classics of urban sound instrumentation. Finally, as in music, the meaning of this repertoire becomes clear when sonic effects are adequately performed and interpreted by both actors and listeners.

Major Effects, Minor Effects

A map plotting the potential field covered by all the various sonic effects described would present us with a very irregular distribution. On the one hand, some effects are well defined by acoustics, but fail to account for numerous other phenomena found in our environment. On the other hand, within certain particular contexts there exists an infinity of different sound events the multidisciplinary description of which, even if limited to the most repetitive phenomena, would take years and would engage a considerable network of observers. Therefore, while we were unsatisfied with an acoustic universality that was too reductive, we also tried to avoid presenting the reader with a chronicle of sonic singularities – a task we leave to the talent of novelists, who often possess an astonishing sensitivity to sound ecology.[26] Following these premises, sonic effects were chosen and placed in a hierarchy according to several criteria:

- the basic effect and its variations (distortion is a variation of filtration)
- effects that always exist in concrete space or in the listening process (For example, reverberation is present in any propagation; synecdoche is the basis of perceptive selection.)
- effects that directly participate in the nature of the urban environment or in cultural processes (For example, metamorphosis is characteristic of the urban milieu; imitation is one of the foundations of human sound-making.)

The editing of the guide thus followed two models: a detailed account for the sixteen effects currently accepted as major effects, and a simple but precise definition for sixty-six other effects that we could qualify as "minor" (which does not imply that they are less interesting or that the repertoire could afford not to mention them). Effects are presented in alphabetical order for easier consultation.

Descriptive Fields and Domains of Reference of Sonic Effects

The sonic effect is often a multidisciplinary object. Our culture has nevertheless differentiated the various sectors of knowledge too strongly for us to make sense of this division. We therefore lead readers from distinct knowledge to the transversal exercise that they will construct based on their own experience.

How can we divide the fields of knowledge crossed over by different effects? In this subject, no border is perfect. Two criteria of delimitation were adopted:

- a clear distinction between scientific domains (For example, we do not use the heading "psychosociology" in order to keep individual aspects – physiology and psychology – distinct from collective aspects – sociology and culture.)
- an organization that facilitates reference to practical experience, so that the reader can rapidly evoke familiar or known situations.

Domains of reference can therefore refer equally to the ensemble of possible discourses on each effect or to the contemporary domains of knowledge and practice through which the existence of a singular effect may be researched.

We may notice that each effect is more easily identifiable in one domain than in others. In the order of presentation, this domain – the primary domain of reference – is given first, immediately following the formal definition. The other domains are listed in a decreasing order specific to the nature of each effect. Therefore, readers using this repertoire as a working tool will eventually be able to use it in a transversal mode, domain by domain. The domains of reference that were selected are:

- physical and applied acoustics
- architecture and urbanism
- psychology and physiology of perception
- sociology and everyday culture
- musical and electroacoustic aesthetics
- textual and media expressions

The description of each effect ends with the enumeration of related effects (which allows us to refine distinctions between them) and opposite effects (which makes the recapitulation of specific characteristics easier).

Between the Lines: Categories of Sonic Effect

A third and less explicit classification allows us to specify different types of relations between the environment and the human listener. The five categories of sonic effects listed below serve to help identify effects and to facilitate the description of a common scheme linking several effects through a particular theoretical approach to the environment. More simply, this taxonomy also allows us to approach sonic effects from a specific point on the two-way loop that connects the physical object to its subjective interpretation. Specialized readers can practice a different transversal reading that brings together effects from the same category. The acoustician, for instance, will be more familiar with the first category, the town planner or the architect with the second. On the other hand, beginning with the fourth or the fifth category provides the sociologist or semiotician with an entry point from which to gradually gain access to a larger variety of acoustic effects.

1 *Elementary Effects*

Elementary effects are concerned with the sound material itself (pitch, intensity, timbre, attack, duration, release, shape of the signal), that is, the mode of propagation of the sound. Deeply rooted in contemporary acoustic knowledge, they are all quantifiable.

Examples: filtration, distortion, resonance, reverberation

2 *Composition Effects*

Composition effects are concerned with complex sound arrangements and are defined by specific characteristics describing either the synchronic or the diachronic dimension of the context. These effects depend on the spatio-temporal flow of the propagation, and they can all be subjected to a physical evaluation of at least one of their components.

Examples: masking, release, cut out, drone, telephone

3 *Effects Linked to Perceptive Organization*

These effects are mainly due to the perceptive and mnemonic organization of individuals placed in a concrete situation. We always locate them through the expression or perception of listeners. Moreover, characters that are specific to the culture and the sociability of reference constitute an integral part of the particularities and the strength of the effect.

Examples: erasure, synecdoche, remanence, anticipation, metamorphosis

4 *Psychomotor Effects*

Psychomotor effects imply the existence of a sound action (be it a minimal movement) of the listener, or a scheme in which perception and motor function interact.

Examples: chain, niche, attraction, phonotonie

5 *Semantic Effects*

Semantic effects use the difference in meaning between a given context and its emerging signification. Decontextualization is always implied, whether it is provoked by shock, humour, or conscious play, or by adding aesthetic value to sound.

Examples: delocalization, imitation

REFERENCES AND ILLUSTRATIONS

As much as possible, references to specialized literature target the most recent or the most fundamental works as well as theses, research reports, and scientific articles. For the other bibliographical references, we prefer to indicate the existence of a single work (a novel, a poem, or an essay) rather than attempting to present all possible varieties of references. For instance, the French poet Henri Michaux is not the only author who describes the ubiquity effect, but the chosen excerpt is particularly eloquent and will likely help readers to perceive the phenomenon through poetic means.

Specific sound experiences taken from sociological surveys may not always be ideal examples. However, they may facilitate comprehension and stimulate a reader's individual experience, evoking other memories or quotations that will even make more sense to him or her. Graphical illustrations are not intended to make visible what is essentially audible. Rather, they recall the intimate and often intrusive relation that images maintain with sounds in our civilization. As mirrors – rigorous in the case of diagrams and acoustical representations, evocative in the case of vignettes, reproductions, situation maps, and architectural sketches – the illustrations should always be seen as invitations to look at sound rather than as substitutes for a lack of hearing. Finally, the sound examples often used in the work are drawn either from world musical culture or from recordings of the urban soundscape.[27]

This edition of the guide includes a two-part list of references. The Thematic Reading List (pp. 195–202) is intended to provide readers with a basic bibliography divided into simple categories that allow easier access to knowledge of the world of sounds. The various categories in this list include works that are not specifically concerned with sound but that provide important information on specific effects. This list provides only author, title, and date of publication. The Bibliography (pp. 203–16) is organized in alphabetical order by author and provides full bibliographic details for all citations in the text, notes, and the Thematic Reading List.

guide to sonic effects

In music, a marking (usually abbreviated as *Accel.*) that indicates an acceleration in the speed of performance, and consequently an increase in the tempo of the piece. One task of a conductor is to determine the precise tempo of a work that he or she conducts. The conductor indicates the movements of acceleration and deceleration of the musical stream based on this chosen tempo. Musical accompaniments for cartoons frequently use the accelerando effect – for instance in establishing chase scenes where image and sound follow the same progression. Apart from the musical domain, we can observe this effect in many animal cries and salvos.

Accelerando

OPPOSITE EFFECT   rallentando

An effect of reminiscence in which a past situation or atmosphere is brought back to the listener's consciousness, provoked by a particular signal or sonic context. Anamnesis, a semiotic effect, is the often involuntary revival of memory caused by listening and the evocative power of sounds.

Anamnesis

Anamnesis, an evocation of the past, refers to situations in which a sound or a sonic context revives a situation or an atmosphere of the past. This effect can span very different periods of time while retaining its intrinsic nature: it can happen on the scale of an entire life –a song that evokes a childhood memory – or a short span of time – for example, when a film soundtrack plays on the exposition of a sound element previously heard. However, the more distant and unexpected the reference, the more the emotion may overwhelm the listener. The effect is not based on the sound or on its meaning. It is rather the listener who gives it an anamnesic value. Two people listening to the same sound environment can develop very different evocations, but these effects could not happen without the occurrence of sound. The anamnesis effect merges sound, perception, and memory. It plays with time, reconnecting past mental images to present consciousness, with no will other than the free activity of association. In its clinical meaning, anamnesis does not refer only to a simple evocation of a memory; it also implies the historical reconstitution of a disease by a patient. In the same way, a sound or a group of sounds may lead to the reconstitution of a whole period of life as it unfolds during the entire updating of a time sequence.

Note that in the sense given to anamnesis here, memory is not necessarily voluntary; in everyday life many evocations happen involuntarily. In music therapy, anamnesis may be voluntarily produced. Evocative types of music are listed for this specific purpose.[1]

PSYCHOLOGY AND PHYSIOLOGY OF PERCEPTION

Anamnesis can be situated at the level of individual psychology, as it is semantic and is linked to the global organization of perception. The particular timbre of a voice recalls a specific person; a certain song allows one to revisit a day in the past; a particular ambiance evokes memories of years past. Thanks to sound, a forgotten moment of our life is restored. Not only is this sound remembered, but all the other sensorial and affective components also cross the threshold of consciousness. All the senses may act as stimuli of anamnesis; sight, taste, and smell as much as hearing.

However sound, and more specifically music, intervenes metaphorically as an open catalyst: the past is not recomposed, with all the details of its authenticity; rather it is presented as an evocation, delimiting a flexible framework that each nostalgia may colour in its own way. Often, the sound sequence that begins this process does not specifically aim to provoke an anamnesis. Between the stimulus and the recalled situation, there is also a perceived and evaluated shift, be it chronological, spatial, or cultural. We will discuss these sociological aspects further, but for now we can say that at the perceptive level, sound acts as a key, opening doors to reunite us with the past; it stimulates images that all of us have hidden at various depths of our psyche.[2]

Note that in scientific literature sound is rarely at the origin of a trauma; more frequently it is one of the ways to explore and find the initial stimulus of the neurosis or the psychosis.[3]

PHYSICAL AND APPLIED ACOUSTICS

We cannot talk of physical criteria in the case of the anamnesis effect. Subjective projection takes precedence over all acoustic transformations and eventual distortions of the initial sound sequence. Consider, for instance, a song that would evoke a childhood memory: for some, the sound colour of the diffusion will be more important for its evocative power than its musical content; the little record player stimulates the recollection just as much as the singer does. For others, a whistled or hummed melody, even totally out of context, will always succeed in awakening memory.

The listening experience may focus on specific details either from the moment that sound was recorded or in the unexpected memories it evokes.[4] In this sense, acoustical conditions participate in creating anamnesis; walks in quite ordinary places – churches, falls, seaside, funfairs – are often propitious to the reappearance of images of a personal or collective nature.

Sound colour has such an influence on emotional response that anything linked to timbre, and notably to filtration, may be likely to induce anamnesis.

SOCIOLOGY AND EVERYDAY CULTURE

Characterized principally by a temporal shift,[5] anamnesis can also combine spatial and cultural shifts. For instance, when a Western adult travels in countries in which she or he encounters traditional activities linked to craft and rural life, various sonic features – particular types of machines, tools, or commercial practices – may evoke the traveller's childhood. Some activities, overtaken by the technical "progress" and lifestyles of so-called "advanced" countries, still exist in other countries, and their encounter during travel may rekindle situations or emotions shifted in time.

Therefore, sound does not necessarily evoke an individual past experience; it can also connect one to a contemporary situation through an entirely different context, another place, another culture.

Although it is essentially subjective, anamnesis also has an archetypal dimension. Specific sounds can produce common references for a given culture: sounds of flowing water, rain, crackling fire, thunder, and singing birds, but also sounds of industrial automatic devices, cars, and urban drones. There are many shared backgrounds over which individual perceptions are laid. Archetypal anamneses are less conscious than others, but they can be just as effective. People working in sonic effects for film know this very well; they select useful sounds for the effect on the audience rather than for a realistic reference to the recorded scene.

MUSICAL AESTHETICS

In a certain way, the aim of a repeat (*bis*) in music, and particularly a *leitmotiv* or a reiterated theme, is to create a sort of anamnesis in the listener. Even if the listener expects to hear a certain theme repeated, musical art consists precisely in the magnification of an emotional path leading to that return.

Film soundtracks are often constructed from characters of the story, a specific theme being assigned to each one. During the film, the evocation of characters may happen through their sound identification, without their presence on screen. Within the logical flow of the story, the spectator integrates this sonic evocation as information or clues. One of the clearest examples can be heard in Ennio Morricone's music for Sergio Leone's film, *Once Upon a Time in the West* (1968), in which every appearance of the protagonists is punctuated by not only a specific melody but also a strongly identified orchestral colour.[6]

The role of music as a stimulus of anamnesis is essential. Undoubtedly music, more than other modes of expression, or even other aspects of the sound domain, possesses an evocative faculty that calls at the same time a feeling and a memory. It can be used as an affective cement to the original scene, which will then be easily revived and enhanced through emotion. "Our day-to-day life is bombarded with fortuities or, to be more precise, with the accidental meeting of people and events we call coincidences. 'Co-incidence' means that two events unexpectedly happen at the same time, they meet: Tomas appears in the hotel restaurant at the same time that the radio is playing Beethoven. We do not even notice the great majority of such coincidences. If the seat Tomas occupied had been occupied by the local butcher, Tereza would never have noticed that the radio was playing Beethoven (although the meeting of Beethoven and the butcher would have also been an interesting coincidence). But Tereza's nascent love inflamed her sense of beauty, and she would never forget that music. Whenever she heard it, she would be touched. Everything going on around her at that moment would be haloed by the music and take on its beauty."[7]

ARCHITECTURE AND URBANISM

Although it can be easily provoked in the sound domain, the anamnesis effect is only rarely confined specifically to the aural sphere. Spatial configuration, and consequently visual perception, sometimes intervenes to favour the emergence of this effect. The senses work together to strengthen remembrance. The acoustics of a space also inscribes its volumetry in the memory. The evocation of a place, even considered solely in its sound dimension, will therefore also be synesthetic.

Any noticeable modification of an architectural or urban context can appear as the divide between past and present. A soundproof wall, for instance, which transforms the sound ambiance of an area, imposes itself as a chronological frontier in regards to anamnesis; there is the state of "before the wall," and the state of "after."[8] A single city can also present many coexisting sound ambiences of different historical origins. In this sense, space is also an organization of potential anamnesis, through its faculty to maintain the presence of different eras.

TEXTUAL AND MEDIA EXPRESSIONS

Language constitutes a particular sonic field in the context of this anamnesis.[9] A language, either because we understand it, or because it positions us as foreigners, carries as much memory as it does meaning. Multi-linguistic situations (movements of populations, human crossroads) evolve in accordance with the spatial map defined by the languages involved, and the affective content that exists in each one. In immigrant families, for instance, languages change depending on what the person wants to talk about, not only at the level of the signifier, but also to particularize or to revive a sociolinguistic climate and solidarity. In such cases, anamnesis is more a common background than a link that connects two sides. This is not exactly anamnesis; more likely it is a contextual effect that calls for active memory.

In poetic evocation, we can also find a similar function for memory. For instance, in *Moravagine* when Blaise Cendras lists the names of cities visited, the tone of their names is sufficient to inspire dreams: "from San Francisco to Sydney via Honolulu and Suwa, Auckland and New Guinea, or from Rotterdam, Antwerp, Hamburg, Dunkirk, Bordeaux, Marseilles, Lisbon, Genoa, to Quebec, Halifax, New York, Boston, Philadelphia, Vera Cruz, Rio, Santo, La Plate."[10]

RELATED EFFECT	phonomnesis
OPPOSITE EFFECT	anticipation

Anticipation

Someone waiting for a sound to appear will "pre-hear" – that is, he or she will actually hear – the expected signal, even if no sound has been emitted. This effect can be observed either in the expectation of an unknown sound, every rustling then becoming a potential sign, or in familiar situations where the listener anticipates in her or his mind, a foreseeable (or *fore-hearable*) sonic context.

If anamnesis is most often an involuntary phenomenon, anticipation, on the other hand, may appear when one expects too much. We may dread a sound, or we may be eager to hear it, but either way that sound seems to be heard without being actually emitted. The anticipation effect is often caused by a specific expectation concerning the sound to appear. It happens as if the desire of the event was creating its own sound envelope. When a child is barely asleep, for instance, the parents listening for crying may have the impression of constantly hearing it. This effect can also be illustrated by the expectation of a car or train passing: every little murmur or noise is interpreted as an announcement of the expected sound. In war, the threat of bombing can also create strong anticipation effects.

In music, two situations are particularly favourable to the emergence of this effect. The first situation is the moment that precedes the performance of a piece: every musician or singer goes through the section he or she will play, either mentally or by humming, like a brief summary of the first sections or a feared passage. The second situation involves all music-lovers and concerns anticipation of the resolution, that is to say the ultimate transition of a development leading to the end of a phrase, a movement, or an entire piece. Before cadences (from the Latin *cadere*: to fall) acquired the sense of "free variation" of a cadenza, they served as figures of musical punctuation, offering points of reference to the listener. The cadence was an anticipation; it announced what was coming right after.

Finally, it seems that the anticipation effect inscribes itself very well in the aesthetics of reception as developed by the Constance school; we may therefore find rich and pertinent correspondences in this theoretical field.[1]

OPPOSITE EFFECTS   anamnesis, remanence

Asyndeton

The deletion from the perception or memory of one or many sound elements in an audible whole. Surveys studying everyday sound behaviour show that the amount of "forgotten" or unheard sound is extremely prominent.[1] The asyndeton effect allows the valorization of a portion of the sound environment through evacuation of useless elements from our consciousness. Asyndeton is therefore complementary to the synecdoche effect. Asyndeton, through its rhetorical origin, refers more to the generic notion of forgetting, whereas erasure is used specifically in reference to practice.

SYNONYM EFFECT   erasure

Attraction

A phonotropic effect in which an emerging sound phenomenon attracts and polarizes attention, be it conscious or not. The magnitude of this effect can range from fleeting comprehension to the complete mobilization of attention. In very busy streets for instance, singers and musical groups try constantly to gain the attention of passersby. These sound situations exert a power of attraction precisely because they are in contrast with the ambient hubbub. When the acoustic horizons of different musicians overlap, there is no emergence effect, thus no attraction. A siren, which manifests itself exclusively in the sonic sphere, and whose source often cannot be located, illustrates the attraction/repulsion duality that characterizes the emergence of certain sound events.

OPPOSITE EFFECT   repulsion

Blurring

The blurring (*estompage*) effect refers to the progressive and imperceptible disappearance of a sound atmosphere. In contrast to the decrescendo effect, the auditor usually only notices the absence of sound once the effect is completed.

RELATED EFFECTS   fade, decrescendo
OPPOSITE EFFECT   emergence

Chain

A chain reaction: one sound event provokes a sonic response, which produces another, and so on. These successive inductions, whether or not they are enacted consciously, can result in a phenomenon of sound escalation. Crowd situations are favourable to the appearance of this effect; the applause that follows a show, for instance, may be started by a small group of people, or even a single auditor, and progressively lead the whole audience up to a manifestation whose intensity greatly exceeds the sum of individual contributions. Sometimes the role of a "claque" appears to be quite useful in inciting movement and maintaining pressure.

Chorus

An electroacoustic effect that consists of mixing a direct signal with a portion of itself, slightly delayed and modulated through a low-frequency oscillator. The variable phase displacement thus produced enriches the original sound by seeming to multiply the sound sources – hence its reference to chorus, sum of individual voices.

RELATED EFFECT   phase

Cocktail or Cocktail-Party

This effect, named by E. Cherry[1] with reference to the sound space in which we can observe it best, refers to our ability to focus attention on the speech of a specific speaker by disregarding irrelevant information coming from the surroundings. In this type of metabolic context, sound components are almost equivalent in intensity and frequency: it is their multiplication that creates the surrounding sound level. "From the physical point of view, one of the predominant elements in the cocktail effect is the spatial separation of noise and speech. In consequence, we know that, on the psycho-physiological level, selective listening is governed by our capacity to discriminate sounds from different sources – that is, by our capacity to localize in the noise."[2]

RELATED EFFECTS   asyndeton, metamorphosis

Colouring

An effect describing the influence of a location, electroacoustic system, or instrument on the new balance of the frequencies of a sound, "coloured" through its diffusion. We speak of the "colour" of a room or the "colour" of a loudspeaker. Colouring is acoustically linked to filtration, but its use remains more popular. To the untrained ear, the colouring of a sound situation is particularly well perceived when colouration changes rapidly. A good example is the clear inside/outside transition of film soundtracks or the entry of woodwind instruments (flute, clarinet, bassoon, oboe) in the musical stream of string instruments.

RELATED EFFECT   filtration

Compression

An electroacoustic effect: a compressor reduces the dynamic range of a signal by raising low-intensity signals while lowering high-intensity ones. Generally speaking, compression makes it possible to raise the average energy of a recording by avoiding the strict use of peak signals in the calibration of its maximum volume. It allows the adaptation of a signal to media supporting different dynamics: vinyl disc, cassette, or compact disc.

RELATED EFFECT   limitation

Interaction between two sound phenomena that seem to be distinct yet connected, without being necessarily engaged in a causal relationship. In architecture, for example, we can observe the reciprocal influences of different reverberations of two adjacent spaces.

Coupling

An effect produced by a progressive increase in the intensity of a sound. This well-known effect, which has specific notation in music, can be found in the most diverse contexts: in the approach of a sound source, the acceleration of a vehicle, the start-up of a machine, the rise of a murmur, etc.

Crescendo

OPPOSITE EFFECT   decrescendo

While the cut out effect describes an abrupt change from one sonic state to another, the term crossfade refers to a more progressive transition between states, accomplished through a decrease in intensity of the first state and increasing apparition of the second. We can experience this effect when crossing a mid-sized square in which reflections from the street or the façade behind us slowly crossfades with sounds from the opposite direction.

Crossfade

OPPOSITE EFFECT   cut out

The cut out (*coupure*) effect refers to a sudden drop in intensity associated with an abrupt change in the spectral envelope of a sound or a modification of reverberation (moving from reverberant to dull spaces, for instance). This effect is an important process of articulation between spaces and locations; it punctuates movement from one ambience to another.

Cut Out

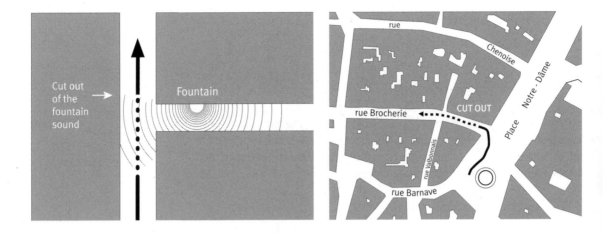

Cut out
of the
fountain
sound

Fountain

rue
Chenoise

Place Notre - Dame

rue Brocherie   CUT OUT

rue Valbonnais

rue Barnave

Figure 1 (left)
Progression of a pedestrian
moving in the direction
of a traffic signal. Once
the listener has passed
the intersection, the
sound source gradually
disappears.

Figure 2 (right)
A pedestrian leaves a busy
urban square, turning left
down a narrow side street:
the more accentuated
the narrowing, the more
clearly the cut out effect
is observed, once the
pedestrian has turned the
corner into the side street.
(This example is located
in the town centre of
Grenoble).

Two types of cut out can be distinguished: the effect can take place at the level of utterance (cutting of a sound source), or it can be determined by conditions of propagation (space organization). In both cases, the cut out effect produces a clear and obvious change in the surrounding sound ambience. The concept of cut-out is particularly concerned with the composition and organization of sound material. Cut out plays a formant role in the perception of space and time by allowing us to distinguish different locations and sequences.

ARCHITECTURE AND URBANISM

Constructed spaces create divisions in the sound environment by influencing the propagation of sound sources and by orienting movement and progression through these spaces. The urban environment, because of its diversity of sound sources, architectural structures, and surfaces, and because of the complexity of its spatial configurations and the mobility of sound sources and inhabitants, appears to be a particularly propitious milieu for the emergence of cut out effects. However, the effect is always perceived in specific, contextualized situations.

The cut out effect is frequently perceived within a movement of either the listener or the sound source. Spatial characteristics thus create cut out effects that are dynamic. To be more precise, it is the relative position of the listener in relation to the sound source that determines the appearance of the effect. Two configurations can be observed. In the

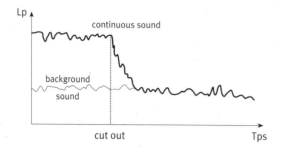

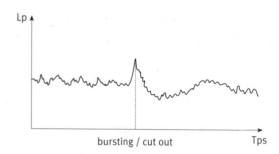

first configuration, the listener is moving (for example, passing through a door or turning at a street corner). In this case, the cut out effect will be produced through a drop in intensity, a change in ambience, and/or the concealment of a sound source. Figure 1 shows a pedestrian passing a street with a fountain. Once the listener passes the intersection, the sound source gradually disappears. Figure 2 shows a pedestrian turning on to a narrow street leading directly off a busy urban square. The more narrow the street, the more clearly the cut out effect is observed. In the second configuration, the sound source is moving (a car, a child shouting) and the emitted sound is suddenly masked or deflected by a screen located between the source and the listener.

We can note two other heuristic situations. With directional sources, the effect can be perceived in the absence of an obstacle, simply because the listener moves away from the principal angle of propagation. Finally, the abrupt interruption of a sound emission, the rupture of a rhythm, or the irruption of an intense sound create cut out effects that do not depend on spatial forms. Figure 3 illustrates a cut out of a continuous or repetitive sound. We find the background sound at its original level. Suppression of a sound can also modify the general tone and will therefore reinforce the difference between the sound before and after the cut out. The drop time or abruptness of the cut out is very important. Figure 4 illustrates a bursting sound that shatters an installed sound climate. This event – a glass shattering – creates a sudden cut out in the sound continuum created by the conversations of people in the bar.

Everyday movements and progressions through an urban space present us with numerous illustrations of the first case. By analogy, we can also consider the closing of a window with the resultant abrupt sound

Figure 3 (left)
Graphic representation of a sound with a fairly continuous or repetitive structure (such as a machine) subjected to an interruption.

Figure 4 (right)
Graphic representation of a bursting sound shattering an installed sound climate: the sound of a broken glass in a bar.

insulation in relation to the exterior, as a cut out effect. Modern conceptions of architecture and urbanism have developed ideas of transparency through fluid and continuous space. These ideas, strongly influenced by the domination of the visual sense, resulted in a sound space that is more homogeneous than in the past, since visual "transparency" usually also allows sound fluidity. The cut out effect is more likely to appear when the space is constant: the width of streets, for instance, plays an undeniable role in the diffusion of sound signals.

The cut out effect has a structuring function that is essential in urban spaces, as illustrated by two typical situations. In the first situation, the perception of limits between different sound locations in the city makes it possible to describe certain public spaces. Cut out effects are often perceptible in neighbouring zones:[1] when moving from a car traffic zone to a pedestrian zone, from a residential area to a commercial sector, from a boulevard to a street, and more generally from an open space to a closed one. In all these examples, the cut out effect is strongly determined by physical changes in the spectral envelope and reverberation, as well as by the transformation of the sound climate through the activities of each location.[2] Yet this relation is not systematic: there exist narrow passages and urban doors that do not necessarily create a cut out effect. Acoustic and visual frontiers are not necessarily congruent. Moreover, one must be attentive to the precise conditions of emergence of the cut out – for example, the sense of progression when the effect is produced in a single direction, and is not symmetrical.

In the second situation, there is an experience of contrast between public spaces and private spaces. Building entrances are spaces that particularly favour the appearance of the cut out effect. Entering a home or a hall, or crossing a courtyard, are everyday practices that produce more or less contrasting cut out effects between spaces of different status. Here, the effect is determined by a drop in intensity that is characteristic to the public/private transition, even if the modification of the spectral envelope that accompanies the movement is also quite noticeable (for example, moving from a reverberant location to a dull one).

From an operational point of view, the invention of architectural forms and spatial configurations that favour the emergence of cut out effects appears to be a desirable goal, insofar as these effects allow and produce a clear and contrasted differentiation of urban and domestic spaces. There are three types of architectural interventions:

1 The "sound door," which consists of positioning constructed elements to be used as acoustical screens in relation to induced progressions. Doors play a fundamental role in the orientation of a progression and in the mutual definition of an interior/exterior relation. This sound delimitation directly intervenes with the perception of a location.

2 The "sound lock," which consists, through acoustical modifications, of creating an intermediary space that unites adjacent locations while separating them. The sound lock contributes to the definition of the hierarchy of spaces by creating a contrasted sound climate.

3 A "sound marking," which takes place in the entrance or exit of the location where we want to produce the effect. This marking can be achieved either through the programming of a certain type of utterance, or the accentuation of the closed character of a space or through its acoustical treatment (for example, by using reverberant materials). In such cases, sound marking strongly establishes identity and recognition of a specific location.

PHYSICAL AND APPLIED ACOUSTICS

We can physically measure a cut out effect based on the sudden cessation of a sound or its disappearance caused by contextual circumstances (for instance, a screen may deflect sound waves). The determining factor in perception of the effect is the period of time over which this modification takes place. Experimental studies could thus be conducted to evaluate minimal thresholds. In the simplest case, it is the relation between the difference in sound levels and the drop time that must be considered if we want to quantify and define this effect acoustically. This applies to any sudden cessation of a sound, or to the appearance of an obstacle between the sound source and the listener.

Acoustic definition of the cut out effect remains fairly general, since any sudden modification of a sound element (intensity, timbre, reverberation, rhythm) can theoretically produce a cut out. When this effect plays on timbre and reverberation, a strictly quantitative evaluation is much more difficult. These sound criteria are not as easy to measure, and the psychophysiological dimension of perception attenuates or amplifies subjective interpretations of contrasts. A small drop in levels may in fact produce a significant cut out effect on a listener.

Because of the natural ubiquity of low frequencies, the cut out effect is observed more clearly with higher frequencies, which are more directional and more easily deflected. Sources for which the spectrum is located principally in a higher register thus favour occurrence of the effect; depending on the relative positions of the source and the listener, the latter may leave the sound field even through confined movement. We know that constructions that block sound waves are efficient in protecting listeners only if they are large enough in relation to the frequencies of the emitted sound; to constitute an efficient screen against low frequencies, which have long wave lengths, a wall must be sufficiently thick and high enough that the waves cannot easily get through it or bypass it.

A cut out effect between spaces may be caused by sound insulation. For instance, some windows can reduce penetration of exterior sounds up to 40 dB(A), so the cut out effect may be particularly evident when closing a window.

PSYCHOLOGY AND PHYSIOLOGY OF PERCEPTION

Our perception is particularly sensitive to change in sensed stimuli; the psychology of perception probably depends on and structures itself around opposites and contrasts. In this sense, the cut out effect is a compositional effect, since it is concerned with sound arrangements. It is also at the origin of other effects, being a necessary part of the relation between different sounds in global sound distribution: the listener moves from one given location (or state) to another, and clearly distinguishes these two specific moments. Cut outs play a fundamental role in structuring time and space (division of time, delimitation of space). As we have seen previously, there is no strict physical description of the cut out in the sense that the drop in intensity and its duration are fixed, indicating "objectively" what a cut out is. We observe that the cut out effect does not necessarily involve high intensities; it can have a similar impact on the listener at lower levels.[3] Certain subjective amplification of cut outs may colour a particular meaning. The memory of an urban progression, for instance, makes it possible to anticipate cut outs and to assign them a symbolic and affective value. The feeling of rupture will thereby be more or less pronounced.[4]

The silence that follows a cut out assumes great importance based on its contrast with sound events preceding the cut. Perceptually, it appears as a radical component of the effect. When a sound suddenly stops, psychological adaptation is not immediate.[5] Cut out through timbre modification (in which intensity does not plays a fundamental role) is more subtle and may sometimes escape the attention of every-day listening.

Sometimes, the cut out effect has immediate consequences on the behaviour of a listener: the level of intensity of the voice can diminish notably[6] and speech may even stop for a moment.[7] Shortly after the cut, a wait, seeming excessively long, can take place: the listener hangs on to the sequence of events, her or his attention having been awakened by the surprising effect of the cut out.

The adaptation of the ear to a new sound environment may lead to a refinement of listening, a better reception of weaker sounds and stronger attention in the initial moments; then, a less vigilant listening attitude reappears. The cut out effect therefore makes it possible to emphasize events following a rupture (when it is actually followed by other sounds). The suddenness of the cut out can also be related to its degree of anticipation: The cut is valued differently depending on whether the listener plays an active part in the effect (closing a door, moving from one place to another, stopping a sound) or is simply a passive receiver of a sound that stops by itself.

SOCIOLOGY AND EVERYDAY CULTURE

Cut out effects emphasize social marking of locations by sounds, while favouring the emergence of "signed" sound milieus. This term designates places in which authors are recognizable and leave sound marks that contribute to the identity of a location. In this sense, notions of districts or blocks, in everyday experience, can refer to divisions between sound spaces. Moving from an anonymous sound milieu – that is to say, a place in which sounds are not assigned to a specific author – to a "signed" place – where human activities are identified and assigned to recognized persons or groups – is quite significant with regards to territorial marking. The role of timbres, propagation, and notably reverberation then acquire all their importance. Individual and collective imagery (or imagination) are easily involved, since the cut out effect can be felt as clearly when a sonic change that is less contrasted on the acoustic level corresponds to a strong social transition. The function of time and space marking through cut out effects thereby plays an important role in individual and collective representations.

Finally, voluntary interruption of an activity, whether or not it is followed by a resumption, is a situation that frequently happens in interpersonal situations.[8] This type of cut is a sort of digression from an ambience; it acts as a temporary interruption of rhythm or as punctuation. In interpersonal relations, this punctuation appears, notably, to create silence.[9] The expression *"couper court aux rumeurs"* (to put a quick end to rumors) illustrates social resonances of the cut out.

MUSICAL AESTHETICS

The idea of cut out is noticeable in music, where it serves as a way of beginning again. The creation of silence is an essential punctuation in musical discourse. It also serves to reactivate attention.[10] Examples may include cutting a musical climate through irruption of a sound in such a way as to emphasize differences, stopping a more or less continuous sound (such as a drone), or damping resonance (cutting the release section of sounds). Changes in mode or tonality also mark a division by creating a new climate.

Note that the first works of *musique concrète* were essentially based on the cut out effect: the manipulation of magnetic tape using scissors was in fact quite appropriate, and the physical arrangement of cut sounds provides an excellent illustration of this effect.[11]

In electroacoustics, "shunting" (*shunter*) amounts to the production of a cut out effect. A slight increase of the level preceding the *shunt* accentuates the effectiveness of the effect, because of the great differences in level between maximum and minimum.

TEXTUAL AND MEDIA EXPRESSIONS

The cut out effect is commonly used in commercials with a *cut* montage structure, often in conjunction with images. With the constraint of saving time, *cut* montage techniques favour the coexistence of many discourses – for example, an actor's dialogue, an off-screen voice narrating the situation, a voice reading a commercial – presented in three different sound styles. The short attention span, easily retained by short-term memory, is used to precisely calibrate the structure of these messages. The radio jingle is a form of cut out: a sudden burst of a sound motif ends what preceded and announces what follows. In poetic language, diction organizes cuts necessary to the articulation of sequences and expression. In the art of classical oratory, the cut out of vocal articulation (*aptum*) was one of the great tools used to capture the attention of listeners.[12] In all these domains, the effect articulates itself through silences and pauses that give the listener a short rest, an interval necessary for the emergence of meaning. According to Gillo

Dorflès, the loss of the interval is a characteristic of contemporary society.[13] The cut out effect is a privileged instrument to thwart continuity, or to avoid homogeneity of sensorial solicitations.

RELATED EFFECTS   digression, erasure, blurring
OPPOSITE EFFECTS   irruption, crossfade

With this effect, the listener's attention searches for a sound that is inaudible, such as the voice of a mute person. The effect is named for Jean-Baptiste Deburau (1796–1846), a famous mime whose trial attracted the whole of Paris, curious to hear his voice. By extension, this effect characterizes the identification of a sound source followed by the observation that once discovered, it is no longer of particular interest.[1]

Deburau

The incongruous intervention of a sound or group of sounds into a coherent situation that was previously experienced, or into a situation where the sonic content is predictable: for example, sounds from the private domain heard in a public space. More or less refined musical gags essentially play on a decontextualization of sound or meaning, as illustrated by the French ensemble Le Quatuor, a classical string quartet that performs in a humorous style, playing on traditional conventions by varying rhythmic and melodic lines and stylistic digressions.

Decontextualization

An effect produced by a progressive diminution of sound intensity. Often indicated in music at the end of a phrase or a movement, a decrease in sound intensity can also be found in varied contexts, whether it is caused by the sound source moving away or by something like a machine stopping.

OPPOSITE EFFECT   crescendo

Decrescendo

In its generic sense, this effect refers to any delay between the emission of a sound and its repetition. Echo and reverberation are thus two types of delay. As an electroacoustic effect, delay can be applied at the

Delay

level of milliseconds; generally it is less than a second. Delay is used to give depth to a sound or to spatialize it in the stereophonic field.

RELATED EFFECTS   echo, reverberation

Delocalization

Delocalization, a form of the ubiquity effect, implies recognition of an error in localizing a sound source. As with the ubiquity effect, the listener does not know where the sound comes from; however, with the delocalization effect, the listener knows exactly where the sound seems to come from, while at the same time being conscious that it is an illusion. There can be delocalization without ubiquity, but there cannot be ubiquity without delocalization.

RELATED EFFECT   ubiquity
OPPOSITE EFFECT   hyperlocalization

Desynchronization

Desynchronization, a temporal decontextualization effect, characterizes the emergence of a sound emission that breaks the regularity of a rhythm or a well-established sound structure, creating a feeling of incongruity. The event may have the same sonic nature as the elements it disrupts, as when someone interrupts another person without respecting the rhythmic alternation of a conversation. The social dimension of the desynchronization effect is crucial. Cinematographic montage also offers a clear field of application for this effect; arranging sounds in a sequence, the rhythmic development must be accomplished while respecting both the acoustic complexity of the scene and legibility of significant sound events. Any discontinuity in the phrasing of the sequence provokes a feeling of desynchronization.

RELATED EFFECT   delocalization
OPPOSITE EFFECT   synchronization

Digression

The digression effect refers to the emergence of a temporary change of sound ambience in a complex perceptive organization that does not seem to affect behaviours or mark memory. Digression is an erasure effect at the level of a whole sequence. The most common example is a phone call that interrupts a conversation, suspends it for a moment, and then allows its resumption at the place where it stopped without altering its content.

RELATED EFFECT   erasure

The dilation effect refers to the feeling of the emitter concerning the space of propagation and the hearing sensitivity of others: the emitter feels that the sound he or she produces will carry and be clearly perceived (diastolic movement). This effect can be anticipatory as well as perceptual. Human ethology is swarming with representative cases of this preventive sound marking: for instance, a person who is not accustomed to using a telephone and speaks loudly as the correspondent is far away.

OPPOSITE EFFECT   shrinkage

Dilation

A distortion of specific frequencies of the spectral envelope of a sound that affects the totality of a sequence. In comparison with filtration, distortion acts through addition rather than subtraction. Distortion manifests itself as an electroacoustic effect, either in an involuntary manner in the electrophonic chain, when saturation is produced during amplification, or as a specific additive intended to voluntarily transform the sound of an instrument such as an electric guitar.

RELATED EFFECTS   filtration, fuzz

Distortion

Physicist Christian-Johann Doppler (1803–53) noticed this effect first with sound and then also with light. The Doppler-Fizeau effect describes a relative anamorphose of the original signal. This perceptive modification is due to a relation of movement between the sound source and the listener that provokes either a compression or an expansion of the sound wave. A sound signal that moves closer is perceived as being higher than it actually is, whereas that same signal moving away will be perceived as being lower. This phenomenon comes from a combination of the sound's speed of propagation and the movement of the sound source. When both the sound wave and the sound source move in the same direction, the perceived frequency rises. When they

Doppler

move in opposite directions, the perceived frequency drops. When there is a sudden change of direction of the source in relation to the listener, the Doppler effect can be accompanied by a complementary effect of approach and distancing.

Drone

The drone (*bourdon*) effect refers to the presence of a constant layer of stable pitch in a sound ensemble with no noticeable variation in intensity. Linked to music in its designation (the drone is a permanent bass note over which other elements are laid), the drone effect can also be observed in urban and industrial soundscapes. Many technical systems generate constant sounds that are close to a drone, even if the frequencies concerned are not limited to the bass range that originally characterized it.[1]

SYNONYMS
teneur, continuum

SOCIOLOGY AND EVERYDAY CULTURE

In everyday life, the drone effect appears principally in the form of humming characterized as a "dull and continuous sound."[2] In ancient times, the first hums were probably linked to physical elements or the natural environment,[3] but were soon augmented by human activities, particularly collective ones: hums of crowds, murmurs of voices, psalmody of prayers.

Mechanical civilization, particularly car traffic, produced an elevation of the intensity of the sound continuum. Road noise is now the object of a precise frequency definition (see "Physical and Applied Acoustics" below). An automobile drone is located primarily in low frequencies. In downtown areas, the urban drone has reached a maximal level because of automobile saturation. Because it is constantly increasing, the level of urban drone has resulted in an escalation of sound powers used to cover it, notably the warning signals of emergency vehicles and alarms. To prevent a continuous increase in sound levels, local regulations often prohibit the use of individual car horns in urban zones. The drone of traffic is now increasing principally in suburban areas and in the countryside, where highways can sometimes be heard more than ten kilometres away, depending on the landscape.

There are important differences between countries in this domain. For instance, we can compare France and the United States. North

American motors are more powerful than European ones, and thus produce frequencies that are fundamentally lower. Also, generalized use of automatic transmissions globally generates a more supple and, in consequence, less noisy driving style. Moreover, the speed limit of 55 miles per hour in most U.S. states during the 1970s and 1980s created an increase of about two dB(A) in identical traffic conditions (flow and percentage of heavyweight trucks) in comparison with France, where the speed limit is 130 kilometres per hour.

The industrial world has generated a large variety of drones, notably where industries were concentrated for a precise activity in a particular region. One example is the mining landscape around Thiers cutlery (at Puy-de-Dôme) where polishers worked on river banks, and the nearby environment of blast furnaces. R. Murray Schafer presents an inventory of typical examples in *The Tuning of the World*.[4]

Drones produced by machines and industrial or construction equipment play a role in announcing the beginning of work for all workers. The start-up of ventilation equipment and compressors in a factory or of a cement mixer on a building site play a role of sound punctuation of working rhythms, even for people who do not directly depend on their functioning.[5] The figurative meaning of the French expression "*avoir (ou prendre) le bourdon*" (in English, "to be down"), describes someone who is filled with a haunting melancholic feeling. Often, the temporary or final cessation of an industry shifts the drone from the proper to the figurative meaning.

Drones that we are subjected to may sometimes result in additional drones, over which we keep a certain control. When coming home from work, for instance, we turn on the radio or the television and thus create a new drone (or background sound). This drone is used to signify one's private territory in contrast to other drones endured throughout the day. This practice not only reveals a way to reject imposed sound elements, but it also illustrates the pressing need to cover silence with a reassuring background ambience.[6] However, when the intensity of a background sound exceeds a certain threshold, mental activity can become paralyzed.[7]

Background sound is used everywhere in closed public spaces to mask disturbing noises, or to create an atmosphere that is considered more comfortable or more suited to encouraging consumption. More and more, these sounds are also being used in exterior locations. Electrophonic diffusion was first used in large stores, shopping malls, hotels, and restaurants. Later on, this practice spread to parking lots of shopping malls, public transportation, and even outside recreation spaces such as ski runs and beaches. Sound ambiences intervene when a certain density of people is reached, as if there is a desire to cover the drone of the crowd so as to avoid individual perception. Sound ambiences are also used in claustrophobic spaces, such as elevators and cable cars, to create an alternative to eventual anxiety.

Languages such as Corsican, Sardinian, and Sicilian allow the utterance of phonetic drones through proper configurations and repartitions of consonants and vowels. In the field of verbal creation, alliteration can produce a drone effect – also used in holorime verses (rhymes that sound the same but are written differently) – with an obsessive resonance.

PSYCHOLOGY AND PHYSIOLOGY OF PERCEPTION

In many sound cultures, there is a connection between the low frequencies and danger, sadness, or melancholy. This is well illustrated by the Western European knell, but also by many warning signals, for example, bells and foghorns, that require broad propagation and therefore must use low frequencies, thus inducing a feeling of fatality.

Drones that are heard constantly (fluorescent tubes, mechanical ventilation, refrigerating equipment, high voltage lines in the countryside) are all aligned on the frequency (and harmonics) of the electrical network (50Hz in Europe, 60Hz in North America). When we ask someone to sing a note spontaneously, the pitch often corresponds to a harmonic of the electrical network frequency. The evolution of lighting techniques, the amelioration of the quality (notably acoustic) of household appliances, and the wider use of low voltage rather than high voltage lead us to believe that this phenomenon will diminish with time.

Some drones are so integrated into our perceptive habits that any modification of their characteristics results in confusion. For instance, the replacement of the burner in a central heating boiler can result in complaints if its sound spectrum is different, even if it is actually less noisy in terms of dB (A). Figure 5 illustrates a comparison of the frequency distribution of the burners in two central heating boilers. When a listener becomes accustomed to a sound of a certain spectrum, this sound will be easier to ignore than a sound of the same type that may be even quieter. This new sound requires a listening adaptation before it is integrated into the familiar soundscape.

In the physiological domain, there is tinnitus – a drone or ringing sound that originates within the ear.

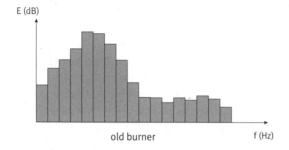 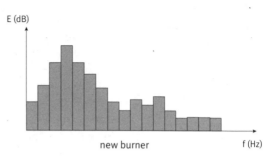

old burner   f (Hz)   new burner   f (Hz)

Both children and adults use a form of linguistic drone: grumbling and mumbling. The general intent of grumbling is to mask the intelligibility of a message in the low frequencies when the speaker does not want to be understood. Mumbling is the oral expression of an intense introverted activity. (Napoleon's grumbling was famous and frightened new secretaries responsible for correspondence!)

Figure 5
Graphic comparison of the frequency distribution of burners in two central heating boilers.

MUSICAL AESTHETICS

On a musical level, the drone may be a consequence of the instruments used, the construction of the music, or the tradition of interpretation. On an organ, for instance, the drone pipes, generally made of wood, are blocked so that they produce a frequency twice as low as that of the same open pipe. Some instruments have a fixed drone: on a hurdy-gurdy or a Hardanger fiddle, it is produced on one or more extra strings; on a bagpipe it is produced by one or more drone pipes. In early treatises, the lowest string on a guitar or a violin was sometimes referred to as the bourdon. The name bourdon is also given to the lowest partial of tower bells.[8] The unique drone on a Jew's harp is produced by the rich variety of overtones in the sound.

In musical composition, a sustained bass note, or a group of low-pitched notes repeated in cycles, can create a drone effect. A note, either in the bass or elsewhere in the texture, that is sustained over several measures is called a pedal point. The term comes from the organ, on which the player can hold a bass note with a foot on a pedal key while playing on the other two keyboards with the hands. A pedal point, most often the tonic or the dominant note, serves as a harmonic foundation; its steadiness creates harmonic tensions that are resolved with the return to the tonic chord. By extension, we also use the terms melodic, harmonic, or rhythmic pedal to describe a group of notes or a figure that is repeated over and over.[9]

In a basso continuo a keyboard instrument or a plucked string instrument (such as a lute or a theorbo) provides a harmonic background and sometimes a lower instrument (such as a cello or a bassoon) reinforces the bass line. The method of notation used for a basso continuo is called a "figured bass." The figured bass first appeared in the late sixteenth century, and consisted of simply a bass line from which the keyboard player would complete the harmony for the accompaniment. Gradually, a system of numbers and symbols was developed, indicating precise chords and harmonic progressions. The continuo musician created a full keyboard part from the single bass line, using the numbers and symbols as a guide.

In the instrumental practices of a wide variety of cultures, musicians develop a continuous layer of sound. With wind instruments, a drone can be continued incessantly by a number of musicians using a relay technique (for instance, Polynesian flute ensembles or Tibetan *dun chen* horns – telescopic instruments more than three metres long) or a continuous breathing technique called "circular breathing." Trance music (for example, that of the whirling dervish) also frequently involves a drone effect.[10] In classical Indian music, modal structures are called *rags*. During the prelude, or *alap*, the musician introduces the listener to the sound universe of the mode. The first appearance of each note is played in a way to emphasize its relation to the tonic degree, which is repeated constantly as a drone.[11]

Among instruments, the sole function of a "tampara" lute is to provide harmonic support for improvisation. Another example is the double *aulos* of ancient Greece, a reed instrument played with two hands that produced a shrill tone.

In vocal music, Gregorian chant clearly emerged from recitative technique of earlier centuries.[12] Monody and recitative are somewhat similar to a drone, notably in a form that integrates psalmody of spoken prayers. The term *recto tono* applied to Gregorian chant indicated that the singers recite on a single tone, thus confirming the importance accorded to stability and permanence.

Many music styles of the twentieth century, particularly those growing from popular traditions, use drone effects either in the strict sense of the use of a sustained bass note, or in a principle of harmonic repetition of a clearly identifiable sequence. Two fields of influence contributed to a renewal of the role of the drone in musical practices. First,

Western musicians and audiences were attracted to Oriental musical forms that preserved the drone in living tradition. Second, the appearance of electronic instruments (synthesizers, samplers, effect processors), the development of which is partly based on filtering sustained sounds, offer a new adventure to a principle that has existed for thousands of years.[13]

ARCHITECTURE AND URBANISM

The drone effect and the environment in which it appears are interdependent factors linked through acoustic propagation. The drone, usually associated with natural elements, with integrated equipment, or with an explicitly human activity, can also reveal the space in which it takes place. The whistling produced by wind passing through doors evokes the physical discomfort of old architecture and a certain climate of anguish often used in cinema. In a chimney, the wind has the more pleasant connotation of a welcoming comfort within a hostile milieu.

In modern habitations, the appearance of fluorescent tube lighting and controlled mechanical ventilation running day and night are the fruit of technical and sanitary "progress." These elements introduce sound continuums that we have judged less damaging than the benefits they bring.

For modern planners, the diffusion of background sound in spaces likely to be deserted, and thus frightening, often appears as an established principle. This form of drone appeared first in the halls of hotels and then in other buildings; it is now used in elevators and washrooms.

The first installations using drones that were not linked to a musical diffusion appeared in exterior spaces. The "soniferous gardens" of the 1970s amplified natural drones (wind, rain, flowing water).[14] Later on, planners wanted inhabitants to hear these arranged exterior spaces from inside their residences. An attempt to selectively decrease the insulation of façades was realized by means of an electroacoustic chain controlled by the inhabitants. This type of electronic porter makes it possible to hear these exterior drones, without the other urban drones.

PHYSICAL AND APPLIED ACOUSTICS

The drone effect can be visualized using frequency analysis. A diagram of energy in function of frequency will present an energy peak at the frequency of the drone. Note that in experimental conditions, this

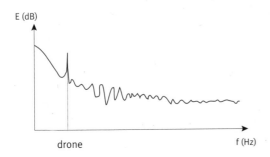

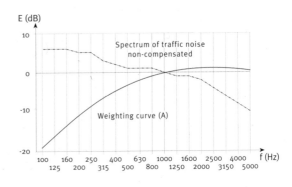

peak does not need to be large to be significant, because the ear is more sensitive to pure sounds than to complex sounds.

Road noise, which constitutes the most significant drone of the urban environment, has been the object of a normalized frequency template. When we superimpose this template to the weighting curve of the human ear (A), the predominance of low frequencies present in road noise can be seen clearly, indicating the great importance it can have in perception.

In Figure 7, the weighting curve (A) represents sound levels of each strip of frequencies, compensated so that each produces an equivalent sound sensation in the human ear. For example, the weighting at 125 Hz is –16 dB in relation to the 0 reference established at 1000 Hz. Therefore a 125 Hz sound with an intensity of 40 dB will be perceived at the same level as a 1000 Hz sound at 56 dB. Since road noise consists mainly of low frequency sounds, it seems particularly intense when we consider that the weighting curve of our perception emphasizes this range.

Dullness

The dullness (matité) effect is the effect to reverberation; absolute dullness implies total absence of reflected sound signals. A room is considered as "dull" when absorbent materials prevent diffusion of reflected waves. The absolute state of dullness is only realized in an anechoic chamber. In such a room, searching for total silence, composer John Cage, could still hear his own circulatory and nervous systems.

OPPOSITE EFFECT   reverberation

Echo, a phenomenon observed in nature, is the simple or multiple repetition of a sound emission, linked to a reflection in the space of diffusion. The term comes from Echo, a mythological nymph condemned to never speak first, but only repeat the last syllables of others. The psychogenetic signification of this effect was underlined as being possibly as important as the mirror stage.[1]

Echo

RELATED EFFECTS   delay, flutter echo, reverberation

A generic effect that includes the totality of sound occurrences that appear in a given context. Often coupled with another effect, emergence not only implies the irruption of a loud sound in a low-intensity context; it also characterizes the appearance of sounds that differ in pitch, timbre, or rhythm. The singuarity of the emergence effect is marked by the affirmation of a new sound rather than the modalities of its appearance, the latter being linked more closely to other effects with which it is combined.

Emergence

RELATED EFFECTS   niche, intrusion, incursion
OPPOSITE EFFECT   blurring

The feeling of being surrounded by a body of sound that has the capacity to create an autonomous whole, that predominates over other circumstantial features of the moment. The envelopment effect is sometimes applied to negative situations, but most often it provokes reactions comparable to bewitchment – staggering, delightful. The accomplishment of this effect is marked by enjoyment, with no need to question the origin of the sound: hence the clear difference between envelopment and ubiquity.

Envelopment

The erasure (*gommage*) effect refers to one or several sound elements in an audible ensemble that are deleted from perception or memory. This selective suppression is a fundamental effect of hearing. The majority of audible sounds in a day are heard without being listened to and are then forgotten.

Erasure

SYNONYMOUS EFFECT   asyndeton

Expansion

An electroacoustic effect. An expander increases a signal over a chosen threshold of intensity, avoiding the disappearance of faint signals in background noise, while increasing the energetic impact of the signal.

Fade

Disappearance of a sound through a progressive decrease in intensity. A fader is a potentiometer that controls volume. In English, the term "fade" also refers to the wave effect caused by fluctuating radio reception, particularly with short wave.

RELATED EFFECTS   decrescendo, blurring, wave

Feedback

Feedback is an application of the retroaction theory developed in the 1940s (by Norbert Wiener, Claude Shannon, and Warren Weaver) that makes it possible to anticipate a current action using past experience as a guide. Feedback, or re-injection, is particularly used in musical electroacoustics. As a controlled Larsen effect, feedback characterizes the sonic loop that occurs between the pickup of an electric guitar and the loudspeaker that amplifies it. The guitarist modulates the Larsen effect created by playing on the orientation of the instrument in relation to the speaker. Thus, the guitarist controls the re-injection of the signal over itself, producing a sustained sound that is often distorted.

RELATED EFFECTS   larsen, distortion, flange

Filtration

A reinforcing or weakening of specific frequencies of a sound. Modification of the spectral envelope can be caused by distortions linked to the mode of utterance, to the space of propagation, or to an electroacoustic filtration that makes it possible to act voluntarily on the response curve.

A filtration effect is perceived when the frequency of a sound that we are accustomed to or that we have heard previously is modified. Various features of the environment separating the source and listener can filter sound. These features may be related to sound propagation through air (atmosphere density, air movement created by wind, lapse rate), or to the presence of obstacles that block the direct reception of a signal (for instance, traffic insulation walls).

MATERIAL	FREQUENCIES (Hz)					
	125	250	500	1000	2000	4000
marble or glazed tile	0.01	0.01	0.01	0.01	0.02	0.02
concrete, unpainted	0.01	0.01	0.01	0.02	0.02	0.03
asphalt tile on concrete	0.02	0.03	0.03	0.03	0.03	0.02
heavy carpet on concrete	0.02	0.06	0.14	0.37	0.60	0.65
heavy carpet on felt	0.08	0.27	0.39	0.34	0.48	0.63
plate glass	0.18	0.06	0.04	0.03	0.02	0.02

Figure 8
Coefficients of absorption of certain construction materials. J.R. Pierce. *The Science of Musical Sound* (New York: Scientific American Library, 1983), 134.

The human hearing system, from the external ear to the brain, is itself a filtering process. Subjectivity also intervenes as a filter that is influenced by the degree of familiarity with sound situations, memory, and possible connotations.[1]

In sound production, filtration is a direct but subtle effect. It makes it possible to control a sonic context by introducing a discreet but well-defined signal without resorting to an increase in intensity. Through a certain economy of means, filtration is one sonic form of adaptation to a defined social and urban milieu.[2]

PHYSICAL AND APPLIED ACOUSTICS

In the journey from sound source to ear, only some of the emitted frequencies reach the listener. When sound is reflected off the ground and surrounding environment (walls, facades, etc.), it loses energy; hence, the original timbre and intensity are modified.[3] Also, high frequencies do not propagate as well as as low frequencies, nor do they travel as far.

Walls on which sounds are reflected have a coefficient of absorption that varies according to frequency, consequently they also act on filtration. A spectrum analyzer allows us to measure the coefficient of acoustical absorption of construction materials.

In applied acoustics, it is fundamental to understand the criteria of absorption of materials used as a means to avoid the poor diffusion of specific frequencies that sometimes appear in certain halls. One famous example is of the opening of the Philarmonic Hall at Lincoln Center, New York, July, 1962 (see Figure 9). The deficit of low frequencies in direct sound coming from the stage is clear. Relative energy

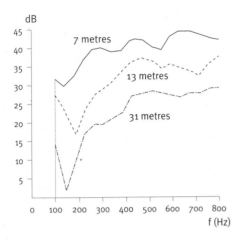

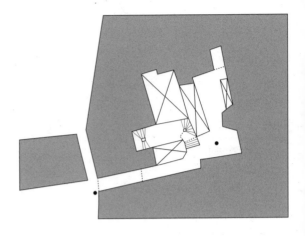

Figure 9 (left)
Relative energy of the
direct sound (in dB)
expressed as a function of
frequency at distances of 7,
13, and 31 metres from the
stage in the centre of the
pit. J.R. Pierce. *The Science
of Musical Sound* (New
York: Scientific American
Library, 1983), 144.

Figure 10 (right)
J.-F. Augoyard, et al.
*Sonorité, sociabilité,
urbanité*. CRESSON
research report, Grenoble,
1982, annexe 2.

of the direct sound (in dB) is expressed in function of frequency at distances of 7 metres, 13 metres, and 31 metres from the stage along the central section of the pit. We can observe a clear trough between 100 and 200 Hz that becomes even more pronounced as we move away from the stage. The shape of the hall, the arrangement of seats, and the surface deficit of the sound reflectors placed on the roof created a strong filtration of low frequencies.[4]

To discover which frequencies are amplified or absorbed, we can record a series of sound signals diffused in a test room through a microphone. The curve that appears on the analyst's screen expresses intensity on the Y-axis and frequency on the X-axis, allowing us to measure the specific level of each frequency diffused in a complex space.

ARCHITECTURE AND URBANISM

In terms of urban configuration, it is well-known that in courtyards of older houses, exterior sounds are attenuated without being particularly filtered. In nineteenth-century buildings, the thickness of the walls provided excellent insulation, so the filtration effect was mostly perceived at doorways. When moving from the inside to the outside of a building, the filter created by a carriage gate makes it possible to anticipate outside sounds; specific sonic qualities that may be more

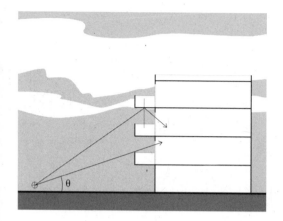

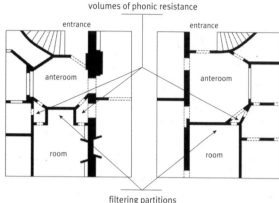

volumes of phonic resistance

entrance   entrance

anteroom   anteroom

room   room

filtering partitions

easily appreciable in direct listening are emphasized so that certain frequencies seem less aggressive to the ear.[5]

In large apartment blocks, sound filtered through the walls separating the units are most often perceived as an embarrassment. By a paradoxical effect of systematic thermic insulation, surveys show that this embarrassment is amplified when the insulation of windows is reinforced.[6]

In architecture, the nature of physical objects that filter sound waves offer numerous possible arrangements of sound environments. Balconies can constitute an initial filtration of exterior sounds, particularly when flowerpots and filled parapets form a screen.[7] Nineteenth-century architectural treatises describe how certain social relations were managed through filtration: "In the 'hôtels' of former centuries there was nothing unseemly about listening to valets' conversations through doors of antechambers or courts." In the nineteenth century, these sounds were not tolerated by home owners who preferred to have a quiet household ("une relation de dépendance sonore tranquille") with their children.[8]

This account of listening arrangements in relation to the evolution of morals is not unique. An analysis by architect César Daly (1864) also shows that apartment waiting rooms were used as sound converters.[9] In 1835, the architect Visconti installed small passageways between rooms and antechambers with one or two doors that acted as airlocks.[10] The

Figure 11 (left)
Filtration effect of balconies. L. Hamayon and C. Michel, *Guide d'acoustique pour la conception des bâtiments d'habitation* (under the supervision of the RAUC; Paris: Le Moniteur, 1982), p. 62.

Figure 12 (right)
Volumes of phonic resistence.

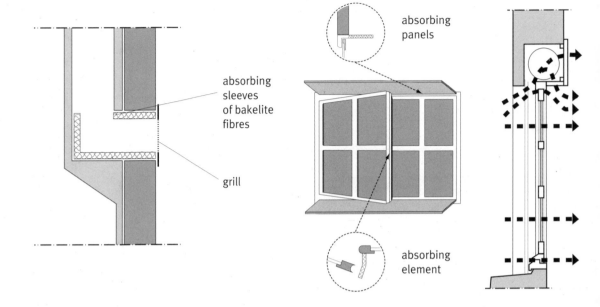

absorbing
panels

absorbing
sleeves
of bakelite
fibres

grill

absorbing
element

Figure 13 (left)
L. Hamayon and C. Michel,
*Guide d'acoustique pour la
conception des bâtiments
d'habitation* (under the
supervision of the RAUC;
Paris: Le Moniteur,
1982), 104.

Figure 14 (middle)
J. Pujolle. *La pratique de
l'isolation acoustique des
bâtiments d'habitation.*
(Paris: Le Moniteur,
1978), 240.

Figure 15 (right)
L. Hamayon and C. Michel,
*Guide d'acoustique pour la
conception des bâtiments
d'habitation* (under the
supervision of the RAUC;
Paris: Le Moniteur,
1982), 105.

distribution of walls and doors separating different spaces of a house thus serves the modes and customs of the time. The filtration effect also plays an active role in any arrangement linked to management and noise prevention.

SOCIOLOGY AND EVERYDAY CULTURE

It only takes filtration of a sound to make a listener feel that there is something strange or modified about a particular listening experience. An open window, for example, will provoke such a feeling for someone who thought it was closed. On this basis, we can assert that the constructed limits of a house function as a zone of spectral transformation and a filter playing on intensity.

We have become accustomed to contemporary sound filters, such as chimneys and mechanical ventilation pipes, and as newer filtration systems appear – for example, the sound from personal audio players present in streets, trains, and buses – they too become part of our daily habits.

In terms of sound production, practices of imitation involving the phonatory system are derived from listening to particular voices such as those of hostesses in airports or well-known singers. Who hasn't tried to sing like Louis Armstrong, to speak "like on T V," or to imitate the nasal voice of Donald Duck? In these cases, filtration is a creative act. Psychological surveys of children show that the more aware they are of their ability to imitate a large number of sounds, the more open they will become to sound creativity.[11] To acquire language, we use specific frequencies privileged by our mother tongue; other languages develop different frequency selections.[12] Therefore, we learn to speak through a spectrum that is related to our culture. To Westerners, the frequencies of some Asian languages may seem quite high-pitched and nasal.

The filtration effect, while participating in knowledge, can also be an instrument of power. After one of the colossi of Memnon (on the site of Thebes in Egypt) was reduced to a pile of rocks (probably due to an earthquake), a moan emerged from the pile every morning. This voice was attributed to an increase in the aura of the colossus that was still standing. Ancient acoustic mythology is founded on these paradigms. Similarly, filtration was used to ensure the power of the oracles. The human voice, speaking through a simple acoustic tube hidden in the pedestal of a statue, sounded so different in timbre that, to the listener, it seemed to come from another world.

Figure 16 (left)
Statue of Memnon.
R. Radau, *L'acoustique ou les phénomènes du son* (Paris: Hachette, 1880), 5.

Figure 17 (right)
R. Radau, *L'acoustique ou les phénomènes du son* (Paris: Hachette, 1880), 63.

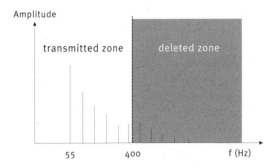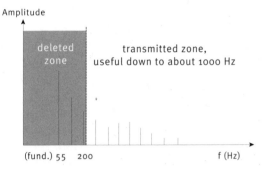

Figure 18 (left)
Filtration of high
frequencies: the pitch is
not modified, but the
timbre is unrecognizable.
Pierre Schaeffer, *Traité des
objets musicaux* (Paris:
Seuil, 1966), p. 190.

Figure 19 (right)
Filtration of low
frequencies: perception
is not modified. Pierre
Schaeffer, *Traité des objets
musicaux* (Paris: Seuil,
1966), p. 191.

Filtration is a major element in recording, amplification and diffusion of music. During the mixing stage, filtration makes it possible to correct flaws in a recording caused by the room or the instruments. In sound reproduction, filtration is a privileged medium for sound modification. Sound engineers can choose between different types of representation: they may decide to use direct acoustic listening as a reference, or they may choose to modify the sound in order to emphasize specific aspects, based either on their own judgment or on the subjectivity of the artist or the producer.

On a technical level, we can distinguish third-octaves, high-pass, low-pass, band-pass, and notch filters. A high-pass filter allows frequencies higher than the threshold to pass; a low-pass filter works the other way around. A band-pass filter allows only frequencies included in a determined range to go through. At the opposite extreme, a notch filter blocks a narrow band of frequencies.[13]

The voice coder (or "vocoder") is a system of speech distortion and recomposition that analyzes the signal emitted by a voice and separates the sounds of the vocal cords and the vocal duct. This technology makes it possible to totally transform the equilibrium of frequencies, bringing the voice closer to an instrumental sonority by disconnecting words from their meaning.

Before electronic instruments popularized these practices, Max Mathews, director of the Laboratory of Acoustics and Psychology of the Bell Group, was able to produce an "electronic violin" that could be mistaken for a conventional violin made of wood, and he could

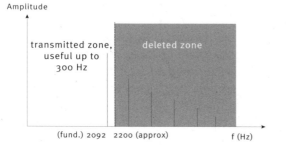

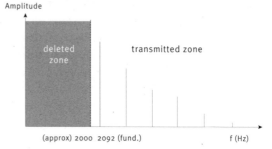

also produce brass sounds using a low-pass filter with a band raised in relation with intensity. The experience of the filtered piano reported by Pierre Schaeffer clearly illustrates these transformations of sound material by an action on its frequencies: "Let's take a low note on the piano (A 1, 55 Hz). With the help of a low-pass filter, we remove the high-frequency zone and the sound quickly becomes unusual, even unrecognizable; the ear appears to be sensitive to any amputation of the high frequencies. More precisely, if we filter starting at 400 Hz, the sound is unrecognizable [see Figure 18]. It can only be identified if we keep it intact up to around 1000 Hz. Let's perform the opposite manipulation: without touching high frequencies, we remove a part of the lows. We can actually remove more frequencies i, without a loss of sound identification. In fact, removal of the low frequencies up to 200 Hz keeps perception of the instrumental origin and pitch of the note intact [see Figure 19]. Let's take a very high note (C 7, 2092 Hz). We observe that the ear is not embarrassed by filtering frequencies higher than the fundamental, providing that we do not actually filter down to that fundamental frequency [see Figure 20]. However, filtration of the lows (just under the fundamental) profoundly modifies perception of timbre [see Figure 21]. In practice, we must keep a distance of about three octaves under the fundamental frequency to avoid transformation of the sound."[14]

With electronic filters we can convincingly modify the timbre of a musical instrument, and hence expand the limits of acoustic instruments. These filters have been used to develop a new instrumentation of "never before heard" sounds by generating artificial intermediary sounds between timbre families.[15]

Figure 20 (left)
Filtration of high frequencies: perception is not modified. Pierre Schaeffer, *Traité des objets musicaux* (Paris: Seuil, 1966), p. 235.

Figure 21 (right)
Filtration of low frequencies: the pitch is not modified, but the timbre is unrecognizable. Pierre Schaeffer, *Traité des objets musicaux* (Paris: Seuil, 1966), p. 236.

The materials used in construction appear as a significant example of filtration and its importance to qualitative perception. Studies of the capacity, by frequency, of a partition to filter air sounds are essential in research on sound recognition. As a general rule, materials are classified by an insulation rating that is globally expressed in dB(A). However, a study completed by the Centre scientifique et technique du bâtiment in Grenoble allows us to conclude that this common practice "does not take into account the capacity of a separation between apartments to allow or prevent the comprehension of conversations from one an apartment to another."[16] The study shows that in terms of sound recognition, the filtration effect acts much more on the qualitative level than on the quantitative one, even if it is correlated to a decrease in intensity.

Filtration can only be distinguished if the reference sound has been heard and memorized. One of the most common modes of perception of this effect involves comparison of "normal" listening with its modified version. When the first compact discs (CDs) appeared on the market, music lovers complained that the sound reproduction included too many high frequencies. The new character of this medium, produced by a modification of spectral distribution of recorded sound and an increased presence of high frequencies, shocked listeners accustomed to another balance and made the music seem too aggressive for them. Slowly the CD player made its way into everyday usage and its technical criteria became the new reference, while older sound reproduction systems appeared to be more muffled and old-fashioned.

Designers of speakers take into account differences of appreciation that exist between countries concerning ideal spectral balance. Many manufacturers have developed speakers with a strong high-frequency concentration for the Japanese market, and medium- to low-frequency predominance for the Western market.

Every technique used in the transmission of sound, and more specifically of voice, uses filtration to great effect. Radio, for instance, uses filtration to make the timbre of voices warmer. Other devices, such as the telephone, that are associated with a strict functionality can sometimes create a feeling of incompleteness, as Marcel Proust has illustrated. He describes a telephone conversation with his grandmother, and although distance separates Paris from Doncières, magically, the voice of his grandmother can be heard. At first seduced, Proust quickly begins to feel an overwhelming deception: the voice he recognizes

Figure 22
A telephone of the 1920s.
R. Radau, *L'acoustique ou les phénomènes du son*, 40.

seems lost because it is different from the voice he remembers, a feeling amplified by the physical distance of the speaking body.[17]

TEXTUAL AND MEDIA EXPRESSIONS

The filtration effect often provides an opportunity for novelists to describe the behaviour of characters who produce or listen to sounds in their environment.[18] For instance, in the writing of Stendhal, filtered sounds create an atmosphere of fullness.[19] The romantic hero in a Stendhal novel will find a medium for reverie. Similarly, sounds softened by the density of the air or reflected on walls of houses or across lakes, allow characters to flee the presence and proximity of people surrounding them. These sounds, which lead to melancholy and resignation, are associated with the character's affective fixation on himself or herself, independent of the listening pleasure the sounds may engender.

For Balzac, filtered sounds are the basis for shaping relations between individuals. They lead to and may even motivate hearing curiosity.[20] It is, however, in the work of Marcel Proust that we achieve a new step toward an understanding of the influence of filtration on individual sound behaviours. The narrator of *In Search of Lost Time* devotes particular attention to the family entourage. Sounds that penetrate through partitions of a room maintain contact, but this contact simultaneously throws the Proustian hero into a state of anxiety.[21] These examples demonstrate that listening through a filtering partition does indeed play a role in behaviour rules, self-reflection, and sonic modes – all practices that Michel Foucault called "practices of the self."[22]

RELATED EFFECT   distortion

Flange

A musical electroacoustic effect in which direct sound is combined with its own delayed reinjection, thus creating a phase effect. By balancing the intensity of reinjection and modulating the filtration of frequencies, it is possible to control the progressive evolution of a sound. This effect was developed in the 1960s from the simultaneous diffusion of the same message over two tape players and the possibilities of desynchronization that this innovation offered.

RELATED EFFECTS   phase, feedback

Flutter Echo

A flutter echo (*écho flottant*) is the localized emergence, in the reverberation of a room, of a specific frequency and its harmonics that remains stationary between two parallel and reflecting walls.

RELATED EFFECTS   echo, reverberation

Fuzz

A musical electroacoustic effect that is synonymous with distortion. Fuzz originally referred to the saturation of a tube amplifier that was pushed to its maximum; later the term was also used to refer to devices of the electrophonic chain that make it possible to obtain and control a similar sonic result. The "fuzz pedal" on an electric guitar allows the player to act specifically on the even harmonics of a sound.

RELATED EFFECT   distortion

Haas

An effect, described by Helmut Haas in 1951, that corresponds to a gap in perception between a direct wave and a reflected wave in order of one to thirty milliseconds. We now call this effect artificial reverberation.

RELATED EFFECTS   delay, reverberation

A musical electroacoustic effect. A *harmonizer* makes it possible to transpose a signal and mixes different pitches created. The chords obtained are often delayed to spatialize each element while making reproduction clearer.

Harmonization

A perceptive effect linked to the sporadic character of a sound source that irresistibly focalizes the listener's attention on the location of emission. When the source moves, the listener continues to follow it. This effect is often found in transmission through solids (for example a marble rolling on the floor upstairs).

Hyperlocalization

OPPOSITE EFFECTS   ubiquity, delocalization

A semiotic effect referring to a sound emission that is consciously produced according to a style of reference. Imitation implies the use of a cultural code that allows recognition of this style in the sound emission. Imitation is found as structure in the global shape of a sound utterance, and it works in a complex way; Imitation implies a sense of intention on the part of the emitter, and to be appropriately perceived, it also requires the listener's knowledge of the reference.

Imitation

Imitation is a semiotic effect because it re-represents particularly significant features of the style of reference.[1] This reference is characterized by a remarkable emission style, or a particular use of certain acoustic parameters that allow its recognition and its differentiation from other sources.

The actual perceptive experience of the sound producer is therefore directly involved in this effect. While the style of reference is presented as a sound element that can be physically evaluated, the imitation does not rely on pure and simple reproduction. The effect exists insofar as there is a reciprocal relationship between the sound element (style of reference) and its interpretation (perceptive and productive activity). Repetition, on the other hand, is closer to an instrumental form that has a mechanical character. Unlike imitation, which plays on sound qualities, the repetition effect is emphasized through the quantity of sequences or fragments reproduced.

As in all Western art since antiquity, sound aesthetics are based on the notion of imitation.[2] In music, painting, and many other art forms, imitation constitutes a common process in our culture. Thus, imitation can be found on many levels throughout the history of Western music. Many compositions imitate nature, human activities, or technical noises in a deliberate attempt to be descriptive.[3] Sometimes instrumentation also relates to the sound environment of the time.[4] Musical language can even mimic certain traits of evolution in the ambient sonic world: for example, the increase of low frequencies and intensity of rock music echoed – and then influenced – similar changes in the urban environment.[5]

The importance of imitation can be found in the co-penetration of musical cultures. Trân Van Khê[6] shows that acculturation of traditional music usually involves the following elements: the adoption of new musical instruments or modification of older ones (for instance electrification); the imitation of vocal and instrumental techniques (vocal vibrato); the adoption of some modalities of performance (for example, the creation of a choir); and the repetition of a foreign musical language (for example, harmonization of traditional modal music). Although imitation refers to a multiform and general process, it can be approached subtly as a sonic effect. For instance, sound designers can force the listener to remember a particular sound necessary to illustrate a situation. Sound designers use aural memory to authenticate sounds that they have been asked to reproduce or create for a film, a radio program, or a television show.[7] The use of a style of reference therefore implies a phonomnesis effect – that is, the capacity to imagine a sound or remember it without necessarily hearing it.

To judge the pertinence of this type of sonic effect, and other effects with a semantic dominance in general, it seems necessary to put the Platonic mode of apprehension of the world into perspective. This mode assumes a referent – a model to imitate or a unit to repeat. Of course this feature is essential, but in many cases (particularly in the application of these effects), the process of imitation or repetition takes precedence over the reference to the original. It is more important to repeat than to repeat *something*. *Mimesis* then appears as one explication among others; imitation cannot be reduced to a simple copy of the model.

MUSICAL AESTHETICS

Imitation challenges the very definition of musical aesthetics. To have imitation in music, the field of musical aesthetics must be extended to include the production of natural sounds, notably those of certain birds. As François-Bernard Mâche writes: "the music of animals and man [sic] cannot be entirely defined in terms of communication ... It is a case where stylistic analysis, whatever its methods, must take over from the studies of acoustic zoology."[8]

We are lead to discover musical aesthetics beyond human experiences. If imitation can be easily observed in this part of the animal world, it is probably due to the important role played by the stylistic element. In François-Bernard Mâche's bird example, we have a zero degree of the imitation effect, for which the imitation of a true style does not necessarily imply a conscious intention from the imitator.

Two other borderline cases involving the relation between sound emission and style of reference may help in specifying the limits of this effect. Sometimes a sound emission can merge with the style of reference to the extent that the listener can no longer differentiate between them. For example, during the credits of the movie *'Round Midnight* by Bertrand Tavernier, the singer's voice is so similar to the trumpet that it is difficult to immediately distinguish either one. Here imitation plays on timbre. This unambiguous referral to Miles Davis' classical interpretation of *'Round Midnight* locates the audience in a specific context, using the mark of an epoch and the style of jazz.

The second case plays on a gap between sound emission and style of reference. Such is the case with a sound excerpt described in the work of Daniel De Coppet and Hugo Zemp concerning the origin of bamboo music.[9] The music of the 'Are'Are is stylized to the extent that it is impossible to recognize the bird song if we do not know the background of this music beforehand. It is through knowledge of mythology, rather than an actual sound culture, that the semantic effect is produced. The semiotic effect thus supposes the recognition of the style of reference and the capacity to distinguish it from its imitation. When the style of a reference concerns a specific musical work or composer (for example, Stanley Kubrick's imitation of the scherzo movement of Beethoven's Symphony no. 9 in the soundtrack for the film *A Clockwork Orange*, 1971), the imitation effect implies a previous musical culture. Sometimes only the initiated will have access to this effect and be able to understand the allusion. In all perceived cases, there is nonetheless an immediate change in sound climate, a modification in the quality of listening.[10] Our attention will focus more on sound as a signifier of the style of reference; a distance in relation to musical production is established.

The development of certain electroacoustic effects is based on the reproduction of imitation with a degree of variation. For instance, the wha-wha pedal on an electric guitar produces modulated sounds in a way that evokes the sonority of muted trumpets used mostly in jazz. In their most popularized developments, synthesizers, and more recently samplers, allow access to stereotypical sounds of existing instruments.[11] In other cultures, the voice itself may imitate an instrument such as the flute. A rapid shift from an instrumental to a vocal sound can create an astonishing continuity of timbre.[12]

SOCIOLOGY AND EVERYDAY CULTURE

In everyday life, vocal utterances are particularly favourable to the imitation effect. Children's games offer numerous examples. Children use a wide range of noise, onomatopoeia, and vocal sounds that represent cars, trains, and other sound-producing objects to give a sense of reality to their miniature toys. The reference sound is that produced by the real machine; the imitation consists of the selection and reproduction of some of its rhythmic and timbral characteristics.[13] The imaginary movement of a machine is accompanied by informative complements. Imitation thus involves a double representation: iconic and indicative.[14] The play function of imitation favours the collective dimension of the game through the articulation of imaginary activity and real activity of individuals.

The voice can also be subtly modulated to account for specific sonic effects produced by diverse techniques of sound transmission and reproduction, including voices for telephone, radio, and television. When modulated, the voice can reproduce distortion and filtration characteristic of certain channels of communication. Combined with a chain effect, an initial imitation may induce others, leading to a collective and self-sustained experience.[15]

The importance of modern communication techniques and mass media favours the emergence of new sound practices, including the imitation effect. A significant part of teenagers' conversations seems to be filled with onomatopoeia, interjection, and deictic words borrowed from the media or cartoons.[16] The same is true of other elements of sound culture. For example, each regional accent imposes its mark on the inhabitants of the area. Newcomers may express their own territory by voluntarily adopting it or not. In any case, the imitation effect activates a feeling of belonging to a group or collective and fulfills a function of socio-cultural cohesion and integration.

Child development, and more particularly the learning of language, offers numerous examples of imitation effects.[17] Before reproducing the content of a message, a baby imitates the essential style of the language. The semiotic effect is immediate as the baby tries to signify his or her intentions. Research on language learning by children in different cultures supports the same conclusion.[18] The prattling of French, Arab, and Cantonese children is differentiated by contrasts in intonation, rhythm, intensity, and frequency. The imitation effect thus plays a role in the socialization of a child. It is a fundamental process through which the acquisition of modes of phonation and perception are accomplished.

Imitation plays an essential role not only in language learning but also in the oral transmission of traditional music. One important psychophysiological mechanism at work is the reciprocity between heard sounds and produced sounds.[19] On a secondary level, this reciprocity intervenes in the hearing of sound produced by the emitter himself or herself. Vocal imitation supposes control over sound emission, which is accomplished using this self-listening process. This theory was developed by Alfred Tomatis who put it into practice in the treatment of problems with phonation.[20]

TEXTUAL AND MEDIA EXPRESSIONS

A singer who imitates a trumpet is not necessarily trying to accomplish a strict reproduction of a sound element; rather, he or she is trying to find a basic sound image that will give the illusion of the presence of the instrument. The same goes for sound designers who create special effect sounds. They excel in finding and selecting the primary principal of each sound through analytical listening. To reconstitute a complex sound situation, sound designers will classify sounds hierarchically, in function of the obtainable degree of realism. Dramaturgical effects can also be created in fictional works: the particular sound of an object (for instance, the noise of wind or the blast of an explosion) can be tightly coordinated with the progression of the narrative.

Strict realism is not always the most effective solution; in fact, the quest for the essential components of a "scene" is often best fulfilled by unexpected sounds. Sound designers accomplish a particular role in the sound domain: to create an effect, to introduce a modification of perception, whether subtle or spectacular.

In a different domain, a style of speech used by one politician some-times leads to real imitation by other politicians. On a more general level, a leader's sphere of influence can be measured through his or her ability to relate a reference style to the surroundings.[21] In terms of media communication, professional imitators choose well-known tar-gets, on whom they confer a surplus of popularity, in a dialectic of the model and the copy, the real and the false.

ARCHITECTURE AND URBANISM

The development of the soniferous garden appears to use sonic pro-cesses directly related to the imitation effect.[22] The introduction of "natural" sounds (of water, leaves, or wind) in an urban milieu pro-duces a particular semiotic effect. The sound designer attempts to create, or at least signify, a countryside atmosphere in the city.[23]

Certain architectural constructions represent an attempt to revive characteristics of a past era. Often, the result is not an imitation but rather the creation of a neo-ancient style that ignores numerous varia-tions imposed by time on physical marks of these eras, as well as the perspective we have upon them.[24] Consequently, it is unlikely that a pastiche or neo-ancient style faithfully reproduces sound qualities of the site of reference.

PHYSICAL AND APPLIED ACOUSTICS

Since the imitation effect is, above all, defined as a semiotic effect, our interest in it focuses principally on sound as a carrier of meaning, a signifier. It is hard to apply acoustic definitions. For instance, research-ers encountered difficulties when dealing with speech recognition.[25] It is extremely difficult to physically express what we call "style." In fact, every acoustic parameter, including rhythm and timbre, can partici-pate in the formation of a particular style of reference.

RELATED EFFECT   quotation

Immersion

The dominance of a sonic micromilieu that takes precedence over a distant or secondary perceptive field. While it is possible that the sub-merged sound element may be heard temporarily, the dominant effect is primarily perceived as positioned above the background sound. Natural contexts offer numerous examples of this effect: listening to snatches of conversation, a song near the sea, or the music of a carousel on a beach. In this specific context, the murmur of the waves creates a permanent setting that gives the impression of containing a primary sonic situation. The urban drone can also create this structure of a permanent framework over which individual sonic activities are superimposed.

Incursion

The incursion (*irruption*) effect refers to an unexpected sound event that modifies the climate of a moment and the behaviour of a listener in a characteristic way. This effect is to time as the intrusion effect is to space. Even with its generalized use, a telephone ring remains an aggressive sound event for many people, not so much because of its timbre, which has softened over time, but because of its unexpected and imperious character: a call not only interrupts the present state, but also dictates new behaviour for a given moment.

RELATED EFFECT   intrusion

Intrusion

A psychomotor effect linked to territoriality. The inopportune presence of a sound or group of sounds inside a protected territory creates a feeling of violation of that space, particularly when it occurs in the private sphere. In some pathological states, voices and sounds are perceived as illegitimate intrusions in the body.[1]

RELATED EFFECT   incursion

Larsen

This effect, named for the Danish researcher Absalon Larsen (1871–1957) who described it in 1871, refers to the loop established in an electrophonic chain between a microphone and loudspeakers that constantly reinjects the signal over itself. If nothing interrupts this cycle, the speakers may blow out when they are used at a high intensity.

RELATED EFFECT   feedback

Limitation

An electroacoustic effect: a limiter prevents a sound signal from exceeding a specified threshold of intensity, thus reducing its most intense sections and peaks. A limiter is also used to augment the average dynamic of a signal.

RELATED EFFECT   compression

Lombard

The greater the intensity of a sound environment, the greater the level of vigilance, regardless of the intelligibility of the signal. In industry, we have observed an increase in attentiveness linked to an increase in the sound level, even when it reaches or exceeds the legal threshold of 85 dB(A) at which occupational hearing loss may start to appear.

Mask

The mask (*masque*) effect refers to the presence of a sound that partially or completely masks another sound because of its intensity or the distribution of its frequencies. This effect, easily demonstrated acoustically, also implies a subjective psychophysiological reaction: the masking sound can be judged as either parasitic or favourable, depending on whether or not the masked sound is perceived as pleasant.

PHYSICAL AND APPLIED ACOUSTICS

In acoustics, the masking effect describes the existence of a sound (the masking sound) that, based on its intensity or frequency, partially or completely erases the perception of another sound (the masked sound) at a lower level. The masking effect can be proactive, simultaneous, or retroactive depending on whether the masking sound precedes, accompanies, or follows the masked sound.[1]

The masking effect reduces the intensity of the masked sound. Extremely ubiquitous, it is found in diverse configurations. Pure and complex sounds can mask other pure or complex sounds; language can also be masked by sounds, noises, or other language sounds. With regard to sounds of other languages, the transmitted message is diminished in audibility.

It is difficult to describe precisely what creates a mask unless there are noticeable differences in levels. Nevertheless, numerous studies on the subject allow us to make some global observations. When the masking is caused by spectral distribution, the effect will be obtained easily if the masking sound is located in frequencies close to those of the masked sound. Inversely, a sound with a precise frequency will be

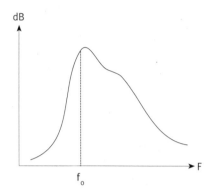

dB

f_0

F

OCTAVES CENTRE FREQUENCY (Hz)	125	250	500	1000	2000	4000
Mask effect	2	6	9	12	13	13

Figure 23 (left)
Mask effect produced by a sound of a frequency centered at f_0.

Figure 24 (right)
Measure of a mask effect due to traffic noise. P. Bar and B. Loye, *Bruit et formes urbaines* (Paris: Cetur, 1981)

difficult to mask using a complex sound consisting of a broad range of frequencies; the sound with a precise frequency will usually stand out enough to be perceived.[2] However, a masking sound with a given frequency can mask sounds with higher frequencies; thus, the masking effect is asymmetrical. This asymmetry varies in direct relation to the amplitude of the masking sound. In Figure 23, note the slope difference between the two sections of the curve (frequencies lower than f_0 and higher than f_0) in a mask effect produced by a sound of a frequency centered at f_0.

In acoustics, when the pressure levels of two sounds differ by more than 10 dB, it is generally accepted that only the loudest sound is perceived. This rule is particularly applied to the addition of sound levels, and allows us to calculate a resulting level within an acceptable margin of error. However, this rule cannot be applied to all sounds. For some types of sound (for example, traffic noise), it may be appropriate to analyze the difference in levels as well as the frequency of the masked sound. The mask effect represents the increase in level that must be given to a masked sound to be perceived as clearly as when listened to in silence. For example, a sound with a frequency centred around 500 Hz at 60 dB will be perceived if the broad band mask sound does not exceed 69 dB (A). Figure 24 gives indications of the differences between the pressure levels of both sounds. At these levels, audibility is almost impossible.

Above a certain sound level, masking reaches extremes that prevent any communication. For example, airport technicians are submerged in the noise of airplanes and wear protective helmets, so they must

Figure 25
Two pure sounds with
an identical amplitude,
de-phased by 180°
(1/2 cycle)

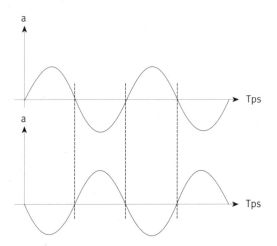

Figure 25
Two pure sounds with
an identical amplitude,
de-phased by 180°
(1/2 cycle)

communicate using arm gestures. At the stock exchange, the hubbub of exchange orders creates an intense sound level that requires everyone to shout louder than their neighbours. Important communications are accomplished with hand gestures.

In recent years, numerous masking processes using cancellation (also known as active acoustic absorption) have been developed. These methods, efficient in specific conditions, allow us to significantly reduce the level of sound through the emission of an analogous but out of phase sound (delayed in time). The addition of both acoustic amplitudes creates phase cancellation, therefore producing a quieter sound. Figure 25 illustrates a simple example of two pure sounds with an identical amplitude, de-phased by 180° (1/2 cycle). In this case their sum is theoretically nil.

ARCHITECTURE AND URBANISM

In this domain, the two types of masking defined above – parasitic and favourable – may induce opposite values. Depending on the context, the same type of sound will produce different subjective perceptions. For instance, fountains create a broadband mask that makes it possible to avoid the perception of the urban drone in a city space. In a quiet location, the same fountain might appear as parasitic. For example, if a fountain is installed in the centre of a closed, paved square, inhabitants may quickly request that it be removed because of sound disruption.

There is a fundamental difference between the transitional listening of passersby and the permanent listening of inhabitants.

The urban drone is an important mask, often perceived favourably as a "cover" against neighbouring sounds. The construction of acoustic screens, which suppress the traffic mask, often reveals these sounds and may paradoxically increase dissatisfaction of inhabitants in the protected buildings. The urban drone also exerts an influence on the level of insulation judged to be necessary between apartments. A building situated in an urban area with large boulevards might be considered to have good sound insulation from neighbouring apartments; the insulation of that same building would be considered poor in a sub-urban region and extremely poor in a rural zone. Acoustic regulations concerning sound insulation between apartments have been conceived for urban zones and collective apartments. These standards are always inadequate for quiet sites and semi-detached houses.

In large department stores, the lack of acoustic comfort due to architectural weaknesses is covered by background music that masks the strictly functional sound events of the building by creating a constant, minimal sound ambience. The favourable or parasitic connotation of this acoustic masking depends on the particular layout and the status of the listener (customer, salesperson, or cashier). Background music used as an acoustic mask in department stores, waiting rooms, or work environments is often seen as sonic makeup. In industrial buildings that accommodate activities generating low frequencies, it is often difficult to maintain discussions or hear everyday sounds. Signals indicating particular dangers, such as the signals for forklifts or swing bridges, must be louder and use precise, audible frequencies.

In other cases sound masking is used to make up for inadequate acoustic insulation (for instance, music in the waiting rooms of doctors or lawyers), or to cover reverberation that is too obvious.[3] Open concept offices use masking produced by the general brouhaha, and complement it with acoustic screens that allow conversations in close spaces (from each side of a desk, for instance) without the distraction of conversations from a nearby office.[4] Finally, sound masking may prevent embarrassment linked to uncontrolled bodily sounds.[5]

PSYCHOLOGY AND PHYSIOLOGY OF PERCEPTION

The notion of masking is observed in several studies on perception, particularly those focused on transmission (telephone, radio). In this domain, two ideas are distinguished: audibility, which is purely acous-

PERTURBING LEVEL OF INTELLIGIBILITY	MAXIMUM DISTANCE FOR NORMAL VOICE	MAXIMUM DISTANCE FOR LOUD VOICE
35 dB	4 m	15 m
40 dB	2 m	10 m
45 dB	1.5 m	6 m
50 dB	1 m	4 m
55 dB	0.5 m	2 m
60 dB	0.25 m	1 m
65 dB	0.20 m	0.75 m
70 dB	–	0.50 m
75 dB	–	0.25 m

Figure 26
Estimation of distances of intelligibility, according to the norm NF S 31.047. Distances are measured from the mouth of the speaker to the ear of the listener.

tic, measurable, and repetitive, and intelligibility, which implies motivation of the individual and considers his or her subjectivity.

Research on the human voice suggests different ratings of speech intelligibility. The French norm NF 31.047 uses the SIL 4 (Speech Interference Level), an average measured on four levels, corresponding to octave bands situated at 500, 1000, 2000 and 4000 Hz. This norm predicts, for instance, that with a perturbing background of 45 dB, a normal voice will be correctly heard at 1.50 metres and a raised voice, at 6 metres.

These studies can be used to analyze the possible range of a student's comprehension in a classroom, but they cannot account for the listener's degree of motivation. Everyday experience demonstrates that with a certain degree of attention, people are able to: listen to a message through a loud background; reconstitute a spoken message of which a section was missed, if the subject discussed is familiar (reconstitution of words or portions of sentences);[6] and complement listening with sight using lip-reading. The masking effect often results in a lack of attention to sound signals coming from different sources. Generally, only the most intense sound is perceived. But if we can manage to reduce this sound or put its predominance into perspective, the other sound components reappear more clearly, sometimes at the risk of creating an unexpected embarrassment or annoyance.[7] Each sonic situation is a complex whole; modification of one component leads to redefinition of a new sound balance and results in a new situation.

Finally, we must mention tinnitus, a hearing perception that is not linked to external stimuli (such as ringing or buzzing), which creates an internal masking that can prevent reception of external sound messages. This phenomenon is permanent in certain pathologies.

SOCIOLOGY AND EVERYDAY CULTURE

The Mask

An analogy to visual masks allows us to extend the study of acoustic masking by emphasizing its anthropological ambiguity. Linked to ritual, the mask hides something or leads one to believe something else; sometimes it hides only to better reveal.[8] We therefore propose the following sonic equivalents to some of the significant social and psychological functions of the mask.

> *The mask and death*: Is background sound (radio or television) not a mask covering the "acoustic nothingness" within which the individual and his or her solitude is immersed?[9]
>
> *The mask and the party*: During carnivals and large town festivals, streets become places of temporary thundering acoustic masking. The usual separation of functions and familiar categorizations of spaces are blurred. The sonic shock created by festivities favours a temporary, playful redistribution of social roles.[10]
>
> *The mask and power*: The shouting of soldiers during battle masks the screams and moans of the wounded, and also gives a form of stimulation to the battle.
>
> *The mask and distinction*: A mask creates isolation and distinction (sacral, or at least social) for the person who wears it. Sonic forms of masking seem to have an analogous function. Thus, the teenagers' search for maximal noise in motorcycles or discotheques may cement a group into a truly isolated sound world. In this category, we also find the oversized sonic ritual of rock shows. Sound power has always been the attribute of the chief; by masking other modalities of sound expression, an unambiguous hierarchy is established.[11]

Masks and Interpersonal Relations in a Settlement

An analysis of acoustic proxemy makes the essential role played by masking visible.[12] Analysis of acoustic limits reveals the importance of the phenomena of overlap (and therefore masking) between sound spaces. Evidently, it appears that an acoustic over-insulation does not represent a systematic answer to neighbouring problems. Even in a theoretically ideal phonic situation, certain noises will always be undesirable.[13] Thus, it is important to maintain a number of sound spaces (some of them used as masks) that allow one to recognize private and public spaces through differentiation.

In a crowd (cocktail party, market, train station hall), diverse sounds act as masks that force the speaker-listener duo to move closer to one another. One can only shift between conversations by moving across the space.[14] Through shouting, children use this effect to isolate themselves from the universe that surrounds them. Also, the modified mufflers on teenagers' mopeds and young adults' cars testify to the sound marking of space and signs of identity affirmation.

We should not consider masking as something that is necessarily undesirable, disruptive, or parasitic. On the contrary, a "parasite" mask functions as a key instrument with which communicating actors (emitters or receptors) can reinforce, inflect, focus, or diversify interpersonal exchanges. Consciously or not, masking is used in a number of situations: to communicate (open-plan offices, children's games); to eliminate a part of what is communicated (in a situation where everything that is said does not necessarily need to be heard, and where the most interesting part is not necessarily what is perfectly audible);[15] to seem as though we are communicating (in situations of conflict, where exchanges become unilateral or are accomplished through a third party); to indicate a refusal to communicate (teenagers' personal stereos or mopeds).[16]

MUSICAL AESTHETICS

Instrumentation plays on masking by using relative characteristics of intensities, timbres and pitch. For example, the cessation of an instrument or group of instruments may paradoxically reveal their previous contribution. Masked key changes can be used to move from one harmonic model to another; the new key, while already present in the transition, is not immediately perceived.[17]

In choral music, vocal play can be considered as a series of masks involving either separate vocal ranges or voices and instruments. In the choral section of Beethoven's Symphony no. 9 (the fourth movement), the chorus often masks the orchestra.[18] In the orchestra itself, the evolution of timbral equilibrium between instruments often proceeds through masking.[19] The latter sometimes determines the rules of the chosen form: for example, in some musical forms a soloist interacts with the accompaniment throughout the piece.

Certain types of computer music have a rich content (based on the juxtaposition of repeated overlapping short grains) that creates a masking effect through the rapid succession of sound impressions.[20] This type of effect, although slightly different from the original definition, is no less important; it corresponds to a phenomenon in which an overdose of sound information leads to a scrambling of possible recognition. Masking can also be a source of stress, created by a lack of control in the face of an information overdose. This idea will be further explored below.

TEXTUAL AND MEDIA EXPRESSIONS

Many authors have observed the masking effect and evoked it in their works. Émile Zola's splendid sonic descriptions of the Halles (*Le ventre de Paris / The Belly of Paris*) and a large store (*Au bonheur des dames / The Ladies' Paradise*), portray the background, murmuring, and shouts of these places. Before Zola, Boileau (in *Les embarras de Paris*)[21] and Juvenal also described the murmur of the city. Viollet-le-Duc, noting differences between the city and the countryside, observed their acoustic consequences, and more precisely the importance of masking.[22]

In media expression, we find what has already been developed in computer music. Media sound has become ubiquitous to the extent that it produces a cerebral sound masking that renders reception of particular sound emissions completely relative. Cinema often uses mediated sound masking, particularly so-called "urban" music such as jazz and rock, to re-create the climate of urban places. Although a radio may be turned on all day (at home or at work, voluntary or not), some people may not perceive or understand news that is broadcast several times a day. A good example of masking in cinema can be found in Bob Fosse's film *Cabaret* (1972). Feeling the need to exteriorize herself, the heroine screams in a tunnel while a train is passing.

Metamorphosis

A perceptive effect describing the unstable and changing relations between elements of a sound ensemble. A classic figure of rhetoric, metamorphosis characterizes the instability present in structural relations that link parts of an ensemble and the resulting possibility to switch elementary components of a totality, so it is perceived as being in perpetual transition. The ancient Greek word *metabolos* (in French "*métabole*") means that which is variable – something that is in metamorphosis. Our considered modification here involves the relation between elements that compose the sound environment, defined as addition and superimposition of multiple sources heard simultaneously.

PSYCHOLOGY AND PHYSIOLOGY OF PERCEPTION

The metamorphosis effect has two fundamental criteria: the instability of the structure perceived in time; and the distinctiveness of the parts or ensemble in a given sound composition. One essential characteristic of a sound environment is its variation over time, expressed by the instability of intensities and succession of sound events. In the urban environment, this perpetual movement may be detected by any sound measurement device – whose needle is rarely still. The difficulty of distinguishing events that are close in time but differ in duration is an essential factor leading to the metamorphosis of a sound milieu; for example, it is difficult for the ear to distinguish elements in a series of fast-paced short-duration events.

The human ear has the ability to perceive multiple sounds as an entity but at the same time, its discriminating capability allows us to listen selectively.[1] To illustrate this process, we might say that some elements are emphasized as "figures" while others remain as "background."[2] If this ability is limited by differences in intensity, this handicap is partially foiled by selective attention: the most intense sound, for instance, is not de facto considered as a "figure."

Someone in a situation of concrete perception, selects figures – sounds on which the subject will focus. It appears that the process implied is a synecdoche (considering a part as a whole). Some sound situations create metamorphosis when everything merges, when no particular sound emerges from a composite ensemble. Such situations may give rise to a perceptive instability between figure and background.

But the notion of figure and background should be used with caution in the sonic domain.[3] The reference to visual perception in which these relations were studied (in particular, the hypotheses from Gestalt theory) seems difficult to apply to the sonic field because of the transposition that this process involves. How does background sound act on figures? Does it distort the figure laid over it, as in some visual representations? In any case, even if the distinction seems to work, the impact of background sound on figures, and reciprocally of figures on the background must be taken into account.[4]

Apart from the relativity that exists between the sound figure and the background, metamorphosis can be expressed through a phenomenon in which each individual sound is indistinguishable and therefore is perceived as a whole. This is what Yannis Xenakis illustrates in his approach to the sound "field," in which a large number of events produce a "single composite and live sound." In the face of such a message, the listener cannot hear events separately but only as a whole.[5] The perception of the ensemble blurs clear distinction of elements; inversely, the effort of discrimination can lead to a loss of global perception.

"Ordinary" listening may sometimes be metamorphic. An absence of perceptive intention allows each sound to be heard simultaneously, with no preference or particular attention. This type of listening is known as floating or disconnected, but can also be called contemplative (in which case, nothing emerging from the environment is perceived as "a single sound").

The metamorphosis effect is related to the ubiquity effect in the sense that it prevents the listener from fixing his or her attention on a particular sound source. But it differs from the ubiquity effect in that each sound is well localized. In a way, metamorphosis is to time as presence is to space: the former is characterized by permanent instability of referents in time (incessant inversion of the relation between sound figure and background); the latter is characterized by an instability of referents in space (incessant questioning of the position of sound sources). From a semantic point of view, in the metamorphosis effect sounds are impersonal (hence the feeling of euphoria), while in the ubiquity effect, they are anonymous (hence a feeling of discomfort).

PHYSICAL AND APPLIED ACOUSTICS

The metamorphosis effect is favoured by any similarity existing at the level of each sound criterion: timbre, pitch, intensity, rhythm, localization. When these parameters are clearly distinct for different and simultaneous sound events, there is a smaller risk of perceptive ambiguity.[6] A fairly continuous sound situation with no marked rhythms favours metamorphosis perception. This is the case with the ambiance of a shopping centre. Another aspect to consider is the propagation qualities of the space in which sounds are emitted: when attacks are not precise, or when reverberation creates an overlapping of sounds, the environment will easily shift to metamorphosis because of deletion of the signs of emergence (attack/release) of singular sound objects.

If timbre and intensity make it possible to distinguish sounds, rhythms are also fundamental elements of location: in a given rhythmical structure (for example, a printing press) the ear can follow one by one and focus on a number of combined movements while identifying the temporal figures of each. Finally, note that the term "background noise" has a precise signification in acoustics based on the stability of a sound situation.[7]

ARCHITECTURE AND URBANISM

Large reverberant spaces intended for the reception of the public often possess acoustic conditions favourable to the metamorphosis effect. The mixing of singular sources is almost always predominant, with none dominating the composition. In a reverberant field, distant sounds are less distinct from each other. Based on impulsive responses of a listening room, criteria of quality are usually determined by the relation between the sound energy of the initial milliseconds and the whole of the energy. This relation must be as high as possible to avoid the metamorphosis effect. This is achieved through the control of early sound reflections (based on the geometric dimension of the space).

Train station halls and shopping centres are characteristic examples: both are reverberant locations in which a density of population produces a multiplicity of sound sources. With the hammering of footsteps at rush hour, pedestrian streets also present a sonic homogeneity that favours the metamorphosis effect. Finally, the same effect can occur when we listen from an elevated location because the height "equalizes" sound sources (in terms of frequencies, by a loss in the high range) and makes the distinction of isolated sound shapes more difficult. The simple experiment of listening to outside sounds from the top of a high building provides an excellent illustration of the function of height in the transformation of a sound ambiance through different perceptions.

SOCIOLOGY AND EVERYDAY CULTURE

Humans model their own metamorphic sound milieus:[8] Vocal metamorphoses – for instance an animated market or a similar situation in which many people speak simultaneously – are clear illustrations. In such communicational sound spaces, transmission of a message is not particularly easy: people try to differentiate themselves from their interlocutors, yet each individual is a producer of this imposing background.

Density and crowds create metamorphosis sound milieus; this is even more so when the space favours diffuse propagation. Undoubtedly, the metamorphosis is culturally significant in the perception of a collective sound environment. The atmosphere of mass or density is sometimes a corollary to this, in the sense that it refers to a co-production of the sound milieu in which everyone creates sound randomly and the totality of the sounds produced can be perceived as an emanation of society. It is here that public space finds its sonic paradigm: what was previously a figure becomes a background,[9] each taking the place of the other in turn.

MUSICAL AESTHETICS

In music, the autonomy of a chord in relation to the notes that constitute it lies precisely in our ability to globalize separate sound elements. A number of sounds emitted simultaneously become one, but it is still possible to select each one in perceptive analysis. This faculty works in consonance, as well as in discord. It is on this ambivalence that Pierre Schaeffer bases his distinction between the physical and sensitive components of sound perception.[10]

In 1890, Karl Stumpf devoted himself to the study of an impression of unity or multiplicity produced by listening to two simultaneous sounds. After a listening exercise, subjects were asked whether what they heard was composed of one or many sounds. The degree of fusion of a chord can be measured by the percentage of errors made by the group: when more errors were made, the chord produced an impression of unity.[11] The metamorphosis effect is accomplished in orchestral compositions in which it is difficult to distinguish basic units of global sound matter. It is also the case when figure-elements quickly follow each other.[12] In music, a perceptive weakening favours the accomplishment of a metamorphosis effect, whether due to cultural factors (musical acculturation or civilization differential) or to factors linked to physical acoustics. The progression of melodic or rhythmic structure leads the listener into a perceptive instability or meta-stability characteristic of metamorphosis.

| COMPLEMENTARY EFFECTS | ubiquity, synecdoche |
| RELATED EFFECT | cocktail |

Mixing

A compenetration of different and simultaneous sound sources. In everyday life, the mixing effect implies close levels of intensity between the diverse sounds present. The effect can be found particularly in spaces of transition that are likely to receive sound ambiences originating in different places. The concurrence of sounds can create indecision; the listener is in a paradoxical situation in which it is difficult to choose what he or she wants to hear. In the context of a musical or cinematographic production, mixing refers to an operation in which all the various instruments, sounds, and noises are mixed together, each attributed a specific intensity, equalization, and effect. Once this intervention is accomplished, the "mixed" sound is placed on a final, generally stereophonic, medium called a master.

Narrowing

The narrowing (*rétrécissement*) effect refers to a sensation that the space is shrinking, which is felt by an emitter listening to the return of a sent message. Characteristic of a reverberating milieu, this spatial perception effect is located in a continuum delimited by reverberation and dullness.

OPPOSITE EFFECT   dilation

Niche

An occurrence of a sound emission at the moment that is the most favourable and that offers a particularly well-adapted place for its expression. The niche (*créneau*) effect, which merges a sound message and a sound context, is one of the key instruments of sound action, and can operate on any component of sound: intensity, pitch, timbre, rhythm.

The context must be considered in two dimensions: spatial and temporal. Spatial context involves opportunities linked to the configuration of the milieu. In most metro stations in Paris, for instance, the elliptical shape of the roof allows two speakers located at the two foci of this ellipse (one on each side of the rails) to hear each other perfectly through the ambient din. The factual or temporal context involves opportunities linked to the moment, the temporality of the occurrence. For example, a pedestrian walking on a street with dense traffic will take advantage of a moment of relative calmness in the stream of cars to hail someone on the other side of the street.

The niche effect, which uses the specific acoustic properties of a given environment, is an instrument of sound action that produces a perceptive physiological effect (emission/reception) through the transmission of a signal. Consequently, the niche implies the existence of two extremes in a chain of sound propagation: one (or several) actors and one (or several) listeners, generally different from each other.

The niche effect plays on the defining parameters of physical acoustics: duration, intensity, pitch, timbre, and rhythm. In general, a sound actor uses many components of the same sound message simultaneously, practising multiple niches. For increased clarity, however, the following analysis artificially separates the elements that characterize a sound.

The *intensity niche* allows a sound actor to exploit an acoustic situation during which a temporary diminution of ambient sound makes it possible to emit a signal toward the listener,[1] either at a level lower than he or she would need to produce at another moment (economy of means),[2] or at a level that is the maximum of his or her acoustic possibilities at that moment, and that would not have been perceived in the preceding context. In these two cases, the aim is an increase in the signal-to-noise ratio.

The *pitch niche* uses spectral distribution of sound. In a particular sound context, a sound actor emits a signal in a range of frequencies such that there is enough sound emerging to be perceived and to capture attention. The street singer or vendor "places" his or her voice in a tonality that allows an optimal output (minimal vocal fatigue for maximum audibility). In large blocks, mothers who call their children through open windows shout in high notes, thus taking advantage of the directionality of these frequencies. In a classroom, as the ambient noise increases, the teacher forces his or her voice to a higher pitch until he or she becomes tired, providing a brutal illustration of the phenomenon. A definite drop in intensity and frequency follows, forcing students to fall silent to understand the teacher. Note that the emitted signal does not have to be louder than the ambient noise; it is actually the difference in pitch that allows the sound to be clearly audible. In this case, the aim is also an increase in the signal-to-noise ratio, but in a precise range of frequencies.

The *timbre niche* is found principally in the domain of music, when the entry of a new instrument creates a variation in sound material in which the elements of melody, rhythm, and harmony are relatively

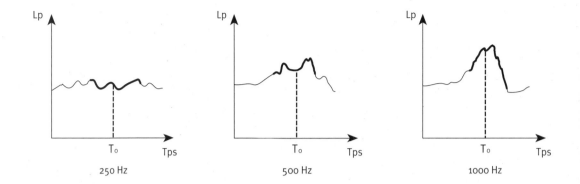

Figure 27
Pitch niche (dynamic level):
increasing of intensity in
function of the average
frequency.

stable.[3] In this case, acoustic intensity is less important; the niche effect is a result of an emerging sound colour. Differences in timbre can favour niches of reversed intensity. In certain situations, a signal will be transmitted more effectively by taking advantage of a high-intensity ambient sound. If we want to have a discreet conversation, it is better to wait for sonic cover to quietly exchange information. For example, students in a classroom can talk to each other more easily without being noticed by the teacher in moments of high sound intensity, such as when outside traffic noise becomes highly audible in the room. The niche effect is thus paradoxically merged with the masking effect.

The *rhythmic niche*, often observed in professional milieus and collective settlements,[4] concerns the emergence of signals linked to chronology. A sound actor who is conscious of the rhythmical punctuation present in an environment will choose the appropriate niche to emit a message, either by making it stand out against the context to individualize it, or by superimposing it to merge with the general ambience.

Sound identification uses a combined form of the niche effect, as in the case of alarm signals (intensity, pitch, rhythm) or pinball machines (intensity, pitch, timbre, rhythm).

ARCHITECTURE AND URBANISM

Here we consider the spatial dimension of the niche effect. The niche is sometimes based on temporal divisions to reinforce sound perception, but for the sound actor it is more a consideration of acoustic propagation in relation to the space in which the effect takes place.

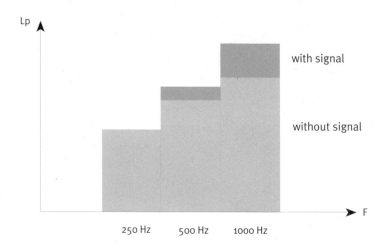

Figure 28
Pitch niche (spectral level).

Lp

with signal

without signal

F

250 Hz   500 Hz   1000 Hz

The acoustic features of a space directly intervene in the creation of a niche effect. In a given place, the choice of a favourable zone of sound emission in relation to the intended receiver is essential. Combinations of reflections created by the shapes and materials of walls and ceilings reinforce the transmission of sound toward the listener. The choice of reflective courtyards, such as those constructed with large concrete blocks in the 1950s, as gathering places corresponds to the selection of a privileged and strategic point of sound propagation, an important tool for distant communication. Reverberation is often used to amplify, to favour, or simply to allow realization of the sound contact.

When a location has a particular geometry, the sound actor will stand at a point that optimizes propagation and the intended effect. This position, sometimes influenced by an intuitive experimentation that is not necessarily based on rational thought, creates a sound transmission that will be more or less favourable either to maintaining the maximal level for the longest period of time (as under an urban arcade or in a subway corridor), or to the best acoustical progress of sound waves by focalization or reinforcement. Street singers and musicians always place themselves at points where the architecture will reinforce the propagation of their music: in a large square, facing a reflecting wall (for example, the Palais des Papes square in Avignon), at the meeting point of several galleries, or in subway corridors.

Figure 29

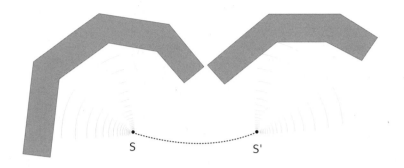

A well-known example of focalization or reinforcement of sound waves comes from the Bible: "Again [Jesus] began to teach by the lakeside, but such a huge crowd gathered around him that he got into a boat on the lake and sat there. The people were all along the shore, at the water's edge" (*The Jerusalem Bible*, Mark IV:1). Here the hill of the bank is used as a terrace, and the sea as a reflector. Another example is a very high (8 to 12 levels) double crique construction in the Arlequin district in Grenoble. When a local association wanted to send out a message about a collection in aid of a house fire victim, the speaker placed himself successively at the points S and S′ (see Figure 29), while orienting his megaphone in each indicated direction, thus assuring the best propagation of sound.

PSYCHOLOGY AND PHYSIOLOGY OF PERCEPTION

By definition, the niche effect only exists if it is actually perceived. But while the niche effect is psychomotor (it is always a sound action), the emergence effect that generally results from it is, on the other hand, of an essentially receptive nature. Consequently emergence is considered as a related effect.

The niche effect, while containing all the information that needs to be transmitted, can be of short duration. It is often used as a warning, to capture the attention of the listener and provoke selective listening. For example, on a construction site or in a very noisy place, someone can try to call another person by calling out the name during a drop of intensity. A whistle serves the same function, but it will call not only the person targeted but everyone present. The listener can then continue to decrypt the sound message in accordance with the modalities of a niche effect, even if it does not emerge from the ambient noise.

According to François-Bernard Mâche, the utterances of animals make excellent use of the positive or negative qualities of the biotope; examples include the piercing call of marsh birds (emitted in an absorbing milieu), or the rich broad modulations of birds in a tropical forest (a reverberating milieu).[5]

SOCIOLOGY AND EVERYDAY CULTURE

The niche effect is a great instrument for social communication. When children place themselves in a particularly reverberant zone of a school courtyard, they reinforce the solidarity and dynamics of their interpersonal relations; at the same time, since they share their games with the surrounding children, they feel a great jubilation to know that they are being heard while hearing themselves. In the same way, a baby who begins to cry after being calmed expresses his or her will to exist and to be recognized by others.

Drummed and whistled languages are complex instruments of cultural communication in timbre and pitch niches that facilitate comprehension over great distances.[6] They are excellent examples of adaptation to specific sound environments. Finally, the rhythmic niche of boiler makers hitting metal in a workshop is typical of a specialized socio-cultural practice. The impact of each hammer must be heard independently of other impacts in order to verify the quality of the blow; hence there is a very clear, almost organized rhythmical alternation.[7]

MUSICAL AESTHETICS

In musical composition, instrumental or vocal emergence is the specific object of a composer's work. By determining the entry and ending of each note, the composer precisely organizes the totality of the work as a series of occurrences while maintaining a balance between event and context. For composers, the niche effect is not an adaptation to an external sound situation but a style effect placed in the music for a future audience.[8]

On the other hand, during performance, the niche effect exists for musicians and singers. One of the principal functions of the conductor is to manage the niches that give access and clarity to the multiple mixed voices. In musical practices linked to improvisation, a dialectical situation is created in which a musician plays when a niche is presented or when its entry has been prepared. Jazz, particularly free jazz, bases progression on the synthesis that arises from the dialogue between the instruments.[9]

With amateur musicians, who may use a common score, a real "struggle" may take place when musicians use intensity and timbre to make themselves heard, or to hear themselves. This situation occurs more frequently when the acoustics of the particular rehearsal hall are not sympathetic to the type of music being played.[10]

TEXTUAL AND MEDIA EXPRESSIONS

Radios commonly use the niche effect by taking advantage of the musical introduction of songs. Timed in advance, the duration of this "intro" allows the host to present the piece while its sound level is automatically lowered (auto-fade or voice-over systems). The presenter ends the comment at the exact moment that the singer enters. Such a modality of diffusion develops as an instituted effect in which songs follow each other seamlessly with speech layered over. Trailers for many radio and television shows and films use the niche effect in a similar way.

RELATED INDUCTOR EFFECT	cut out
RELATED INDUCED EFFECTS	irruption, chain, emergence
COMPLEMENTARY EFFECT	synecdoche
OPPOSITE EFFECTS	drone, masking

Noise-Gate

A musical electroacoustic effect that involves the establishment of a threshold of intensity, literally a "gate," below which the signal is automatically cut. The cutting rate of the sound intervenes directly on attack and release, making it possible to retain only the most dynamic impact of a sound.

Perdition

A semantic effect that might also be called the "dereliction" or "loss." This effect is linked to a feeling of perdition, in the double sense of a soul in distress and the dissipation of a sound motif. The sound seems to be emitted for nothing, for everyone to hear but requiring no answer. It is a sound without destination, absurd in the etymological sense; its entire expression is simply a sign of powerlessness. Often characteristic of extreme suffering constituted principally of tears and moans, this effect accompanies life situations that are violent or painful.

An acoustic effect that desynchronizes the cycles of two simultaneous emissions of a sound signal. Phasing is in fact a de-phasing effect: two cycles that are identical but begin at two different points of their curves, or two cycles that begin together but do not have the same duration.

RELATED EFFECT   chorus

This effect refers to a sound that is imagined but not actually heard. Phonomnesis (*phonomnèse*) is a mental activity that involves internal listening: examples include recalling to memory sounds linked to a situation, or creating sound textures in the context of composition.

Close to anamnesis because of its inner, rather than sonic, nature, the phonomnesis effect consists of imagining a sound. In this case, it is not a sound situation that stimulates a memory process, but rather a lived situation that engenders an inner and silent listening. There is no strict causality between the lived and the imagined sound. The latter can be expressed in multiple ways: the remembered tune, the mental elaboration of that same melody interpreted by instruments of different timbres, the invention of sound images, musical or not.

Phonomnesis remains one of the great methods of composition, since a theme – before it is actually played, whistled, or hummed – is a mental act. Some musicians cannot compose without actually listening, but others elaborate their works in exterior silence.

At a less professional level, the creation of a sound from memory, in the absence of a sound signal, is quite widespread. The simple reading of a description of the sonic universe is enough to stimulate the imagination, which will evoke an ensemble of sounds necessary for the veracity of the story. Listening is an act that can sometimes be totally mental and silent. Graphic sonic effects, characteristic of strip cartoons and real phonomnesic indicators, transpose the sonic world into the visual field, in which the occupied surface and the shapes of letters combine to illustrate or invent the intended effect.[1]

Unlike anamnesis, which often occurs in an unexpected way, the imagination of sound characterized by the phonomnese effect is most often voluntary. But in some cases, when a sound situation stimulates an evocation that engenders the resurgence of a sound phrasing, there can be a shift from one to the other. If the latter appears only in fragments, phonomnesis takes over to recompose it. When we look for a theme, for instance, we may find that it is easier to reconstitute it by re-imagining the timbre of the original instrument than by some abstract means. Between melody, harmony, rhythm, and timbre, a means of organization draws itself up to re-grasp a sound structure.

RELATED EFFECTS   anamnesis, anticipation

Phonotonie

This effect, also called the phonotonic effect, characterizes the feeling of euphoria provoked by a sound perception. Sometimes it induces a behaviour directly, such as a renewed activity, a collective movement, or a reflex gesture. Musical listening often plays this functional role in individual or collective work.

Print-Through

Print-through (*empreinte*), or pre-echo, is an electromagnetic effect that characterizes the reproduction, during storage, of a dynamic signal on the near turns of a magnetic tape on a reel. Listening to the traced turns preceding the original signal creates an effect of anticipated echo. To avoid the disadvantages of this effect, magnetic tapes are usually wound onto the reel backwards for storage; this will not avoid the print-through phenomenon, but it does place the effect after the signal, making its presence more discreet.

Quotation

The emergence, in a contemporary context, of a sound fragment for which the semantic reference is confirmed. Contrary to imitation, quotation (*citation*) is a textual reprise and does not imply distance. It is easily identifiable in musical and verbal contexts, but it can also be observed in the everyday sound environment. This semiotic effect can range from homage to burlesque. The quotation effect will always be accomplished in the scope of a known cultural product; it is conventional and is recognized in a given culture. This excerpt of another expression is accompanied by signs that make it possible to recognize the original source. While the imitation effect stimulates a style of reference, the quotation effect is located at the level of the content, the sonic figure. Reprise, another related effect, differs from quotation because it repeats a sound motif in an identical way. Reprise implies a self-reference, since the pattern that is re-played has its founding in the work itself.

RELATED EFFECTS   imitation, reprise

In music, a rallentando (rall.) marking instructs the musician to re-duce the speed, or tempo, of the performance. and Ritardando (rit. or ritard.), another Italian marking has the same meaning. Ritenuto (rit. or riten.) indicates a more sudden or extreme slowing of the tempo.

Rallentando

OPPOSITE EFFECT   accelerando

Release (*traînage*) is an acoustic effect that describes the residual dura-tion of a sound, from its cessation until silence or background noise. This period of time is variable, depending on sounds and spaces of propagation, and includes diverse modes of progressive disappearance of a signal through different frequency zones. In electroacoustics, we also speak of release as the duration of the extinction of a sound once its emission has stopped. Release should not be confused with rever-beration, which concerns the diffusion space.

Release

A continuation of a sound that is no longer heard. After the extinc-tion of both emission and propagation, the sound gives the impres-sion of remaining "in the ear." Remanence is neither an anamnesis (sounds heard in the present that evoke the past), nor a phonomnesis (remembered sound without physical listening). Remanence does not involve deep and early memory. It is simply the mnestic trace of barely subsided sound signals. This effect is often used in music: the perma-nence of a tonal or modal climate of reference; the impression of hear-ing a continuous drone; or melismatic movements that make an absent sound virtually present.

Remanence

PSYCHOLOGY AND PHYSIOLOGY OF PERCEPTION

The remanence effect is a perception of a sound for which the object and cause has just disappeared. There is no actual creation of a per-ceived sound, as in a hallucinatory process.[1] However, this effect comes clearly under the domain of sensorial illusion. Short-term memory intervenes through the reproduction and transformation of the prime sonic cause.[2] Whether this is during sleep, awakening, tiredness due to hyperacousia, or a "surrender," in a very cultivated and mastered way, to musical listening, it is always a matter of para-conscious percep-tion. The sound that produces a remanence effect intercepts in us what escapes from the state of waking. More or less short in duration, this effect does not allow the intrusion of a memory, and it is not reminiscence even if it involves pleasure or displeasure surreptitiously. Awakened by the buzzing of a mosquito, we still hear it, even though it has momentarily disappeared from our perceptive field. The displeasure thus created probably participates in remanence.

To illustrate this effect, we could cite the numerous furtive experiences of subjective and often recurrent sound perceptions that we are conscious of after the event: the musical air that wakes us up and follows us all day long; the melody suggested by a few notes at the cinema that we prolong naturally without knowing it; or sounds heard during sleeping. Dream or reality, we cannot know without an exterior witness. Pierre Sansot tells the story of a rugby touch judge who would hear the "booings" and "cheers" of the public only the day after, and who collected in a way a "treasure of hearing" – exemplary remanence![3]

It all happens as if the sound really existed. The remanence effect borders on hallucination, and we may wonder if the strange and fascinating sound perceptions that accompany the consumption of LSD, heroin, or other drugs are purely hallucinatory, or if they simply amplify and transform sound, music, and voices through an excessive remanence.

From a strictly physiological perspective, remanence does not initially differ from tinnitus. Yet a ringing in the ear is more insistent, more significant. This ringing, often symptomatic of a deficiency in the hearing system, manifests itself independently of any sound cause. It persists, regularly or intermittently, over months and even years. This is far from the remanence effect. In fact, with the exception of certain specific situations (for instance, tinnitus that appears after a rock show where the intensity was very high, but quickly disappears), the comparison is exhausted.

MUSICAL AESTHETICS

R. Murray Schafer used the remanence effect extensively as an element of composition in a number of soundscapes he recorded. The fog horns and buoys that start the sequence of the entrance into Vancouver harbour provoke a remanence so strong that the rest of the soundscape remains profoundly impregnated.[4]

Tonality is an extremely systematic application of this imperceptible sliding between physical resonance and mnestic traces. In fact, to define the tonality of performance of a piece is to give it a scope of reference, a secure basis, a system of reference that locates it from beginning to end. Accidentals and complementary tonalities can be understood only through their reference to the original tonality. Fundamental notes of the chosen tone (tonic, mediant, dominant) become encrusted in listening and remain present as harmonic structures, even though partially muted.

In traditional modal music, the physical absence of a tone of reference or a sustained note does not prevent remanence. Paradoxically, their absence makes them even more present, because they possess the power to give the tone. While waiting for the return of the basic tone, opposites meet, and the remanence effect is transformed into an anticipation effect, the pre-perception of the return of the tone of reference or the drone.[5]

SOCIOLOGY AND EVERYDAY CULTURE

Certain sounds and certain climates favour remanences typical of urban society: ambiances related to a drone, the passing of a train or plane, noise from industrial machines. Silences can even, paradoxically, be "heard" against the noise that appears. When they occur abruptly, cut out effects often create a feeling of uncertainty of sound perception. This may happen through the silence that supercedes the uproar of large boulevards as we leave them to turn down a protected alley, or through the stopping of a pneumatic drill. Events that are marked on the sonic level leave mnestic traces and resonate "in the ear," including, for example, rhythmic slogans of demonstrators, or screams from a fight taking place in a quiet district. These remarkable sound events, which inspire memory, lead initially to a strong remanence and may subsequently provoke a phonomnesis effect.

PHYSICAL AND APPLIED ACOUSTICS

The remanence effect is a purely subjective phenomenon. We cannot observe it and measure it from an acoustic point of view. On the other hand, remarkable conditions may favour and even systematically provoke remanence. For example, a prolonged vibration can lead to so strong an enrichment of the prime sonic cause that it will render the cause unrecognizable and will favour a remanence effect.

Sudden variations of intensity also facilitate the emergence of this effect.[6] This is the case for the interruption of a sound in a relatively quiet and stable sonic climate: think of sounds such as a siren or a scream that interrupt our activities or rouse us from torpor. Such sounds have a tendency to continue after the original sound level is reinstalled.

Reverberation and release effects may favour remanence. Singing and music performed in a strongly reverberating location such as a cathedral persist "in the ear." When the fade of a sound is extended in time to reach silence, the moment of its cut is not pronounced. It is through the uncertainty of listening linked to this sudden diminishment of the sound signal, that remanence overtakes perception.[7] Sound levels characterized by a distinct frequency may also become encrusted in the ear as a remanence: sound from fluorescent tubes, buzzing of insects and, more generally, any permanent or interrupted drone.

TEXTUAL AND MEDIA EXPRESSIONS

If different musical forms play on the remanence effect, we can consider that this effect, strictly defined, intervenes in any attempt at sound communication. From a stylistic point of view, alliterations are favourable to a remanence effect, whether the reading is silent or not.[8] Advertising music is intended to be easily memorized. Thus, when the first notes of a known commercial jingle are diffused, they act as an immediate invitation to prolong the musical phrase. Sonic hammering, in all its forms, directly induces the remanence effect.

RELATED EFFECTS anamnesis, drone

OPPOSITE EFFECTS anticipation, erasure

Repetition

A reappearance of similar sound occurrences. The repetition effect works on two levels: on one hand, it marks phenomena of automatism involving subjection; on the other hand, it characterizes phenomena of return, reprise, and enrichment by accumulation.

In a strict sense, the repetition effect is defined as the feeling of reappearance of sound occurrences perceived as identical. Repetition – being both a composition effect (an object that we listen to) and a psychomotor effect (an object that we produce) – does not describe a priori a particular sonic content. Any sound or group of sounds, simple or complex, may be concerned. Also, the repetition effect determines neither a specific system of perception nor a typical psychomotor context: multiple attitudes may be related to it.

Two series of examples conveniently illustrate this effect. The first series includes the multiple sound events of everyday life that are reproduced at variable intervals, and that may belong to the domain of habits and customs or to more exceptional, or even unusual contexts. They create both the rhythmic framework of everyday life, punctuated by repetitions that remain unnoticed, and unusual occurrences that the repetition reveals as extraordinary. Everyday life does not choose between valorization and trivialization, and so allows us to illustrate a first structural bipolarity of the repetition.

The second series emanates from musical composition itself, the temporal specificity of which resides precisely in the voluntary organization of the "return" (in the large sense of the word), symbolized by the reprise.[1] It consists in the re-presentation, after a development, of an initial theme. The reprise as such is thus a repetition effect (even if the reproduced sound unit has a certain duration). There is a great temptation to oppose reprise and repetition: the former refers to an active dimension including active listening, the consciousness of the event, and a strong positivity; the latter refers to the automatic, mechanical, and even obsessive character, a quantitative accumulation at the limit of the consciousness and a certain sonic poverty.

But on the strict level of acoustic physics, it is quite difficult to accurately distribute sound events between these two polarities. For example, the hammer on a building site and that used in a concert of *musique concrete* are often made of the same metal; the water drop that obstinately hits the sink may be a torture, but can also become a rhythmical support for dance by playing the role of a metronome; the ring of a telephone can be dramatic or full of hope; some choruses are unbearable, others lively. In the perceptive field, repetition cannot be separated from its context, whether we consider it as an effect of composition or as a psychomotor effect.

Apart from any sonic or contextual articulation, the repetition effect involves a second, potential and permanent, structural bipolarity.[2] The negative pole reveals a submission to an external event, the repetition of which is passively suffered by the listener. This sound phenomenon can be either conscious (and can then become obsessional), or it can punctuates the unfolding of life, unnoticed through habits (revealing its mechanical or automatic dimension).

By opposition, the positive pole emphasizes the revival, the new beginning of something.[3] The repetition/reprise then appears as a re-appropriation, a recovering. To restate is to produce a difference (contrary to the negative pole for which to repeat is to reproduce the same). In a chronological evolution, the positive pole perceives the repetition as a return that includes, as valorization, the time that separates the sound motifs. The reprise integrates and condenses all that lead to it, like a recurrence, a sedimentation.[4]

Examples and evidences oscillate in the tension between these two poles.[5] But from one pole to the other, we must never forget the principal dimension of this effect: it is repetition that confers importance to unforeseen sound occurrences. Emergence happens by isochronia, through a periodical return of the motif or the sound, thus defining a configuration. In this sense, repetition partakes in the temporal organization of complex sounds. It is a generic category in the group of "chronophonic" effects.

SOCIOLOGY AND EVERYDAY CULTURE

In a sociological perspective and in everyday life, the repetition effect is characterized as a phenomenon of communication, or at least as an element of information. It often serves as a link between different actors, either to establish a contact and confirm it, or to ensure a precise transmission. When interlocutor B, for instance, repeats the sound signal that he or she just heard from emitter A, contact is clearly established. Everyday life multiplies situations in which the repetition effect can be observed in a certain social mobility where connections are made through the sonic field.[6] The rhythmic unfolding of everyday life goes through a familiar/singular determination, of which the primary material is the repetition effect. In a known space, sounds are located and expected, even unconsciously, and are part of the usual setting which, once forgotten, clears the present consciousness. At the same time, each sound is barely recognized as such, as if we measured in a fraction of a second its capacity to emerge from the common framework. In fact, repetition often appears in the form of a "mechanical" echo that does not require reflection.[7]

The role of repetition in education exceeds the single scope of a sonic effect, but we must emphasize its importance, particularly in reference to learning languages, in which certain exercises use the automatic part of repetition exclusively (for example, drills in which a small group of words is repeated until the pronunciation is correct). Imitation and repetition thus conjugate, in a general psychological attitude. Musical teaching, of course, also integrates this aspect of the control of progress by the ear in the instrumental gesture. Linked to a dragging effect, applause is based on a simple repetition. It clearly shows movement from individual response to the collective, since on the sonic level, it does not matter what somebody claps on; what matters is adhesion to common movement. In fact, in a sequence of applause, despite the isochronic phases clapped, repetition tends to disappear into a homogeneous mass that approaches the wave effect.

At very different scales, the repetition effect is one of the tools for locating periodicities of the world. From a ticking clock to a factory siren, an angelus bell, a train whistling at regular hours, or bird songs heard every morning and evening – an indefinite variety of sounds constantly define time.[8] Many soundmarks assume a synchronization role for action: by presenting a sequence composed of a regular repetition, a soundmark proposes (or imposes) a formal framework to activity. Soldiers who parade with the sound of drums are a typical example, but dances linked to music, diverse ringing sounds (door, telephone, alarm) that induce an answer, and many other situations proceed with the same regularization of the social "chronophony" and "synchrophony" that accompany all activities of human beings.

PSYCHOLOGY AND PHYSIOLOGY OF PERCEPTION

The repetition effect is a constitutive factor of our perception of the world. Our consciousness of bodily rhythms such as breathing or heartbeats makes us aware of the necessity of repetition that also marks physiological time. Bodily cycles that have sound manifestations punctuate biological life by expressing its formal framework and thereby establishing a perception of reference.[9]

In the perceptive domain, the principal role of repetition seems to reside in the offering of marks for the organization of a complex message. Take the example of a functioning printing press. For the uninitiated, a press seems to produce only an indistinct uproar. Extended listening makes it possible to appreciate the details of the sound material and its components. On the level of the global mechanism first perceived, refined listening reveals diverse rhythmic cycles of different durations, the movement of cams that establish temporary delays before a new cycle begins. After a moment, attention may flit from one sound element to another, or encompass the whole of the sound field; it can penetrate a sonic logic that at first may seem inaccessible. In this example, it is the decoding of repetition effects that makes the message comprehensible. The ear tries to capture the units reproduced over a given frequency, and classify them according to temporality, as if it were positioning their occurrences and locations on a grid. If we move around the press, certain elements will stand out at specific locations, masking those heard before or revealing others. For the professional printer, listening provides a permanent indication of current good functioning of the press: any sonic discontinuity in the complex game of multi-repetitions, the precise roles of which are clearly understood, acts as an indicator.[10]

When the repetition effect is produced by isolated or less complex sound objects, the process of accumulation becomes essential. Deleuze and Guattari developed the hypothesis of an active ethnology.[11] There would be no pre-existing territory marked by an animal – only a trace or an olfactory, sonic, or visual expression – thus the territory would be defined by the perception of others. The repetitive whistling of a bird in different locations assumes this role exactly. The territory is defined by a certain number of repetitions, and perceived by others as a spatial shape. In this sense, there may be a smaller difference between the third and the tenth listening than between the first and second; at that moment, there is a qualitative change of degree: we move from an anecdotal occurrence to a significant series.

Repetition is one of the key expressions of any social life through the integrative role of habit forming. First listening establishes a reference, a basis for comparison: never again will there be a perceptive innocence over which the sound object, unheard up to that point, is inscribed. At the same time, this initial listening is fragile, since it cannot put into perspective the details of the global shape. Successive listening brings a progressive sedimentation that allows mastered apprehension of structure and the sometimes complex comprehension of the play of elements.

MUSICAL AESTHETICS

Repetition is so much rooted in our perceptive life that it also weaves into our expressive dimension; we could almost define music as the art of organizing repetitions. Throughout the history of music, we can observe four elements involved in the principle of repetition: the note, the textual reprise, the variation, and the sequence. These distinctions do not cover all musical genres completely, nor do they correspond to a strict chronology, but they can be observed in many different musical forms.[12]

The Note

Each musical system defines a number of intervals and organizes the appearance and return of every note. In the Western world, for instance, there is a system based on tonality that favours a particular group of notes – the tonic chord – on which the melody is based; complementary chords (for example, the dominant and the subdominant) are added to this fundamental chord at specific moments. Thus, in musical composition, harmony dictates the reappearance of notes that are repeated even if this is not perceived as a repetition effect. This nuclear scale is essential, but it acts more on the subconscious mind of the listener than on his or her sphere of reflection. The evolution of twentieth-century Western music might be described as a multiform attempt to escape the law of repetition and to create other forms and rhythms of reappearance or non-repetition.

The Textual Reprise

Beyond the nuclear dimension, of which the unit of reprise is the note and which acts in a semi-conscious mode, the traditional dimension of the reprise is related to phrasing: the "air," the "chorus," the "theme," the "melody." The repeat sign in a music score indicates that the same passage is to be replayed strictly, although the repetition may be altered by nuances of performance without being transformed: it is the return of the same. There are two basic patterns of reprise: the immediate repetition of a passage (for example, AAB), and the return to the theme after a development (for example, ABCDA). In a song that has a systematized chorus-verse-chorus alternation, when we hear the chorus a second time, it is "something previously heard." The chorus is also valorized by the simple fact that it is repeated and because it is charged with all that happened since its first appearance. It is thus like the first, and much more.

A large part of pleasure in listening to music resides in these reappearances and in the way that the composer manages this nostalgia for the moment of return. This dimension was largely developed in the nineteenth century; examples include Beethoven's circulation of themes and Wagner's use of the *leitmotiv*.[13]

Variation

To the second level of analysis – the textual reprise – we now add the domain of variation, since the progression from one to the other is gradual and offers no rupture. Throughout *Bolero*, Maurice Ravel repeats the same theme, adding to it and constantly enriching it in a strong crescendo so that the music evolves without ever losing sight of the original melody. The entire sonic range is in movement but the bass remains stable. Quite often, variation paints a continuous melodic and harmonic structure with different colours. It can also effect a movement away from a theme, introducing larger and larger distances, playing with the original landmarks, improvising on with them. At this point, we exceed the strict bounds of the reprise – an almost identical restatement of a clearly enunciated motif – and enter a formal framework in which it is the structure that is reproduced, as if a single skeleton receives different bodies: each body develops its own individuality while retaining the family likeness.[14]

The use of harmonic and rhythmic archetypes partly defines a style. The further we move from an epoch or a country, the more these archetypes impose themselves on listening and mask individual distinctions: to an Westerner, Chinese music often appears as uniform since the pentatonic scale seems to take precedence over details of composition. What appears to be repeated is thus clearly related to the formal framework and acts on a large scale in extremely sparse schemas.[15]

The Sequence

In Western music, the reprise calibrates itself for the most part through phrasing, but in a number of other traditions, systems of repetition are based on more reduced sound cells that we might compare to a word or a group of words. For example African or Indonesian music based on percussion develops according to a succession or tangling of sequences, often incomprehensible to people of a different culture, but rich with multiple significations for listeners who can decode the sedimentation and changes.

Repetitive music, which was influenced by music from other traditions, particularly Oriental, appeared in the United States during the 1960s and propagated itself around the world as an autonomous trend, uniting diverse experiences in a similar framework based on the repetition of sequences. The principle of this compositional technique is based on the juxtaposition and repetition of very short sound cells, the agglomeration of which creates a scenery in which everything is in vibration, but which nevertheless seems, as a whole, almost immobile. The listener focuses either on the totality, and assists in the slow evolution of "sonic wallpaper," or on the micro-events, grasping the logic of repetition, the game of ruptures and appearances. Here, repetition as a criterion of sound is also a guide for perceptive organization because it establishes multiple connections between form and content.[16]

Greek mythology attributes the role of repetition to the nymph Echo. Because she could not speak first, she would only repeat the last syllables of her interlocutors. Echo was in love with Narcissus, but could not reveal her feelings to him. On one hand, for mythology, the terrible enslaved dimension of repetition is clear. It is a punishment inflicted by Hera, a mythic signification of two great hauntings of man: the loss of meaning and alienation.[17] On the other hand, beyond the borders of the sonic domain, Milan Kundera defines repetition as one of the keys for human happiness.[18]

Can we consider television and radio, which constantly churn out jingles and titles, or broadcast the same song all day long, as part of the same perspective? Here the repetition effect still reveals the guiding principles: the comfort of reunion and the enslaving reproduction of the same.

The whole domain of electrophonic recording is based on industrialization of the repetition effect: through compact discs, cassettes, or vinyl discs, an original can circulate in millions of copies and be heard at the same time on thousands of different media, in thousands of different ways.[19]

ARCHITECTURE AND URBANISM

Repetition is a key factor in the definition of context. It is through the location of its characteristic sound units that an environment is recognized as familiar, peaceful, hostile, or aggressive. The repetition effect takes place on two levels: the doubling of occurrences in a given periodicity, and their confrontation with memory. Every soundscape, whether in urban or rural spaces, organizes multiple repetitions that punctuate its weave: the passing of cars, shouting, mechanical noises, bird songs, insects, atmospheric sounds. However, the repetition effect is perhaps not the best criterion of approach for these situations. Repetition is so inherent in these that its use may proceed from tautology.[20]

Although architecture and urbanism sometimes involve repetition effects, and even produce them – as in the organization of traffic noise by circulation lights – they appear not as major domains of reference but more as systems of diffusion, propagation, or absorption of sound units that they contain but do not generate. We must note, however, that in neighbour complaints, repetition is a key criterion: continual barking, footstep sounds, electric devices. Insulation is thus perceived as a way to cut ourselves off from the repetitions of others.[21]

Echo is a phenomenon of repetition made particularly spectacular by certain configurations of the natural environment. Simple or multiple, echo illustrates the first shift between the emission and the hearing of a signal: thanks to the echo, the idea of sound conservation and recording was born.

PHYSICAL AND APPLIED ACOUSTICS

Echo is the first "natural" manifestation of repetition, and of a type of repetition that depends on the physical space of diffusion. Spatial and acoustic configurations create an effect of redoubling of the sound source. In this case, the doubling of the signal is exclusively due to the space of propagation, but the repetition effect can be provoked in many other ways as we have already seen.

Outside of this natural phenomenon, the physical context intervenes in the sound material, producing a progressive amplification or diminution of intensity, thus altering frequencies and colouring the sound. Electroacoustic music proposes numerous techniques that make echo and repetition accessible. From the simple reproduction of a signal (reverberation) to multiple echoes rhythmically spaced, a great variety of additional effects have been used to colour music of the last forty years, popularizing delays and organizing sonic space.[22]

RELATED EFFECTS   niche, echo, reprise, wave

Reprise

A musical marking indicating the strict repetition of a sound motif (phrase, chorus, air). The reprise may take place either immediately after the exposition of the theme and be quickly repeated, or after one or more developments. The reprise does not imply any modification of the original motif but may be performed by another instrument, or at different octaves.

RELATED EFFECT   repetition

Repulsion

A psychomotor effect referring to a sound phenomenon that produces, in an uncontrolled or conscious way, an attitude of rejection and behaviours of flight, whether mental or real. There are numerous examples in the human and animal worlds: for cats, the crumpling of an aluminum sheet; for humans, a high pitched squeaking produced by chalk on a board or a metal point on a hard surface.

OPPOSITE EFFECT   attraction

The resonance effect refers to the vibration, in air or through solids, of a solid element. The production of resonance requires a relatively high acoustic level and a concordance between the exciting frequency and the object put into vibration. Modal resonance refers to the phenomenon of standing waves in a three-dimensional space. Note in everyday language the term "resonance" includes any acoustically observable sonic effect, particularly reverberation.

Resonance is a general physical phenomenon found in all periodic sinusoidal movements, particularly in mechanics, acoustics, optics, and electricity. The identity of the role of certain elements make it possible to perform studies by analogy, referring to a general system that includes the actual case of resonance at the sonic level.

For the phenomenon of resonance to manifest itself, the periodic sinusoidal movement must fulfill the four following conditions:

1 The system must have a characteristic frequency.[1]
2 It must be maintained with a constant energy input (because of the loss of energy due to friction, which must always be taken into consideration).
3 The loss of exterior energy must be low enough that the transmitted energy remains superior or equal to the internal loss of the system.
4 The exciting frequency must be equal or almost equal to the characteristic frequency of the system.

Under these conditions, theoretically resonance produces an infinite gain in amplitude. At least in the normal mode, corresponding to the lowest frequency, called the fundamental. Other modes are multiples of the fundamental and are more and more damped, as shown by the Curie curve (see Figure 31). Some situations illustrate this general phenomenon well: a swing set in motion by rhythmic impulses that have the same frequency; a heavy bell pulled progressively by appropriate rhythmic tractions on a rope; or the well-known example of troops

Resonance

Figure 30
Mechanical, acoustic, and
electrical application of the
general phenomenon of
resonance.

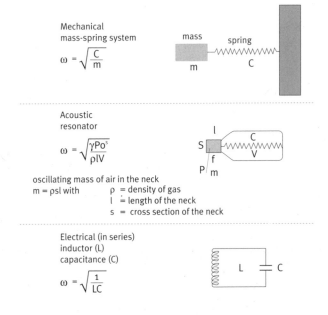

Mechanical
mass-spring system

$$\omega = \sqrt{\frac{C}{m}}$$

Acoustic
resonator

$$\omega = \sqrt{\frac{\gamma Po^s}{\rho l V}}$$

oscillating mass of air in the neck
m = ρsl with   ρ = density of gas
                 l = length of the neck
                 s = cross section of the neck

Electrical (in series)
inductor (L)
capacitance (C)

$$\omega = \sqrt{\frac{1}{LC}}$$

crossing a suspended bridge in step, transmitting a dangerous amplitude leading to a rupture.[2]

Resonance, perceived as a prolongation and thus interpreted as an
amplification, has also been described as being the origin of echo.

PHYSICAL AND APPLIED ACOUSTICS

We must first distinguish two types of resonating chambers:

– chambers of dimensions that are smaller than the wavelength from
  which the standing waves that act as elastic springs are constituted.
– chambers in which one of the three dimensions is the same as or
  larger than the wavelength.

Helmholtz Resonators
Helmholz resonators correspond to a scientific concept developed by
the great nineteenth-century physicist Herman Ludwig Ferdinand von
Helmholtz that made it possible for him to calculate the intensity of a
periodic sound.[3] A resonator consists of a chamber of volume (v) connected to a sphere by a neck characterized by its length (L) and its cross

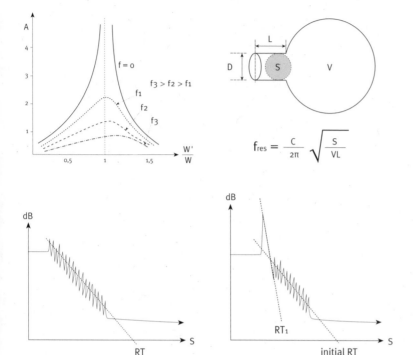

Figure 31 (top left)
Resonance: Curie curve.

Figure 32 (top right)
Helmholtz resonator

C= speed of sound in the air
S = cross section of the neck
L = length of the neck
V = volume of the cavity

Applying the Rayleigh
correction to L gives
L' = L + 0.8 D where D is the
diameter of the neck

Figure 33 (bottom left)
Closed neck: irregular
curve (RT 100 Hz)

Figure 34 (bottom right)
Open neck: two curves,
regular decrease (RT 100
Hz)

$$f_{res} = \frac{C}{2\pi} \sqrt{\frac{S}{VL}}$$

section (s). The system acts as a mass-spring device, with the air in the chamber as the spring and the air in the neck as the mass. Studies on applications of these resonators in the acoustic equipment of rooms have demonstrated that:

– The rear volume can be of any shape that is something like a sphere.
– When it is embedded into a wall, there is a lowering of the resonance frequency in the order of 10% to 15%.
– The installation of an absorbent material in the bottom of the cavity results in a lowering of the resonance frequency by 5%.

The installation of absorbent material in the neck allows for an absorption that is maximal for resonance. When the neck is closed (neutralized resonator), the reverberation time (RT) curve[4] is quite irregular (characteristic modes, reflections), but the average slope corresponds to the RT of the empty room. When the neck is open (resonator in action), the level increases for the first few milliseconds and then abruptly but regularly decreases; as the decreasing slope becomes less pronounced and returns to the gradient of the initial RT, irregularities are attenuated, making the slope more steady.

This two-slope decrease results in an early decay time (EDT)[5] that is much shorter than the RT, which explains the increased perception of transients in a reverberating milieu when the effect of the first slope is around 5 dB, the separating capability of the ear being of 50 milleseconds for speech. Resonators thus act as cavities coupled to the principal room. The result is determined by the relation of the RT between resonators and the room.

- If the RT60 of the resonator is longer than that of the room, the listener will have the impression of natural amplification and an excellent reproduction of transients.
- If the RT60 of the resonator is shorter than that of the room, the EDT of the room is then much shorter than its RT, which allows a good intelligibility of transients and gives a weaker global RT.

Diaphragm Resonators

Diaphragm resonators are generally light panels, perforated or not, mounted on a peripheral framework that is fixed to a wall, creating a hermetic space between the panel and the wall. This space is often damped with mineral wool. Subjected to an acoustic wave, the panel shakes under the spring effect of the air contained in the resonating space, transforming some of the acoustic energy into kinetic energy. The absorption is maximal at the resonance frequency of the system, according to the following formula $f = \dfrac{600}{\sqrt{md}}$, in which m = the surface mass of the panel in kilograms per square metre and d = the distance from the wall to the panel in centimetres. The absorption curve of these panels is generally less selective than that of a resonator.

Now let us consider volumes in which one of the three dimensions is equal or larger than the wavelength from which the standing waves are constituted. This phenomenon specifically concerns double walls. An ensemble consisting of two simple walls separated by a strip of air behaves like a mass-spring system with a resonance frequency of the formula $f_{res} = 84 \sqrt{\dfrac{1}{d}\left(\dfrac{1}{m_1} + \dfrac{1}{m_2}\right)}$, where m = surface mass of the panel in kg/m^2 and d = distance from the wall to the panel in centi-

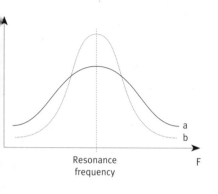

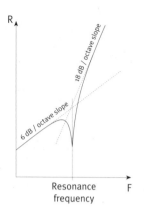

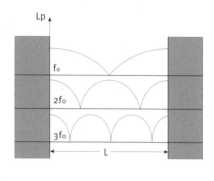

metres. However, this phenomenon can also be applied more generally to room acoustics.

In the case of a room with parallel walls, further standing waves manifest themselves. The resonance frequencies, which are called "characteristic modes" of the wall-air-wall system, correspond to multiples of the lower, fundamental, frequency. Standing waves produce a non-uniform acoustic field since the difference between antinodes and nodes may be in the range of 60 dB. Each pair of parallel walls thus possesses characteristic frequencies that combine to create other characteristic frequencies. These frequencies are classified in three families according to the Rayleigh formula: $f(m, n, p) = \dfrac{C}{2} \sqrt{\dfrac{m^2}{L^2} + \dfrac{n^2}{W^2} + \dfrac{p^2}{H^2}}$

- *Axial characteristic frequencies* correspond to the characteristic frequencies of parallel walls, and so are parallel to each of the three axes of the room: $f(m,0,0) = \dfrac{mC}{2L}$ $f(0,n,0) = \dfrac{nC}{2W}$ $f(0,0,p) = \dfrac{pC}{2H}$
- *Tangential characteristic frequencies* refer to frequencies constructed from two families of axial characteristic frequencies. They are of the type $f(m,n,0)$, $f(m,0,p)$, or $f(0,n,p)$, thus contained in a plane parallel to one of the sides of the room.
- *Oblique characteristic frequencies* are all the other frequencies of a general form $f(m,n,p)$ with m, n, and p being non-nil. Since they are neither parallel to a side nor contained in a plane parallel to one of the sides, they are oblique standing waves.

Figure 35 (left)
Movement of the curve of absorption of a diaphragm or a resonator.

Figure 36 (middle)

Figure 37 (right)
Standing waves between two rigid reflective walls (R = 1, a = 0).

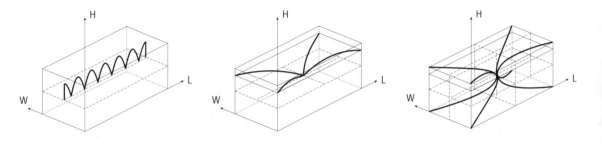

Figure 38 (left)
Axial characteristic
frequencies.

Figure 39 (middle)
Tangential characteristic
frequencies.

Figure 40 (right)
Oblique characteristic
frequencies.

D. Mercier et al. *Le livre des
techniques du son* (Paris:
Eyrolles, 1987) vol.1, 77–81.

Axial characteristic frequencies carry twice as much energy as tangential ones; tangential frequencies carry twice as much energy as oblique frequencies. The goal of the acoustician is to obtain a uniform acoustic field and a regular density of the modes through proportions of optimal dimensions of the room.[6] The resonance of a room corresponds to the excitation by a sound of all these characteristic modes, its reverberation being the decrease of these characteristic frequencies.

ARCHITECTURE AND URBANISM

Between two parallel walls, a system of standing waves – and thus resonance frequencies – is established. This phenomenon can often be observed in urban milieus, particularly in streets. In figure 41, resonance continues with multiple reflections off the even surfaces of the buildings, resulting in an increase of the sound impulse. In figure 42, the sound, diffracted because of the different facades, loses part of its impulsion and thus its "aggressiveness." Often is it rendered unintelligible, and is transformed into murmurs. The phenomenon of resonance can be found in interior locations. The "ear" of Denys, the tyrant of Syracuse, famous for its acoustic properties, was a device that allowed him to hear from outside what his prisoners were saying inside. Its configuration was similar to an ear canal. Natural sites or enclosed spaces such as caves also have resonant properties, and these characteristics have been known since prehistoric times.[7]

In the field of architecture, the use of resonators goes back to antiquity. The oldest Helmholtz-type resonators, called *echeas*, were used in Greek and Roman theatres. These resonators were described by Vitruve, a Roman architect in the first century BC, but there are no extant graphical representations; however, his description did stimulate the imagination of architects. These *echeas*, or brass vases, were tuned to

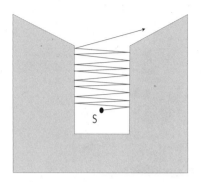
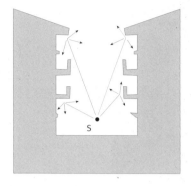

⊥ impulsive sound
⊥ reflected sound
⊥ absorbed sound
⌒ diffracted sound

the fourth, fifth, and octave.[8] Two types of vases were used simultaneously:[9]

– The vases placed beside the stage, close to the actors, the dimensions of which could be important (170 centimetres at the Nova theatre, in Sardaigne) were used for amplification at the source.
– The vases placed near the audience, produced a Haas effect – that is, a delay in the perception in the order of 1 to 30 milliseconds – that we now call artificial reverberation.

Up to the end of the seventeenth century, acoustic vases were often used by architects, as demonstrated by clay pottery found in Roman churches.[10] The shapes and dimensions varied greatly, but they were generally less than 25 centimetres tall. They have been found embedded in walls, at the base of arches, and sometimes even in the ground. More recently, this method was used in 1948 by the architect André Le Donné in the reconstruction of the arch of Notre-Dame du Rosaire in Le Havre. (Hundreds of ceramics were embedded in the concrete arch. Later, the church was transformed into apartments; the space located under the vault is now the attic.) The usefulness of these resonators has been revived today because their invisible and easily reproducible features make them convenient solutions in both acoustic and architectural contexts.

Figure 41 (left)
Section of a modern street.

Figure 42 (middle)
Section of an older street.

Figure 43 (right)
Profiles of a variety of acoustic vases.

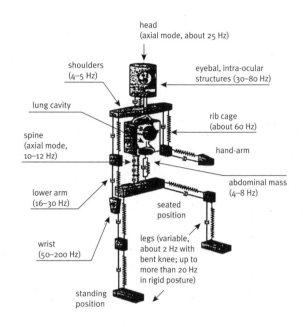

Figure 44 (left)
Notre-Dame du Raincy
(architect, Auguste Perret).

Figure 45 (right)
Resonance phenomena
of the human body.

Until about the 1950s, the analysis of the behaviour of the bodies of musical instruments led through analogical reasoning to the design of singular devices, especially with regard to concert halls. The hall was thus assimilated into an instrument, with vibrating walls. Another technique used in churches was in the installation of cables, like immense violin strings, that were designed to absorb sound. Even the shape of halls has sometimes been traced to the model of a musical instrument.[11] The orchestra pit was also considered as the "instrument" of the hall and was the object of much research.[12]

In 1923, in the church of Notre-Dame du Raincy, Auguste Perret used the principle of coupled volumes, by conceiving a double vault, the air space of which was linked with the nave through a system of stone railings.

PSYCHOLOGY AND PHYSIOLOGY OF PERCEPTION

From the physiological point of view, the human body is subjected to many resonance phenomena. At the level of low frequencies, the body as a whole can be considered as a group of spring-mass-damper subsystems. Depending on the length of the waves implied, these systems

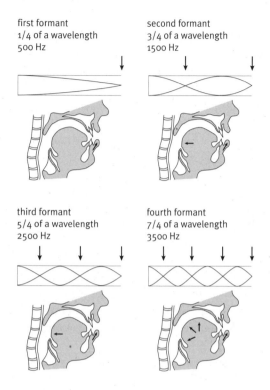

first formant
1/4 of a wavelength
500 Hz

second formant
3/4 of a wavelength
1500 Hz

third formant
5/4 of a wavelength
2500 Hz

fourth formant
7/4 of a wavelength
3500 Hz

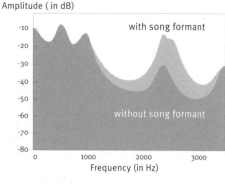

Amplitude (in dB)

with song formant

without song formant

Frequency (in Hz)

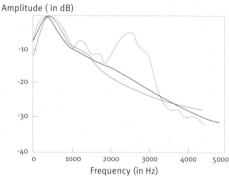

Amplitude (in dB)

Frequency (in Hz)

can develop kinetosis (motion sickness), or vascular and articular diseases; this is the case particularly for operators of vibrating machinery such as chainsaws or pneumatic drills, the use of which is strictly legislated.

The ear is also the centre of a number of resonance phenomena (outer, middle, and inner ear), since it is a chain of reception and transmission based on mechanical systems put into forced vibration by a variation in pressure created by sound.

The human vocal system, on the other hand, can be compared to an instrument, since it comprises a source of energy (air from the lungs), an oscillator (the vocal cords) and resonators (the pharynx and the mouth). The vocal canal is thus a resonator possessing four or five important resonance frequencies, referred to as "formants."

Singing uses a supplementary formant, called the "singer's formant," located between the third and fourth formants (between 2500 and 3000 Hz). The singer's formant is produced uniquely by resonance, with no

Figure 46 (left)
The four formants of the vocal canal.

Figure 47 (right)
Role of the singer's formant in the amplitude of voice.

supplementary effort, by lowering the larynx, which corresponds to an extension of the vocal canal. This formant by increasing the amplitude of the voice, makes it possible for a singer's voice to be heard over a large orchestra. Of course, the art of singing cannot be reduced to morphological configurations; Alfred Tomatis and Marie-Louise Aucher have clearly demonstrated that singing is actually a synthesis of hearing and phonation.[13]

SOCIOLOGY AND EVERYDAY CULTURE

From an etymological viewpoint, the word "resonance" comes from the Latin verb *resonare*, meaning "to sound again." We can trace the noun resonance back to about 1150, but the adjective form only appeared in the mid-sixteenth century. It was originally used to describe acoustic phenomena. In the seventeenth century, confusion between the French verb *résonner* and its homonym *raisonner* (to reason) developed to such an extent that common French proverbial phrases grew from the ambiguity. For example, we say a person whose ideas are confused is "a bit cracked," or "raisonner comme une pantoufle" or "comme un tambour" (talks through his/her hat).

A common expression based on resonance, "to be on the same wavelength," found an unexpected continuation when Pierre Le Gouzic demonstrated that each living organism is in vibration and has a specific speed. On this basis, he attributes specific wavelengths to given names.[14]

TEXTUAL AND MEDIA EXPRESSIONS

Resonance has always fascinated humans. It seems to combine two fundamental dimensions: first, the potential for power that sounds possess, and second, the capacity to act at a distance using sound as an intermediary. In a way, resonance is a myth of strength, symbolized by the power of sound. "Come and hear: Rami b. Ezekiel learned: In the case of a cock putting its head into an empty glass utensil where it crowed so that the utensil thereby broke, the payment must be full, while R. Joseph on the other hand said that it has been stated in the School of Rab that in the case of a horse neighing or an ass braying so that utensils were thereby broken, only half damages will be paid" (*The Babylonian Talmud*, baba kamma, fol 18 c. n.). "When the ram's horn rings out (when you hear the sound of the trumpet), the whole people must utter a mighty war cry and the town wall will collapse

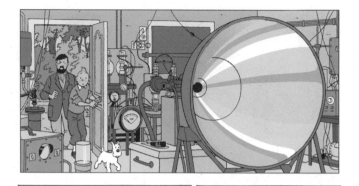

Figure 48
"Ultrasound weapon"
in Hergé, *The Calculus
Affair*, 1954. © Hergé/
Moulinsart 2006

then and there; then the people can storm the town, each man going straight ahead." (*Bible*, Joshua v). There are many other expressions of the power of sound, including the glass broken by the high note of an opera singer, or the Kïaï, the famous mortal shout of martial arts.

The adjective "resonant" is often used to describe a place filled with sounds of exceptional amplitude.[15] By metaphor, resonance is also used to refer to the effect of representations of the mind.[16] The term can also refer to a person who amplifies sensations, ideas, or theories, and is thus a resonator. Another accepted use of the word "resonator" refers to a modern scientific concept concerning acoustic vases that was defined by Helmholtz in 1868. Today however, the term resonance is not used in the theory of acoustics because it involves an ensemble of phenomena, and thus is too imprecise.

The development of science has allowed researchers to demonstrate that resonance is a physical phenomenon that can be applied to all sinusoidal periodic movement. The term is used not only in acoustic practice, but also in electricity, mechanics, optics, physics, radiology, and theoretical chemistry.

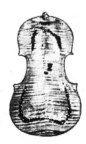

Figure 49 (left)
Violin body: nodes and
antinodes shown by
powder.

Figure 50 (right)
Violin body: nodes and
antinodes shown by laser
interferography.

MUSICAL AESTHETICS

The use of resonators is a basic principle in the construction of musical instruments. Most often, resonance involves the transformation of mechanical energy into aerial vibrating energy through the intermediary of a "resonating body." For instance, the strings of a violin are stretched tight along an almost fully enclosed wooden body. The sound depends on the transfer of energy from the vibrating string to the body, and then to the surrounding air. The body is constructed of plates, all of which have characteristic frequencies due to the resonance of the wood and the enclosed air space. Chladni used a very fine powder to detect the nodes and antinodes, and thus to determine the characteristic frequencies of a violin body (see figure 49). Laser interferography is a more delicate method but it produces more comprehensive results (see figure 50). Variations of tuning among these different modes seems to be the indispensable element for the production of a great violin.

Resonance is a phenomenon that makes it possible to characterize a location that can be emphasized and used for itself in music, when a note or a chord is followed by silence. The link with the continuation of a composition can depend on the resonance of the concert hall.[17] This effect is then somewhat similar to reverberation.

On another level, Pythagoras, knowing that any object moving at a high speed produces a sound, believed that the planets turning in their orbits produced a concert of consonance. This concept – "the harmony of the spheres" – is based on the fundamental law of musical media that is applicable to any phenomenon.[18] All elements enter into resonance because of this universal tuning of microcosm and macrocosm.

| RELATED EFFECT | reverberation |
| OPPOSITE EFFECT | cut out |

A propagation effect in which a sound continues after the cessation of its emission. Reflections of the sound on surfaces in the surrounding space are added to the direct signal. The longer these reflections conserve their energy, the greater the reverberation time. In everyday language, reverberation is often referred to as the "cathedral" effect, or by extension, as echo.

PHYSICAL AND APPLIED ACOUSTICS

The notion of reverberation is linked to a measurement of the time it takes for a sound to decrease by 60 dB. Etymologically, the word comes from the Latin verb *reverberare*, meaning "to strike back, to reflect."

In the displacement of a sound from its source to the ear, only a small part of the sound energy travels in the most direct way. A large portion of the sound energy follows indirect paths, as it is reflected on the ground and the environment of the milieu: walls, ceiling, facades. Since these routes are longer, reflected sound energy takes more time than direct energy to reach the ear. This discrepancy is the basis of reverberation. Thus we can distinguish direct energy from reverberated energy; this distinction can be easily visualized by emitting a very short signal (Dirac impulse) at a specific point in a room while recording the sound intensity over time in another part of the room. In the series of lines produced by the recording, the direct energy line and the reverberated energy lines can be clearly distinguished. The lines of reflected energy arrive after the direct energy line because their sonic path is longer. Also, their intensity is generally lower because a part of the energy has been absorbed by reflection(s) on surfaces and, due to the distance, by the air. For example, organ builders listened to the reverberation of a church by knocking on the ground with a stick before designing the adaptations for an instrument. The ear integrates these different signals, which are merged by perception into a single sonic effect: reverberation.

The phenomenon that we just described in time can also be characterized in space: if we place a constant-power sound source in a closed or semi-closed space and measure the intensity of the sound source while moving away from it, we can see that the sound normally decreases within a certain distance. Beyond that distance, the intensity does not decrease further. This distance, which depends on the space, is called "critical distance" (CD). Critical distance is independent from the power of the sound source. Within the critical distance, we are in the direct field of the sound source; beyond the critical distance we are in the reverberated field of the given space. In fact, depending on

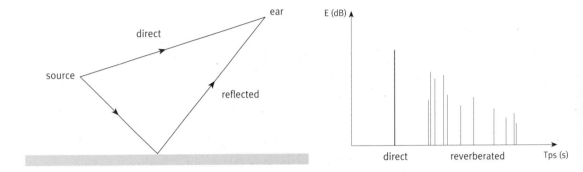

ear

direct

source

reflected

E (dB)

direct   reverberated   Tps (s)

Figure 51 (left)
Direct and indirect paths of
sound energy between the
source and the ear.

Figure 52 (right)
Measurement of the
intensity of direct and
reverberated sound
energies.

the characteristics of the room, and when we move far enough from the source, the combined reflections can produce a sound level higher than that of the single direct sound.

An essential effect in architecture, reverberation led to the development of a physical measurement commonly used: reverberation time, symbolized by "RT60." Reverberation time is defined as the time that it takes for sound intensity to decrease by 60 dB, once the emission has stopped. Reverberation time depends on the frequency of the sound, and measurements are most often done by octave bands or third-octave bands. Reverberation time is generally more important in lower frequencies than in higher ones. The analysis of the RT60 curve as a function of frequency allows one to identify particular acoustic specificities of the considered room. The RT60 increases in proportion with the volume of the room.

Reverberation can be predicted by calculation using several formulas developed by Sabine, Eyring, and Millington.[1] These formulas are obtained by simplifying the hypothesis of a similar basic equation, and thus obey strict conditions of application. Since these modes of calculation involve absorption rates of materials for which the only measurements are imperfect individual qualitative estimations, they are only indications of the subtlety and the nuances of hearing perception.

Other indexes applied to reverberation that were created after RT60, include:

- initial reverberation time, commonly referred to as early decay time (EDT);
- coefficients of speech intelligibility in a given space for a given language (RASTI and STI);

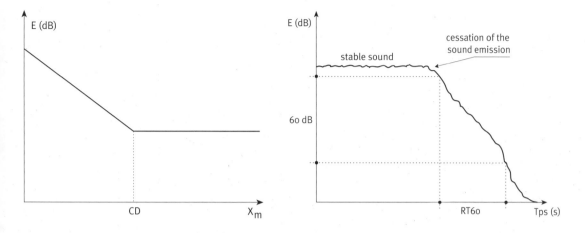

Figure 53 (left)
Measurement of the
critical distance (CD) after
which intensity does not
decrease.

Figure 54 (right)
Measurement of the
reverberation time (RT60).

– lateral energy fraction (LEF): a ratio in which the energy arriving in the first 80 milliseconds is compared with energy coming after that point.[2]

In ordinary speech, people often substitute the word "echo" for reverberation, but acoustics clearly distinguishes the two effects through the criterion of onset.

ARCHITECTURE AND URBANISM

The reverberation of a location is conditioned by urban (yards, squares) and architectural forms (rooms, halls), as well as reflecting materials (concrete, plaster, glass, marble) and absorbing materials (carpet, glass wool, Helmholtz resonators). Spatial forms determine significant reverberation in some specific locations: the centre of a circle, the foci of ellipses, parabolas, and hyperbolas, as well as all the volumes of revolution engendered by these curves.

In architecture, the control of reverberation is important. Reflecting surfaces increase reverberation. Materials develop different absorption capacities depending on the frequency of the sound:

– To limit reverberation in lower frequencies, we use diaphragmatic absorbers: thin panels installed a few centimetres away from a surface.

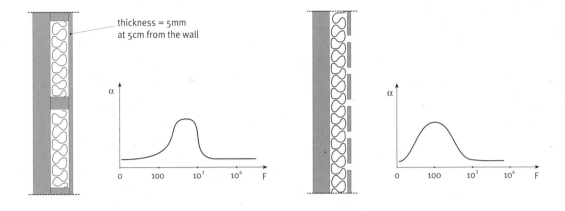

thickness = 5mm
at 5cm from the wall

Figure 55 (left)
Limitation of reverberation
in the low frequencies
using a diaphragmatic
absorber.

Figure 56 (right)
Limitation of reverberation
in the mid-frequencies
using Helmholtz
resonators.

– To absorb sound in the middle frequencies, Helmholtz resonators are favoured: a plate with small holes where the sound enters and becomes trapped.
– To absorb sound in the higher frequencies, fibrous (glass wool) or porous (foam) materials are the most efficient.

The natural environment also features reverberant (cave, water, rocks, forest) and absorbent (grass, snow) milieus and elements.

PSYCHOLOGY AND PHYSIOLOGY OF PERCEPTION

In everyday practice, reverberation is omnipresent; even if measurements indicate weak physical variations, the correspondent hearing perception may be strong. The average listener tends to valorize reverberation when he or she becomes aware of it, sometimes having the impression that sounds are interminable. In fact, because of air and material absorption, reverberation is always mediated. If reverberation was infinite – if sounds did not fade away and were never absorbed – a single sound would "circulate" constantly and the sound level would increase to infinity, making all communication impossible. Although limited, the reverberation of large spaces such as churches or concrete and glass buildings may illustrate this lack of intelligibility.

On the other hand, in a totally absorbent milieu it is difficult to be aware of space. In an atmosphere of quietness and absence of sound, our impression quickly becomes unpleasant. We can hear our own heartbeats, and body sounds acquire incredible proportions. These

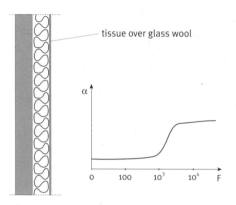

Figure 57
Limitation of reverberation
in the high frequencies
using fibrous material.

tissue over glass wool

impressions can be experienced in an anechoic chamber (an experimental space in which all reverberation is eliminated): the space seems to be squeezed in on itself, narrow and stifling, even if its physical volume is large.

Blind people listen for subtle variations in the reverberations from the sound of their canes in order to find their way and to detect a wall or an angle they are approaching. From this point of view, large, empty places are unsuitable for good perception of the sonic space. Reverberation frequently plays a role in our perceptions:

- the perception of the presence of something or someone beside oneself (through the modification of the reverberated field)
- the feeling of "collectivity" and the sharing of social communication (through the envelope it creates)
- the propensity toward a narcissistic attitude as a sound mirror in situations of individual sound productions (singing or whistling in a bathroom, for instance).[3]

MUSICAL AESTHETICS

The vocabulary used by a musician or a listener to refer to the acoustics of a performance or listening space (bright, dull, clear) can partly be correlated with specific physical measurements of reverberation.

Leo Beraneck was the first to demonstrate a relation between great musical works (symphonies, operas, particularly those of Richard

Wagner) and the reverberation time (RT60) of halls traditionally considered as good that he measured.[4] In these places, reverberation is perceived as an enrichment of the musical production of the orchestra. It seems that composers intentionally play with acoustics (and thus with reverberation) of halls chosen for a performance.[5] Gregorian chant also uses the long reverberation effect of abbeys to produce a virtual polyphony.

Electroacoustic practice acts directly on the control of reverberation. First, sound recording is done in studios that are acoustically treated to be very absorbent. In fact, for full control, reverberation is usually added electronically at the mixing stage, since it is impossible to remove it from a magnetic recording. In order to test different types of reverberation, it is thus necessary to record a sound as "dry" as possible – that is, with very little reverberation. The mastering of a sound recording involves the control of reverberation.

SOCIOLOGY AND EVERYDAY CULTURE

Reverberation is socially perceived as an indication of solemnity and monumentality. It signifies volume and large size. This monumentality can be sensed as functional and inherent to the use of some locations (cathedrals, concert halls) or as unpleasant and residual for others (train station halls, concrete underground parking garages). Reverberation is also perceived in terms of "resonance," a term referring, in everyday speech, to reverberation in general. Through its architectural representation, reverberation is easily associated with various functions of power (religion, justice).[6]

In the domain of culture, reverberation is synonymous with a crowd. It is linked to large ritual or solemn gatherings in churches or sacred caves. Reverberation also plays a role in large press conferences, where, paradoxically it reduces the intelligibility of the message. In large spaces, a poor sound system may emphasize the shortcomings of natural reverberation.

Every epoch is characterized by specific types of reverberation linked to specific places, but a history of this effect remains to be written. Even if we consider the example of cathedrals, which are the oldest large enclosed spaces in the West, it is extremely difficult to have a precise idea of the diverse acoustics they contained because of the evolution of interior decorations and arrangements. The original reverberation is still unknown, and would be quite difficult to reconstitute.[7]

Reverberation is abundantly used in media expressions: horror and science-fiction films, westerns, and advertisements emphasize the connection of reverberation to large spaces, even if the location is often not adapted to such an effect (desert, interplanetary space). Reverberation can also refer to sociological aspects emphasized in the preceding locations (power, justice).

RELATED EFFECTS   coupling, echo, filtration, modal resonance, release, flutter echo

OPPOSITE EFFECT   dullness

Rumble

An effect characterized by the inopportune whirring of a phonograph's motor, picked up by the needle and added to the musical signal, literally creating a "rumble."

Sharawadji

An aesthetic effect that characterizes the feeling of plenitude that is sometimes created by the contemplation of a sound motif or a complex soundscape of inexplicable beauty. This exotic term, introduced in Europe in the seventeenth century by travelers returning from China, designates "the beauty that occurs with no discernible order or arrangement. When Chinese people visit a beautiful garden that strikes their imagination because of its absence of design, it is commonly said that its 'sharawadji' is admirable."[1] This virtual order, imperceptible and present, produces fascination and is breathtaking. The sharawadji effect is unexpected and transports us elsewhere, beyond the strict representation of things, out of context. In this brutally present confusion, we lose both our senses and our sense.

Although the beauty of sharawadji allows the greatest fantasies in design – fantasies that tend to favour the rapture of imagination – we will focus here on the most ordinary elements of the urban sound environment where unexpected beauty appears only through a rupture in the context, the sonic and musical codes of reference. The article by Louis Marin, which is the inspriation for the name of this effect, invites us to enjoy an idle walk in the "garden, parasite of the domain."[2] By analogy, we evoke the sonic wandering of the astonished and wonder-struck stroller listening to the multiple sounds of the city, the cacophonous parasites that defy classification. Undoubtedly, to define the sharawadji effect, we need to define some modalities of the sublime.

AESTHETICS

The sharawadji plays with composition rules; it diverts them and stimulates a feeling of pleasure in the perceptive confusion. Apparent disorder constitutes the necessary, although not exclusive, condition of the sharawadji effect. Distortions, incongruities, imbalances, and irregularities all diverge from canons of beauty but nevertheless exert such an attraction that the eye or the ear gives way to pleasure. Artifice disappears: the neat shape with discernible contours and composition is opposed to the formless shape that hides its artistic elaboration from eye and ear.[3]

To the uninitiated ear, contemporary music follows no rules and even represents the negation of compositional craft. However, in the contingency John Cage seeks through random methods,[4] happenings, and other diverse performances, we can hear the disappearance of artifice. Unbridled and unintentional structures disrupt the nature–culture binary and reveal new forms of life beyond their disorder, which paradoxically can be completely fabricated. Thus technological and industrial sounds can become more natural than any imitation of nature. It is this blurring of the edges of aesthetics, this shifting at the frontier of art itself, that defines sharawadji.

Art is not always where we think it is: during a performance by Nicolas Frize at the Gare de Lyon in October 1987, we heard screaming and moaning signals of locomotives that stimulated memory and suggested the strangeness of the "dernier-cri" trains. The sharawadji affirms itself in contrast with the very banality it is based on. Sharawadji sounds belong to everyday life, to a known musical style. They become sharawadji only through decontextualization, through a rupture of meaning.[5]

The feeling of pleasure, an element of the sharawadji effect, is dynamic rather than passive. An internal tension maintains the contradictory poles of this beauty in the consciousness of their limits and in the surpassing of these limits. And this tension, the sustained and contained attention to what is presently taking place, to the emerging sonic form, is mixed with pleasure and animates it.

With the sharawadji effect, we participate in the actualization of an impossible potentiality, and we hold our breath to so as not to prevent its accomplishment. The transported imagination becomes powerless and thus accesses the unlimited, the immeasurable.[6]

This feeling of pleasure of an aesthetic nature is a matter of the sublime rather than the beautiful, in the sense that Kant distinguishes these two judgments. Satisfaction relative to the beautiful is not thwarted and can lead to a calm contemplation. On the other hand, the initial gesture of the sublime is a disruption, a "momentary inhibition of the vital powers," to use Kant's terms, and we find in Kant's definition of the sublime of nature, the "formless," disorder, uproar, and chaos.[7]

Why should we call it the sharawadji effect, instead of the sublime effect? Because the sharawadji of Julie's garden is subtly sublime, without splendour or theatricality. It is the sublime of the everyday, the invisible but present exception of the ordinary. And it is in this sense that we designate sounds – strangely discordant in relation to their context, a brouhaha, a sonic muddle – that magically and suddenly transport us elsewhere.

The sharawadji is a semantic effect insofar as the sound material loses its sense. But the surprise is such that it seizes the mind and no sense can supplement this loss; a circumstantial effect of sense and of going beyond sense.

SOCIOLOGY AND EVERYDAY CULTURE

Although sharawadji remains a subjective effect, soundscapes, particularly urban soundscapes, have the power to produce this sensation because of their unpredictability and diversity. To some people, thundering sounds of a technological or industrial origin may suggest a worrisome yet beautiful strangeness:[8] Consider a four-stroke diesel motor, the troublesome starting of a motorbike, or the sounds heard when entering a factory yard. Another example is the sonic role of barges in *La rose des vents*, by Pierre Mariétan (82–3). The din or racket of carnivals, demonstrations, or children's games all disrupt sonic rules. Three criteria – discontinuous rhythms, high intensity, and low-frequency sounds – in any combination, may stimulate a sharawadji effect.

The sonic richness of nature can also create a sharawadji effect. The rumbling of thunder or the fury of a volcano, which illustrate the sublime of nature in Kant, generate fear but also pleasure for one who feels safe. If power and sound intensity contribute to a loss of orientation, quieter sounds may also cloud our minds and rise to the cosmic level; for instance, the wind – the great sonic paradigm of humanity according to Murray Schafer[9] – or the singing of whales. In the countryside, the sharawadji effect can be produced through silence, when all the activities of animals momentarily stop at the same time.

Sounds become sharawadji less by their excessiveness than by their implausibility. Coming from an unknown and uncontrolled elsewhere, it is their strangeness that opens the unlimited. Didn't the first radiophonic "bip-bip" evoke extra-terrestrial sounds? The voice of E.T. has shattered many children, and we can imagine the emotion that would provoke listening to a pulsar coming from elsewhere. In the same way, in Shanghai, the din of crickets that apparently took up residence in a single tree created a surprising discord with the ambient noise of the city. Some of these examples may suggest that sharawadji is created by novelty, but in actual fact, a sound that is too strange makes it impossible for us to maintain a controlled relation with the milieu in order to fire the imagination. The beauty of Pygmy music, for instance, can surprise, unsettle, and transport. But if unfamiliarity with this culture produces an astonishment favourable to sharawadji, extensive sonic and musical knowledge will not always inhibit the effect.

PSYCHOLOGY AND PHYSIOLOGY OF PERCEPTION

Sharawadji is a subjective effect: as with any aesthetic judgment, only subjectivity may declare that it is under the hold of the sharawadji, to which it will attribute a universal value.

Acousmatic Position
Objective elements of sonic decontextualization (for instance, the crickets in Shanghai or the song of a drunkard) do not necessarily provoke the sharawadji effect. Circumstances in which it is made possible are always specific. If dreaming or worried, we may be completely deaf to the environment. On the other hand, during travel our minds can combine receptivity, attention, and perspicacity to become receptive to novelty and sonic fantasy.

Attraction–Repulsion
Under the sharawadji effect, the mind is set in motion despite a certain fear, a certain discomfort. Attraction and repulsion are linked, but we know that the feeling of pleasure wins without, however, suppressing

what holds us back. Julia Kristeva analyses the abject and comes to consider the sublime. These two poles proceed out of the same impossibility to name the object, to produce the desired bearer of meaning. And the sharawadji that leads beyond meaning still shares similarities with the sublime: the emotion that transports us seems to come from a memory that precedes meaning.[10] Sharawadji, a semiotic effect, can manifest itself at the behavioural level by a temporary breathlessness, a hesitation between attraction and repulsion.

Inside–Outside

The characteristics of sound lend themselves to the emergence of sharawadji. Imperceptible, it crosses partitions, flows around obstacles, and penetrates ears that are helpless to stop it. Often unpredictable, sound disrupts our spatio-temporal perceptions – that is, it endangers protective boundaries.

Among the ideas proposed by Edith Lecourt to account for the psychic phenomena linked to sound is the "self-sound interval," which expresses the relation that the "self-sound identity" maintains with the present environment. Our minds and moods conceive the constant fluctuations of this interval in relation to environmental contexts. But more fundamentally, the control of sonic experience depends on an identity acquired in the remote period of childhood, in close relation with the group to which we belong.[11]

Thus it seems that sharawadji, a semantic effect, requires a supple and usually controlled relation with the environment. If not, there is a risk that the characteristic dizziness of the perceptive confusion of sharawadji will be transformed into anguish and will not permit this experience of coming closer to what is outside of us. Contemporary music research might make use of this interval, experimenting with its limits.[12]

False Sharawadji

There are sounds that abolish inside–outside limits by exercising a violent attraction while maintaining listening despite ear pain. Rock concerts, for instance, allow immersion through high-intensity sound. But this apparent sharawadji is more passive than active. In this respect, Edith Lecourt believes that both rock music and mellow synthesizer music express a desire for "sonic bathing" and a "quest for ties" to reinforce the "sound envelope."[13] The notion of sharawadji does not directly concern feelings provoked by these musical works, even if they sometimes lead to the sublime. By placing the listener in a prepared situation, a concert organizes expectation and presents the unexpected in a more supple way than with the sharawadji effect.

MUSICAL AESTHETICS

The term sharawadji is appropriate to refer to the unintentional "music" produced by city sounds; however, it is more difficult to apply this term in the domain of structural and composed music. Only a few of the handful of works that we would spontaneously associate with sharawadji predate the last century. Some were judged as cacophonous in their own time (for example, works by Berlioz); others (for example, works by Mahler), through their rupture of intensity, develop a vertiginous romanticism. Still others continue to astonish the ear with their pleasant and creaking mystery (for example, the fifth symphony, *New England Holidays*, by Charles Ives).

However, the introduction of noise and silence in contemporary music, the abandonment of the cadence, and the rejection of intention correspond more clearly with sharawadji (Luigi Russolo, John Cage). Such work on temporal structure is on the leading edge of musical composition and shades its foundation. For instance, indetermination created by repetition–variation (Arnold Schoenberg), or by the association of random events (John Cage), can open the way to an infinity of sharawadji, but can also result in meaninglessness.

Also, the computer allows an exploration of psychoacoustics favouring sharawadji, such as the "paradoxes of timbre and pitch" by Jean-Claude Risset, in which upward and downward movements meet continuously.[14]

PHYSICAL AND APPLIED ACOUSTICS

Certain acoustic parameters seem to favour the sharawadji effect. As mentioned previously, the three criteria are high intensity, low frequency, and rhythmic irregularity. According to Luigi Russolo, it is the complexity and acoustic richness of certain noises that explain their incredible beauty.

ARCHITECTURE AND URBANISM

No space could prevent the emergence of a sharawadji effect, but none will necessarily produce it. One analogy with loss of perspective, because of the confusion between poles that is characteristic to the sharawadji effect, is Escher's 1951 lithograph, *House of Stairs*.

TEXTUAL AND MEDIA EXPRESSIONS

The beauty of advertisements is often overly formal and intrinsically linked to the message. How can we lose sense when everything combines to express an actual single sense? On the other hand, the construction of audiovisual clips tends to create a feeling of excessiveness and formal rupture.

INDUCING EFFECTS	cut out, delocalization, incursion, metamorphosis, synecdoche, presence
RELATED EFFECTS	attraction, repulsion

Suspension

A semantic compositional effect characterized by the feeling of non-fulfillment of a heard sound sequence: the sound seems to be suspended, awaiting continuation. This effect leaves the listener in a state of uncertainty, indecision, or powerlessness. In its aesthetic dimension, suspension corresponds to the principle of incompletion of a work; in its psychosociological dimension, it refers to waiting. Sound signals and sonic punctuation (jingles) are types of tamed suspensions.

OPPOSITE EFFECT	digression

Synchronization

A psychomotor effect by which the rhythm of appearance of a sound phenomenon determines the beginning of an individual or collective perceptive or motor activity. Synchronization is one of the major forms of chronophony in social life – that is, of punctuation of time by sound.[1]

RELATED EFFECT	chain
OPPOSITE EFFECT	desynchronization

Synecdoche

For someone listening to a complex sound ambience, the synecdoche effect is the ability to valorize one specific element through selection. Selective listening, a fundamental capacity, is involved in all everyday sound behaviours. It is produced by simple acoustic vigilance, by the determination of a predominant functional criterion, or by adhesion to a cultural schema establishing a hierarchy.

The synecdoche effect is complementary to the asyndeton effect and is necessary to its existence: the valorization of certain sounds necessitates partial or absolute deletion of the other sounds.[1] These two effects, concerned with perceptive organization, are at the basis of any interpretation of the sound environment because they make it possible to create a gap between the physical sound of reference and the object of listening. In this sense, they are at the basis of the idea of the sonic effect itself. As rhetorical effects, these two paradigms can also be found in other domains of human activity.[2]

PSYCHOLOGY AND PHYSIOLOGY OF PERCEPTION

From the point of view of information theory, it is easy to demonstrate that every individual has a maximal limit of apprehension of information that is smaller than the flow of sound sources in our environment: To perceive is to select.[3] The incapacity to deal with too large an amount of information constitutes one of the major causes of stress. The current orientation of studies on stress focus on the feeling of submersion that generates anguish and is felt by a subject incapable of assimilating an ensemble of complex information.

The valorization of one or many sounds is accomplished through selection, which implies minimal activity on the part of the listener. Our intention to hear is decisive because we actually hear only what we want to hear.[4] Synecdoche thus refers directly to the etymology of the French verb *entendre* (to hear), in the sense of *tendre vers* (to tend toward), or *avoir l'intention* (to have the intention of).[5] In most cases, the voluntary selection of sounds is achieved by a recognition of these sounds, made possible by ear training. The most common example of the shaping of mind and ear is probably the learning of language by children.

The synecdoche effect differs from the notion of emergence, which refers primarily to physical phenomena (in terms of signal-to-noise ratio) and which excludes the activity of the listener. The most convincing and best known examples illustrating the selection of a signal in a stream of information and the intention to hear are often found in studies on speech. The search for a useful signal also appears in situations of danger. In this case, intent listening is strongly developed.[6]

The synecdoche effect refers directly to time perception by establishing continuity in our everyday experience. By emphasizing the permanence of certain sounds or by playing on their importance to memory, synechdoche structures our apprehension of time; it introduces us to the experience of duration by organizing sound perception.[7] At the same time, valorized sounds vary across time and succeed each other. The move from one valorization of a sound to another produces discontinuity in individual lived experience. The synecdoche effect operates in our perception of time according to the continuity–discontinuity binary. The two poles come into being in this effect.

Physiological mechanisms related to the valorization of sound have yet to be discovered. It appears, however, that such a phenomenon can only be analyzed in its psychophysiological complexity.[8] The synecdoche effect may create pathological problems. When a single temporal continuity is involved and valorized sounds remain invariant, a phenomenon of fixation is produced. The same sounds stay present in the mind of the subject, existing in a phantasmatic state.[9]

Finally, note that the synecdoche effect does not refer exclusively to perception. Sound production is also involved, since the valorization of sound must also be involved in expression. Any intentional sound production is based on choice and the form of emission of particular sounds.

SOCIOLOGY AND EVERYDAY CULTURE

The culture to which an individual belongs has an important effect on which sounds are valorized. In professional culture, notably, synecdoche appears in a functional way. For example, in building activities and public works, occurrences of hammer sounds for the bricklayer and the noise of the speed gear of the crane for its operator will receive a particular attention that is related to the work itself.[10] In fact, research in this domain integrates the social dimension more and more, particularly the signification of sounds acknowledged as embarrassing. The partiality of sonic interpretations remains closely linked with culture.[11] To a certain extent, the synecdoche effect affirms itself through significant sounds for a given culture, language being their archetype.

Sonic symbols exist for inhabitants of a place, understood through listening.[12] These symbols are located at a microsocial scale and bring coherence to the perception of the district. Thus, the synecdoche effect allows a structuring of space at the sonic level. It favours the marking of places by associating sounds with them: whether it is a human voice in a large boulevard or the jingling of a metal plate in a market, perceptive organization takes into account local particularities. The notion of the soundmark is located more at a macrosocial level and also involves the synecdoche effect, both in perception and in sound production. According to R. Murray Schafer, "The term soundmark is derived from landmark and refers to a community sound which is unique or possesses qualities which make it specially regarded or noticed by the people in that community. Once a soundmark has been identified, it deserves to be protected, for soundmarks make the acoustic life of the community unique."[13]

The soundmark constitutes the sign of a cultural specificity. It is possible to list particular sounds for a given city. In this way, cultural dimensions of the synecdoche effect are underlined: cultural codes participate in the structuring of perception, and the valorization of certain sound productions accounts for the condition of a community at a given moment.

What are the social conditions favourable to the emergence of this type of effect? We have already seen that situations of danger provoke an accentuation of hearing intention. It seems, in fact, that any situation of waiting or vigilance favours the emergence of the synecdoche effect. Among examples of selectivity, a particularly common case is that of parents who are awakened by the cries of their child, while other more intense sounds (such as traffic or the noise of neighbours) produce no effect on them.

Here, we are likely observing one of the primary functions of the ear, sometimes called the "primitive ear."[14] We can imagine our ancestors, threatened by many perils, surrounded by darkness or semi-obscurity, always sleeping with one eye (and two ears) open, able to rely only on their hearing to catch survival messages and signs of danger. Initially, listening to sounds and recognition of a specific sound (a man, an animal, a thing?) is the fundamental guesswork of primitive man, the most skillful technique; we still observe it in certain populations.

Whether listening is "primitive" or "cultural," the synecdoche effect is part of the relationship between the individual and his or her (natural or social) environment, by underlining its fundamental characteristics.

MUSICAL AESTHETICS

The synecdoche effect can be found both in musical listening and in the process of composition. The distinction between everyday listening and intentional listening makes it possible to be precise about the modalities of musical perception.[15] In everyday listening, the synecdoche effect emphasizes the dominant perception of a given music; in intentional listening, the valorization of sounds is defined beforehand, and the effect becomes a technique of conscious listening.

A musician's listening participates in the definition and constitution of the musical domain. At the same time, by making a clear distinction between musical and non-musical sounds, it contributes to its rigidity.[16]

At the level of sound production, the synecdoche effect is observed in composition techniques: the use of an ostinato or a *leitmotiv* are good examples. Some musical styles, such as process music, are constructed from very simple phrases. The repetition of a similar sound cell tends to impose it as a dominant figure subjected to diverse subtle modifications. The longer the duration of performance, the stronger the expression of the motif will be.[17]

The synecdoche effect is used in the performance of a work. Whether in a jazz improvisation or a classical concerto, the voice of the soloist must be emphasized. The volume of each instrument will be specifically controlled so that the sonic mass of the group or the orchestra does not mask the notes of the soloist. The analysis of a concerto score reveals the use of nuances characteristic to each instrument to favour the performance of the soloist. A musical nuance principally describes the degree of power or restraint that must be accorded to sounds during performance. By extension, nuances characterize each aspect of interpretation, including the intentionality of the musician; they therefore exceed the strict domain of acoustics.

Finally, the production of soundscape compositions is based largely on the choice and valorization of certain sounds over others.

TEXTUAL AND MEDIA EXPRESSIONS

The job of a sonic effect designer is similar to that of the soundscape composer, in the sense that the designer must select sounds that will allow the better illustration of a situation. Whatever technique is used, the choice between one sound and another is the first act in the construction of a sound organization.[18]

In a different domain, the history of sound recording and mixing reveals hierarchical systems that succeed one another to determine the different levels of intensity and presence between musical instruments. For instance, if a singer is placed in front of the accompaniment, the voice can be clearly situated as soloist, but if the singer is integrated as a sound element among others, the voice will merge into the group. Depending on the epoch and the musical fashion, a particular instrument may play a predominant role in the "sound" of groups and variety music. The sound mixing thus reflects the social and cultural status of various instruments at a given time.[19]

On a more general level, the sociocommercial phenomenon of a "hit" repeated all day long on the radio can also be analyzed in terms of sound synecdoche. The systematic repetition of a song by a group of stations confers a special status. The song will momentarily mark our everyday soundscape and will punctuate our day. Finally, for textual expression and novels in particular, sound elements mentioned in a description alert us to the specific listening of the author. The use of a specific sound event to express the ambience of a scene is not an arbitrary choice; it highlights elements that are important for the author in the perception of the atmosphere.[20]

ARCHITECTURE AND URBANISM

We cannot speak of an actual synecdoche effect in the domain of architecture (since this effect is primarily perceptive), but we can discuss factors that favour its appearance. We know that the conception of concert halls implies choices made according to their sound qualities, particularly in terms of sound propagation. The decision to absorb or reflect a particular frequency by a certain coefficient, for instance, gives the hall a character that will favour the perception of high, low, or middle frequency sounds. The acoustics of concert halls can thus alter the importance accorded to the perception of a particular frequency.

The use of personal stereos ("walkmans") in public spaces can be seen as a caricature of the synecdoche effect: here, the selection between sound messages takes place not at the level of post-listening perception, but through a radical closure to the sound environment, the univocal character of the heard signal, and often through the ostentatious display of this voluntary retreat from the world.[21]

PHYSICAL AND APPLIED ACOUSTICS

Obviously, synecdoche cannot be observed in this domain since acoustics as a scientific discipline, by definition, excludes perceptive interpretation (its object of study being physical aspects of sound). On the contrary, in certain situations, this effect can contravene the laws of acoustics, as is the case with the rule of the 10 dB contrast. This rule determines the threshold below which there is no discrimination between two signals, but for the listener who is looking for a weak signal and manages to perceive the sound through synecdoche, this law may be infringed.

COMPLEMENTARY EFFECT   asyndeton

The Tartini effect refers to the production of a sound that is physiologically audible, but that has no physical existence. It looks like a sonic hologram. In psychoacoustics, this phenomenon is also sometimes described as "combination tones."[1]

This compositional effect exists under very specific conditions: for instance, it is possible to hear a fundamental frequency reconstituted by the ear based on listening to two or more of its harmonics: a mixture of tones of 1000 Hz, 15000 Hz, and 2000 Hz, for example, will "provoke" the sensation of a 500Hz tone.

Although he was not the first to observe this phenomenon, the Italian composer and violinist Giuseppe Tartini (1692–1770) is known for his extensive exploitation of this psychoacoustic effect. During the Age of Enlightenment he aroused much curiosity, as is revealed in contemporary dictionaries and treatises on music and harmony, and he remains a fascinating example of unconscious psychic process.2

In his *Trattato di musica* (1754), Tartini describes this phenomenon and its interpretation in a musical performance as a trill that requires a particular virtuosity in terms of the precision and performance of intervals. The mystery of the effect – according to legend, Tartini had a dream in which his own G minor violin sonata (1713), also known as the "devil's trill," was performed for him by Satan – remains a fascination for contemporary audiences, kept alive not only in the performance of Tartini's compositions but also in electroacoustic works based on the same principle. The psychoacoustic illusion has become a sonic hologram.

The magic of this 'diabolical' effect still amazes musicians, philanthropists, and thinkers, while inspiring technological and instrument-making research. For instance, we can now produce organ stops of large dimensions (32 feet) even when the physical space does not allow for such large pipes. New possibilities of simultaneous diffusion through loudspeakers has also given rise to a large number of works on sound localization, particularly with the production of combination

Tartini

tones that can be precisely localized even though they do not physically exist.

The effect is even more effective and powerful when the harmonics are ultrasounds (non-audible sounds) produced by piezo-electric speakers. The diffusion of two tones of 200 and 201 kHz, for instance, will produce an audible sound of 1 kHz. The reality of this sonic hologram and the precision of its interference trajectory are astounding, according to researchers such as Elwood Norris and Peter Fryer.[3]

And as with any thinking concerning magic, power shadows knowledge. Since the 1960s, a number of military and crowd-control applications based on combination tones have been designed: a non-audible stimuli can produce a second non-audible sound, the effects of which can be formidable: nausea, discomfort, disorientation. It seems that from the time of Tartini's dream, Satan has played a role in this effect.

RELATED EFFECT   remanence (analogous perceptive process)

OPPOSITE EFFECTS   filtration (by attenuation), erasure

Tremolo

A fast pulsation characterizing the diffusion of a sustained sound, in the form of multiple repetitions articulated in discontinuous frequencies. Tremolo actually cuts a signal into square signals, whereas vibrato leads it into a sinusoidal movement (frequency continuity). In music, the term tremolo is used mainly to refer to the rapid repetition of a single note, whereas the word trill is used to indicate a fast pulsation between two adjoining notes.

RELATED EFFECT   vibrato

Ubiquity

An effect linked to spatio-temporal conditions that expresses the difficulty or impossibility of locating a sound source. In the major variant of this effect, the sound seems to come from everywhere and from nowhere at the same time. In a minor variant, sound seems to come simultaneously from a singular source and from many sources. Beyond the simple phenomenon of sound reflections that limit localization, the ubiquity effect opens the way to the metaphysical dimension of sound.

Diffused, unstable, omnidirectional sound presents an intrinsic tendency toward ubiquity – in fact it is impossible to delimit or materialize the "location" of a sound.[1] Inversely, the notion of ubiquity, immaterial in principle, could not be better evoked than by sound – it cannot be seen, it does not "manifest" itself, and it uses other sensorial channels to be revealed, among which hearing seems to predominate.

There is therefore a fundamental link between sound and ubiquity. Certain sounds are in fact more "present" than others: any "sound background" – an urban drone, the purring of a machine in a reverberant room, or the bodily hum of an organism – can be described as a ubiquitous sound in the very literal sense that it comes from everywhere and nowhere at the same time. But these different sounds do not produce an effect; rather, they are characterized by the fact that we forget them and no longer hear them. The sound itself is ubiquitous, but there is no ubiquity effect. For the ubiquity effect to occur, we must consciously look for the source location of the sound, and fail, at least for a moment, to identify it. A background sound will only produce a ubiquity effect at the moment of its emergence, either because the listener suddenly enters the space (the arrival of a stranger in a city, getting off a train or a car), because there is an erasure of other sounds (the reappearance of the urban drone at night when neighbouring sounds fade), or because we perceive the onset of the emerging sound (start of a machine in a shop).

Where does the sound come from? Etymology answers *"ubique"* – which means "from everywhere" or "from there as well," thus from anywhere, and from nowhere. The ubiquity effect is an effect of space – and this is perhaps its fundamental characteristic.

The listener is in search of information. The ubiquity effect is based on the paradoxical perception of a sound that we cannot locate, but which we know is actually localized. The sound of the sea, for instance, is ubiquitous, but since we know that there is not localizable source, it does not produce a ubiquity effect. Often it is important to know where a sound comes from; sometimes, it is vital information that we need to determine whether to flee, to attack, or to remain motionless.[2] The uncertainty produced by a sound about its origin establishes a power relationship between an invisible emitter and the worried receptor. The ubiquity effect is an effect of power – and this constitutes its second major characteristic.

ARCHITECTURE AND URBANISM

Because of their particular conditions of propagation favouring the delocalization of sound sources, urban milieus and architectural spaces are the most obvious locations for the emergence of a ubiquity effect.

The presence of various screens and walls that act as masks and reflectors, the solid transmission of many impact sounds, and the diverse mobility of numerous sound sources all constitute favourable factors found in urban settings and architectural spaces. We must therefore distinguish the role of spatial configuration and the role of the listener's position in this space.

Spacial Configuration

The ubiquity effect is intimately linked to the reverberation conditions of the location. Schematically, we can assume that the more reverberant a place is, the more opportunities there are for the ubiquity effect to appear, due to the increase in relative importance (in number and intensity) of reflected sounds to direct sounds. For instance, a single momentary sound can create a multitude of reflections and delocalized echoes that may lead to a ubiquity effect. Consequently, this effect appears particularly in closed spaces (such as squares, streets, underground parking garages, halls, corridors) built of reflecting materials such as asbestos, reinforced concrete, glass, or metal.[3]

The effect can also appear in dull or slightly reverberant spaces. But since direct sounds become predominant, the sources must be multiple, dispersed in space and condensed in time. In this case, the ubiquity effect is linked to a phenomenon of hyperlocalization of simultaneous or almost simultaneous sound sources between which we must, but cannot, choose. The dull and muffled spaces of open-plan offices often develop an acoustic in which there is hyperlocalization of numerous sound sources, which are made equivalent and are then difficult to discriminate (keyboards, telephone, conversations).

In certain situations, these conditions are superimposed and there is a paradox between delocalization and hyperlocalization. We do not know, for instance, if the sound comes from left or right, up or down, inside or outside. Reverberant intermediary spaces that also direct sound in specific directions (buffer zones, access catwalks, stairs, corridors, sills, landings, intersections), are very favourable spaces for the emergence of this phenomenon.[4]

The Position of the Listener

From the point of view of the listener's position, we can distinguish, in a natural or an urban environment, two main situations.

In the first situation, the listener is immersed in a ubiquitous sound environment, and the effect is linked to the multiplicity (real or imagined) of the surrounding sources (the listener does not know where to look). For example, a pedestrian or a cyclist stuck in urban traffic; the situation being vital, this effect may appear: it can be linked to random interference due to variations in the relative mobility of sound sources represented by all motor vehicles. The effect will become even stronger as the listener moves closer to points of convergence between direct and/or indirect sounds: foci or geometrical centres of all concave spaces.

In the second situation, the listener is placed outside the sound environment, and the ubiquity effect is linked instead to distance and to the modifications imposed by the environment on propagation times. In air, a longer duration of propagation is accompanied by a diminishment of sound due to the differential absorption of high frequencies: since these frequencies help to locate sounds, elevation leads to a certain sound ubiquity. This happens particularly in situations of dominance or physical prominence: perception of sounds in a valley from an elevated point, or perception of street sounds from the top of a tall building.[5] On the other hand, in water or through solid, the speed of propagation is increased. For example, the solid transmission of impact sounds (drill, hammer, footsteps, etc.) in concrete buildings. In this second situation, the origin of the sound is located in a somewhat defined scope, but we do not know from where it comes inside this field – the listener does not know where to look.

Architectural Conception

From the point of view of architectural conception, no recipe can be presented. We usually try to avoid the emergence of the ubiquity effect since it often causes anxiety. Architects nonetheless often use it for explicit means of control, through the transformation of a "panopticon" into a "panaudible."[6] The ubiquity effect also used, in a more implicit way, to express the symbolic power that consists in making any spectacular space a ubiquitous space. In sacred architecture such as cathedrals, the organ, the choir, or the preacher's voice illustrate this symbolic power. The church can also represent an instrument, and the congregation is, in a way, inside the resonator. In institutional state architecture (particularly in large reverberant spaces of neoclassic architecture), voices of the jury in a court (sometimes invisible from the hall) are also mysterious. We also find it in central-stage concert halls, antique theatres, and large stadiums. This is the case, to some degree, with any location associated with power and representation.

In fact, on a practical level, a hall in which we cannot locate sources is a failure. We might expect that such a criterion would be extended to the conception of urban space and the arrangement of territories.

PHYSICAL AND APPLIED ACOUSTICS

From a strictly physical point of view, we can only define the ubiquity effect through tendencies, based on the different factors of localization of the sound source. In fact, there is no strict acoustic definition of this effect. Certain physical characteristics favour its perception, or contribute to its shaping, but do not necessarily provoke it. Two types may be distinguished.

Acoustic Properties
The important role of sound frequency is supported by the fact that higher frequencies are easier to locate than lower ones, which can thus be considered as more "ubiquitous." The role of intensity is very important: high amplitude creates a loss of localization, a feeling of exhilaration; we say that loud sounds can drive one mad (threshold of pain, neurophysiological saturation of receptors). A strong intensity affects direct and reflected sounds. The "doubling" of intensity will appear louder as the intensity of the direct sound is increased. For example, with a clap of thunder in a mountain kettle, the ubiquity effect appears to be linked as much to the reverberation effect as to the intensity of the sound itself.

At the other extreme, silence is ubiquitous – it is actually often frightening. Silence, as we know, is a relative notion and a healthy ear will quickly perceive, after a moment, sounds that were inaudible in a previous sound context. The ubiquity effect seems here to be linked more to a cut out (strong drop of intensity) than to silence itself. Certain experimental sounds could also be considered as ubiquitous. These include white noise (because of a confusion of frequencies) and clicking (because the shortness of the sound makes it difficult to identify the level, intensity, and location).

Propagation
Among the characteristics linked to propagation, we distinguish those concerning the space of propagation itself: certain locations 'preserve' more than others. The higher speed of propagation in water or solids makes these milieus more ubiquitous than air, since the probability of simultaneously receiving close and very distant sounds is greatly

increased.[7] In air, we can also explore the acoustic properties of fog.[8] In addition, we can distinguish characteristics of obstacles to propagation, such as screens and spatial configurations.[9]

Masks, filtration, and distortion can contribute to a ubiquity effect, but only if we do not know what the original sound was or if we are not used to it. A simpler situation would be a listener placed on one side of a wall and a sound source placed on the other: here, the listener is in the "shadow" of high frequencies and the penumbra of low frequencies. Because lower sounds are less easily localizable, the multiplication and tangling of sounds in this situation tends to produce a ubiquitous perception.

The fact that the acoustic properties of the sound and the propagation space are insufficient to explain the ubiquity effect emphasizes the important role of the complex conditions of perception.

PSYCHOLOGY AND PHYSIOLOGY OF PERCEPTION

Ubiquity, by its very definition, supposes active listening rather than a simple stimulus/answer schema. If there is a "sound object," it cannot be immutably perceived by a passive receptor organ; it is constructed and "realized" by an active ear that creates it as such. It is therefore specifically through an emitter–receptor interaction that the ubiquity effect can be described.

Concerning the listener, we have already seen that the ubiquity effect can be produced in various ways. First of all, with a multiplicity of real or illusory sound sources, differences appear between speech and other sounds. In the case of a single sound, it seems that a slight phase difference in speech is perceived as an echo, while the same difference for another sound will be perceived as a second source. In the case of the synchronous emission of several sound sources, it appears that speech is more difficult to discriminate than other sounds, which implies that speech has a more ubiquitous tendency. (The means of segregation by the ear between simultaneous emissions are based on the synchronization of harmonics belonging to the same source, and an analysis of their periodicity).

The ubiquity effect can also be produced by a displacement of real or illusory sound source(s): "If we bring a sound to both ears using telephone receivers, and if we increase the intensity in one of the receivers, the subject has the impression that the sound source turns toward that side; in such an experience, a difference of intensity creates the illusion of a displacement of the source."[10]

For the receptor, the ubiquity effect can also appear through an ear deficiency. Physiologically, three systems of localization can be affected. The first system uses the difference of intensity between the two ears – a system of localization based on the masking effect created by the head when a sound is lateral. (This works mostly for high pitched sounds because the wavelength is shorter than the width of the head). The second system of location is based on the phase difference or temporal shift of arrival between the two ears – a system of localization used to locate lower-pitch sounds (rate difference inferior to a half-wavelength). The third system is based on a difference of spectrum, and is made possible by the outer structure of the ear and its pinna.

We can presume that a deficiency of the first two systems of location, caused, for instance, by deafness of one of the two ears, would create a strongly ubiquitous perception. A sound coming above us is more "ubiquitous" than a source emitted on the horizontal level, where our ears are located. We may then question whether the ubiquity effect is stronger with children, because the voice of the father or the mother comes from above. However, in monaural listening, localization is always possible through spectral discrimination, and, in cases of extended deficiencies of the other two methods of localization, this discrimination seems to become more sensitive through habituation.

Consequently, there is no ubiquity effect that we can attribute solely to a physiological pathology; it is rather in the interaction between the emitter and the receptor that we must look for the co-determination of this effect. We can, however, claim that the ubiquity effect appears when the conditions of perception are such that the receptor is incapable of realizing a sound object.

This is particularly the case when poly-sensorial interpretation is not possible, which happens not only in acousmatic situations but also when the relation between sound perception and the other senses becomes ambiguous or unusual.[11]

It is also the case when spatio-temporal conditions of listening place the listener in a paradoxical situation in relation to the source: more specifically, the ubiquity effect can be linked to a paradox of perception: the closer the sound source, the less localizable it is. For example, in industrial or workshop environments, it often happens that the sound of a tooling-machine is well localized through the sound perception over distance (perhaps from the back of a shop), but near the machine a ubiquity effect is possible, which poses safety problems. Security alarms are problematic in terms of localization: from far away we know the origin of the sound; from closer, on the other hand, we often do not – hence probably a cause of their effectiveness (to create panic). The paradox becomes extreme when the listener is unaware that she or he is actually the sound source (the most banal example is probably the derealized echo of our own footsteps pursuing us at night through a reverberant urban space), or when the listener believes that he or she is the emitter of a sound that cannot be found.[12] In such cases, the listener is simultaneously emitter and receiver.

On a psychomotor level, the ubiquity effect may have diverse consequences. One case involves enjoyment: in some situations, the subject can find pleasure in the ubiquity effect, ranging from simple rest or a feeling of calm created by natural sounds (sea, birds, crickets) or human environments (murmur of the city, which is sometimes compared to the sea in literature), to a liberation and catharsis (crowds, collective games, musical trance) in which the ubiquity effect may be considered as a type of drug (if the effects are not felt under the actual influence of alcohol or drugs).[13] But these exaggerated situations are more related to what we call the envelopment effect.

As a general rule, however, the ubiquity effect implies discomfort and anxiety for the person who perceives it (or else the listener would not wonder about the origin of the sound). This anxiety may range from a simple faint feeling to the most uncontrollable panic, including feelings of flight, aggressiveness, or inhibition, perhaps marked with paranoia.[14] The relentless attempt to locate a sound while being powerless in the absence of possible feedback may in fact easily result in the perception of a harmful and voluntary intentionality of the sound, directed towards oneself.[15] This might induce a variety of behaviours including submission, anticipation, fascination, or fear. It can also lead the listener to search for, and likely not find, where the frightening sound is coming from.

But independent of factors of enjoyment or anxiety, the ubiquity effect can also induce motor behaviours, notably when the emission is identified as a particular signal, while the uncertainty about its location leads to an uncertainty about the concerned addressee.[16]

SOCIOLOGY AND EVERYDAY CULTURE

The world of games presents good examples of the ubiquity effect: games such as hide-and-seek, hunt-the-slipper, or blind man's bluff provide occasions for children to disorient the "victim" with screams. More generally, we can examine how games based on what Roger Caillois calls mimicry and ilynx (respectively linked to principles of simulacrum and vertigo)[17] are associated (or not) with ubiquitous sound production (rounds, counting rhymes, plays of echoes, masks and role games, costumes and voice imitations) or perceptions (turns, swings, carousels at fairs, hang gliding) all of which are aimed at either producing an illusion (such as delocalization) or maintaining a somewhat prolonged feeling of dizziness.

But the use of the ubiquity effect is not limited to play; it can be more strategic and determined. For instance, ubiquity is a classical principle of hunting in a variety of cultures: examples include hunting with hounds and various methods for "beating the bush" by surrounding the area with beaters.[18] It is here that power – the second major component of the ubiquity effect – intervenes. Beyond the gratuitousness of play, the ubiquity effect is used by design in pragmatic or symbolic exercises of power.

This leads us to establish a distinction between the ubiquity sonic effect (which we have considered above) and the "effect of sound ubiquity" (which constitutes a broadening of the strict definition). In the ubiquity sonic effect, the sound occurs first, and is perceived as ubiquitous. The sonic effect produces the ubiquity, in the sense that the receiver does not know where to look for it; consequently it is the spatial aspect that determines the effect, through a phenomenon of sensorial perception. In the effect of sound ubiquity, the sense of ubiquity or disorientation comes first, and is perceived through the way it is manifested in sound. The ubiquity effect "is produced" by the sound, in the sense that it makes use of the sonic medium to "produce itself." Thus, it is the semantic aspect that becomes decisive, through the expression of power, either real or imaginary.

These two aspects of the same effect are evidently complementary and sometimes even indivisible: for the receiver to be, in fact, ignorant about the origin of a sound is already to "be possessed." This is how myth works in an oral society; it is also how rumours work. These phenomena are characterized by the impossibility of knowing the source or origin of a story that is carried from one individual to another, and which exists only because it is told and retold. At the same time, to not know where a sound comes from is almost to believe in the manifestation of a superior force or a transcendental power: God,[19] the State, Nature, the Father.[20] On the other hand, for the sender, the exercise of power consists in making its voice heard without being detected: to control, listen, inspect,[21] with no chance of being controlled, listened to, or inspected (or perhaps to show only what is intended to be presented); such is the strategy of power.

If the ubiquity effect introduces a fundamental asymmetry between the sender and the receiver, the power that takes advantage of it is based on a rupture of the possibility of exchange: on the one hand, listeners are placed in the exclusive position of receiver (they cannot emit in return, since they do not know where to turn or who to speak to), and are forced into silence.[22] On the other hand, the reversibility of the ubiquitous process is attributed only to the sender[23] – notably through the control of media.

TEXTUAL AND MEDIA EXPRESSIONS

The role of media can be described using the previous distinctions.

The Sender

For the sender, the ubiquitous character of media systems constitutes a major stake of power. Empires spread through the extent of their road system – that is, they were defined by the speed of transit of speech and information. Today, states still attempt to maintain some control over communication networks; radio and television play a social link by diffusing the "great narratives of legitimization" of power to their audiences. In totalitarian regimes, this control is accomplished in an authoritarian way. Through monopolization of the broadcast of messages, the voice of power becomes ubiquitous, because it is diffused everywhere and the power is itself perfectly identified and localized.

In democratic regimes, however, power requires a formally distinct third party to accredit its discourse and to ensure a connection between democratic power and the public. The media assume the role of the "intermediary narrator." Consequently, as shown by Louis Quéré, the speaking authority is split between power and media. This division leads to a disappearance of the actual narrator (it is neither the power nor the media narrator that speaks) and a similar splitting of the receiving body: the account of the media is aimed toward both the power it serves, whose desires of power it must fulfill, and toward the public, whose desires are different.[24]

The totalitarian ubiquity of the broadcast and transmission of information is substituted for or added to the feeling of ubiquity of the receivers, who do not know the origin of the transmitted message (it is, and at the same time it is not, the voice of power). The feeling of ubiquity is linked to the disconnection of a significant relation of cause and effect between a determined place of emission and a determined place of listening, but the appearance of an "effect" still depends on the awareness of this situation by subjects who perceive it – a realization that is generally only temporary.

The Receiver

For the receiver, these splitting effects are multiplied with technological and anthropological mutations that concern not only the narrator and the receiver but also the referent and the type of discourse.

From the viewpoint of technological development, the progressive establishment of new networks of communication[25] provides possibilities of interactivity that were inconceivable a few years ago, and that make improbable any exhaustive control of networks while making the fantasies of power accessible to anyone linked to the principle of ubiquity of communication networks.[26]

From the viewpoint of sociocultural evolution, factors including the diversification and fragmentation of lifestyles, the desynchronization of familial activities, the mobility of professionals, the fragmentation of the nuclear family, the multiplicity of cultural references, and the rise and multiplicity of forms of subjectivism all lead to the psychological impossibility of referring to any "stable objective authority."

This is what media change expresses. "Today, the voice of great narratives also becomes inaudible. It is relayed by a multiplicity of voices, the voices quoted by the media. We may characterize the narrative production created by media in three ways: disseminated, miniaturized, and polyvalent."[27] These three aspects may be seen as characteristic of today's media ubiquity: dissemination of cultural references through the multiplication and diversification of channels; miniaturization of programs (real-life stories, testimonials, particular histories, videos); and polyvalence, through the generalized equivalence of programs and possible permutation of radios.

The ubiquity effect is thus double and paradoxical. On one hand, technology allows an increased openness to the world (technical ubiquity is the ability to communicate anything to anywhere and from anywhere, at any time, and with anyone). On the other hand, it risks the development of a phenomenon of rejection by closing in through the fragmentation of references (feeling of ubiquity: to not know what to communicate, where to communicate, and with whom).[28]

These behaviours and representations of ubiquity concern us here only insofar as they are based on the sonic transmission of information (radio, television, telephone). However, we must note that ubiquity sonic effects (in the perceptive sense) can be intimately linked to these representations and behaviours: the successive refinements of the remote control, distance programming, "audiovisiophony," vocal synthesis, and voice-activation, for instance, continuously enhance the possibilities of emergence of such an effect in the most common situations. Examples include the ability to change location through a simple commutation, to call our own answering machines, or to listen with headphones and not know whether the sound is real or recorded.

MUSICAL AESTHETICS

The ubiquity effect is intimately linked to the technical possibilities offered by concert hall and public address systems as well as by the successive discoveries of electroacoustics. In fact, the equipment of a hall makes it possible to exploit ubiquity as a power effect (to take the microphone, to diffuse information, discretely or ostensibly), or as a spatial effect (the electroacoustic creation of spatial trajectories).

Technical evolution in sound involves not only refining the quality of reproduction, but also improving listening conditions so that we can get as close as possible to "natural" or "real" conditions. The ubiquity effect then appears in two forms: in the multiplication of sound sources (loudspeakers) and their dispersed distribution in space;[29] and, in the ambiguity introduced by the increasingly perfect simulation between the recorded sound and the reproduced sound (we no longer know what the sound of reference is).

The use of the ubiquity effect for aesthetic purposes does not necessarily require the technical means of electroacoustics, but it has become more and more common in the domain of shows and theatre. The ubiquity effect thus appears as an implicit, underlying principle in either the staging or the composition of a work.

The ubiquity effect is now part of common practice in contemporary theatre: for example, when actors are spread out in different sections of the theatre, or when spectators are asked to move during the performance. There is a questioning of the status and the role of the stage, and a further questioning of the status of the spectator, who may become a listener if he or she does not know where the action will move to, or even whether he or she is spectator or actor.

This use of ubiquity is also widespread in contemporary music, which sometimes employs analogous techniques of decontextualization by distributing musicians or even whole orchestras to different locations in the hall or the surrounding space.[30]

Such stagings are however not characteristic of only of our time; they are also found in the tradition of carnivals and fêtes,[31] which are themselves ubiquitous. The carnival, as a place and time of negation and inversion of normal social relations, and as a place and time of "transgression of the obligations and prohibitions of everyday life" – as shown by J.-P. Dupuy using the Girardian theory of mimetic crisis – is based on a process of "panic" or scrambling of social differences. This lack of differentiation introduces a "total confusion of demarcations and compartmentalization" in which the multiplicity of orchestras, dance contests, and processions play a determining role.[32]

These stagings also evoke antecedents in very diverse works of classical Western music. Numerous examples can be found in religious music, which exploits the acoustic possibilities of large cathedrals with choral scores that seek to express supernatural voices and the power of the afterworld.[33] Other examples appear in opera, beginning in the Baroque era (Jean-Philippe Rameau, Charles-Antoine Le Clerc, Marc-Antoine Charpentier),[34] and in other genres.[35]

Certain principals of musical composition favour the emergence of the ubiquity effect. From a temporal point of view, it usually appears through simultaneity. Performance involves the simultaneity of playing or retransmission in different points of the real space. Composition involves the simultaneity of different tonalities which, by signifying or referring to different spaces of reference, can play on different "levels" of sound spaces. In this respect, the diminished seventh chord no doubt plays a particular role. This chord is composed of three minor thirds, which means that all three inversions of the chord have the same distribution of intervals. "The diminished seventh chord, being constituted of equal intervals, has no determined tonal label ... In harmonic progressions, the diminished seventh can lead at will to many different tonalities. For the same reason, if it is used in isolation, considered as an absolute, it has an ambiguous sound, an atmosphere of discomfort or anxiety, that it the perfect choice for mysterious or fantastic effects. Lyric theatre provides many dramatic examples, including the chord we hear in Mozart's opera when the statue of the Commander appears in Don Giovanni's door."[36]

Some compositional principles prepare a ubiquity effect through succession, blurring differentiation through the use of repetition,[37] recurrence,[38] and looping.[39] These techniques are based on a loss of orientation in the progression of the musical motif. If the ubiquity effect comes from an uncertainty about space perception, it is doubled by an uncertainty about time perception.

Undoubtedly cinema has made the most aesthetic explorations of the unsettled frontiers of time and space in complex relationships established between image and sound. Synchronicity or non-synchronicity, visibility or non-visibility of sound, dubbing or non-dubbing of an image, can create paradoxical relations in the space-time continuum of the film – relations that are similar to the ubiquity effect. We must note that since most movie theatres are monophonic, there can only be "semantic" sonic effects: the sound source is unique (placed behind the screen so that sound can "follow" the image everywhere inside its frame), so there cannot be an effect in the strict and perceptive sense of the term. The spectator, however, is located in several places simultaneously: the space of the theatre where he or she is sitting, and the spaces presented in the film.

Theatres equipped with stereophonic sound and a large panoramic screen can move sounds from one side to the other to reinforce effects of war scenes or hubbub. Michel Chion distinguished between three types of sound in cinema:

- *onscreen sound*: sound that is synchronized with the image: We see the sound source on screen, whether it is the voice of an actor or the sound of a car.
- *offscreen sound*: "the cause of which is not simultaneously visible in the image, but which remains located in our imagination at the moment when the action presented, and in a contiguous space to the one shown"[40] (for example, outside noise in an inside scene).
- *nondiegetic sound*: "which emanates from an invisible source, located in another time and/or another location than the one shown in the image"[41] (the "off" sound of film music, and the voice-over of a narrator are the two most conventional uses).[42]

There is an implicit progression from one type of sound to another, from the least ubiquitous visualized sound to the most ubiquitous acousmatic sound: onscreen sound is most often perfectly located, while a voice-over is literally a voice that comes from nowhere and everywhere at the same time. But this does not necessarily produce a particular effect on the spectator.[43]

We now return to the problems of definition raised in the preamble. For an effect to take place, as stated, the sound must interrogate, it must establish a paradox between localization and non-localization, between temporal linearity and temporal non-linearity. The previous distinction allows us to distinguish three ways of using or producing a ubiquity effect. In the first case, the sound can say that it is onscreen without saying where it is inside the frame. It is not located (and this is what interrogates), but we know that it is localizable somewhere inside the frame.[44] In the second case, the sound may say that it is offscreen without specifying which external space it is located in. It is not visually localizable, but we know that it can be located somewhere offscreen (in a space that has been shown or at least suggested by previous action and images).

In the third case, the nondiegetic sound must not appear as such, to create an effect (or else it is conventional and has no reason to astonish apart from the moment of its emergence). It is not localizable, but we cannot be sure of that and we nevertheless try to find it. The most characteristic example of this type of situation corresponds precisely to what Chion calls "acousmêtre intégral" – a voice that has not yet been seen but is still susceptible to appear at any time in the frame.[45]

Moreover, borders between these three situations may be blurred, and effects may double each other if the director establishes doubt about the nature of a heard sound: onscreen, offscreen, or off.[46] Where is the sound coming from? asks the ubiquity effect. This question may double itself: first, is it onscreen, offscreen, or nondiegetic? Then, if this is determined, other questions appear. If a sound is onscreen, we question: Where is the sound inside the frame? We know that the subtle worrying noise is in a car, but we cannot see if it comes from the rear-left, or the front-right). If a sound is offscreen, we question: In which space of reference is it located? We know that the siren of the emergency vehicle is coming nearer, but we cannot see which street it will emerge from. If a sound is nondiegetic, we ask: How can we bring this unthinkable sound into a determined space of reference? The subjective voice-over instructs the driver to brake before an invisible obstacle, which saves him from an accident at the last moment.

And if these three questions, single or combined, can constitute the stakes of a film, it is because they also cover the most ordinary situations of life experience.

RELATED EFFECTS   delocalization, envelopment,
                                                    metamorphosis, telephone

COMPLEMENTARY EFFECTS INDUCING THE UBIQUITY EFFECT	imitation, dullness, repetition, reverberation
COMPLEMENTARY EFFECTS INDUCED BY THE UBIQUITY EFFECT	decontextualization, derealization[47]
OPPOSITE EFFECTS	deburau, hyperlocalization, synecdoche

Vibration that affects a sustained sound. Vibrato consists of a continuous modulation of intensity or pitch allowing one to enrich a sound. The control of vibrato required for the human voice and for string and wind instruments is one of the great characteristics of performance style.

Vibrato

| RELATED EFFECT | tremolo |

A composite effect in which a continuous high intensity sound gives the listener an impression of facing an ensemble of sound materialized in the shape of a wall. This feeling of solidified sound, accompanied by a feeling of powerlessness and crushing, can be easily experienced at a rock show or when facing an urban street with multiple lanes of dense traffic.

Wall

A compositional effect describing a sound or a group of sounds that we hear following a curve of intensity, the shape of which is analogous to the shape of a wave and consequent undertow: crescendo, maximal point, fast or progressive rupture of the sound, and decrescendo. These cycles, spaced by metronomically quite long intervals (a few seconds), follow each other according to a variable or regular frequency. When the period of the cycle is shorter, we describe the effect not as a wave but as a phase or a musical fade.

Wave

The wave effect, which is composed of diverse elementary effects (phase, filtration) that we might also call the undertow effect, is based on an aquatic metaphor that has an explicit image of reference. The sound progressively intensifies, spreads out, is suspended – giving the impression of a quasi-stop – and then starts the cycle again.

We can distinguish two types of wave effect. The first type is linked to the source, to the morphology of the emitted sound. This type of wave effect is like a wave in the ocean, which produces and defines a sound curve that accurately describes the characteristics of this effect. When the source itself is organized as a sound wave, it is clearly a compositional effect.

The second type is linked to the conditions of propagation of the sound; the source remains unaffected but is potentially governed by other effects. A sound continuum carried by the wind to a listener, for instance, is modulated by gusts that create *crescendos* and *decrescendos* following the same shape as a wave. The result is closer to a particular type of masking that we might call "dip wave effect." In this case, an acoustic screen is temporarily established between the source and the listener; the perception of the effect depends on the position of each element – source, screen, listener – and the wave effect results from their spatial situation. The displacement of one of the three elements may cancel the effect. The metaphor of the wave effect and its aquatic reference operate on a visual level as well as on a sonic level: the graphical representation of the wave as a broken sinusoid describes this effect as precisely as listening to multiple variations of the sea.

ARCHITECTURE AND URBANISM

Whether it characterizes a sound source or modulates the perception of a continuum, the wave effect is a typical environmental effect. Atmospheric elements in the environment, provide remarkable examples: in addition to the ocean in its different forms, wind often creates this effect as both a sound source and a sound carrier. Gusts of wind, with or without rain, follow the same sound cycle as a wave.

The wave effect finds its archetypal image in natural elements, particularly the sea, from the description of its cycle to the potential submersion it possesses.[1] The scale of concerned sounds often greatly exceeds the framework of individual listening. The hearing subject is the peaceful or frightened witness of a sound rhythm that surpasses him or her both in space (through a tendency to submerge) and in time (by offering no way to modify its progression). In this sense, the wave effect plays on relativity by placing the listener in a framework where he or she has no control, the only way out being to move away.[2]

To work as an effect, the cycle of the wave must be relatively stable. Even if the intensities differ from one period to the next, the difference between minimum and maximum must allow identification of a constant structure, according to everyday listening criteria. The configuration of locations is essential for the propagation of the wave effect, both in the position of the sound source in relation to the listener and as an amplifier or muffler of a message. Any industrial continuum (such as factories or trains) can create a wave effect through wind. Places that are particularly reverberant will add to the amplitude of the wave.[3]

PHYSICAL AND APPLIED ACOUSTICS

The precise measurement of a sound wave indicates that the structure of this effect is primarily based on a variation of intensity. It is fluctuating volume that characterizes the wave effect. Other complementary variations, such as the appearance or disappearance of certain frequencies or the progressive modification of timbres, may be added over this basic evolution. It seems however that these secondary criteria cannot create a wave effect on their own. Intensity is always a necessary variation.[4] In fact, the wave effect is related to the resonance of the location, and its amplitude varies according to it.

The wave effect develops as a discontinuous permanence. It does not subdivide time in a clear fashion, as is the case with its sudden drops and appearances of the niche effect. On the contrary, the wave creates a sinusoidal rhythmicity, developing a crescendo followed by a drop with no actual interruption of the message. Even a period of quasi-silence is totally integrated into the wave cycle. The wave is always defined on the basis of a sinusoidal signal, but the connection between maximal and minimal intensities may adopt very different forms: constant progressive, rupture, constant *crescendo* / abrupt *decrescendo*.

But if there is no rupture of the continuum, the wave effect can still be articulated around a type of break in regularity. The maximal point is a moment at which the sound material collapses, as if folding back on itself – giving a momentary impression that it will cease – before it finally begins a new cycle. There are many differences between wave shapes; their common denominator is periodical fading: the fluctuating animation of a drone. The rhythm is not definite; rather it is a cyclic envelope with a duration of one to thirty seconds on average. Shorter than a second, vibrato takes precedence over wave effect; beyond thirty seconds, the cycle is perceived as a series of isolated sound events.

In the field of perception, the wave effect acts essentially as a sign of localization and contextualization in two opposite directions: the uncertainty about the origin of the sound source in space, and the feeling of potential submersion.

Uncertainty about sound origin, which also evokes the presence effect, includes situations linked to hearing perceptions for which the absence of visual references makes it difficult to identify the sound source location. The listener perceives the regular but micro-cyclical flow of a source, the distance of which is difficult to evaluate. Most distant sounds that approach us or that we move toward are perceived through a wave effect, first by bursts, then more and more steadily. One good illustration of this perceptive progression is approaching the sea at the top of a cliff, without seeing the shore until we are quite close. Another example is walking through the streets of a city toward a gathering crowd that is heard first in momentary bursts, then by waves, until we finally plunge into the sound.

In the hollow section of the wave, the listener may have the impression of almost losing the message and its continuity. But the link immediately reappears with the following wave. This sensation is even stronger when meaning intervenes in the perception. A clearer example of this situation is the reception of radio shows a long distance away: the wave variations follow an actual slow-wave pattern, going from a clearly heard signal up to a scrambled sound and quasi-silence during which the listener concentrates so as not to lose the thread of the speech. This specific wave effect linked to short-wave radio reception is also known as fading.

In many everyday situations, discreet wave effects situated away from the listener can be identified. In some cases, the listener may be immersed in a fluctuating sound continuum, plunged inside the actual wave. In a phase of great amplitude, the wave has a potential to submerge or physically cover the listener. Then comes the "vague" threat of the breaking. It all happens as if the danger could be materialized if the undertow does not take place: if the peaks of the sinusoid are connected and there is no decrease, drama is accomplished. In this sense, the undertow is an eternally restated reprieve. All sound continuums, whether natural or urban, can reach such a level of intensity that they appear as a materialization of danger for a specific moment. In this case, the wave effect is actually the consciousness of survival: even if there are only moderate decrescendos in each period, there is constant hope for the appeasement of the situation.

The wave effect introduces time into the perceptive field. By establishing a cycle, the wave harnesses the sound stream, imposing its rhythm and limits. The threat of submersion it possesses is therefore more a sensorial counterpoint than a plausible danger. By repeating the same sound event without strict imitation but through the reproduction of the same formal framework, the wave effect pads accidental traits and opens the way for habit or custom. Therefore its perception is for the most part unconscious when it is part of the everyday sound domain. Only exceptions linked to the appearance or the disappearance of a sound message may stimulate consciousness.

SOCIOLOGY AND EVERYDAY CULTURE

Metaphorically, we could say that the wave effect pertains to the collective order of the world, and even to the domain of number. It can only exceptionally be applied to single sounds. Atmospheric elements (sea, wind) or urban continuums previously mentioned (factories, highways, traffic) refer to the layering of multiple sounds to allow a wave effect. A single car passing is only an occurrence; it requires a stream to create this effect. On the other hand, human voices or the roaring of some types of animals can singly imitate the wave effect.

In the same way, human sound manifestations developed in waves are mostly observed in structured or informal meetings: applause, schoolyards, street demonstrations, sports gatherings, crowds, funfairs. Acoustic and perceptive criteria of the wave effect – notably the distance between these and the listener – can also be applied to these sound sources.

However, one particular instance is contrary to the factor of distance: the sound participation of the listener in the wave effect. At concerts, demonstrations, or sport events, clamors of a crowd may modulate according to this effect, often combined with the chain effect. Here the submersion previously mentioned becomes an individual self-immersion in collective movement. The rhythmicity of the effect offers a context of expression and amplification in which everyone has access to the collective wave. The combinatory character of the wave effect is then fully exploited. Acclamations at a stadium, a concert hall, or an arena often describe this sound undulation, the peaks of which seem to keep increasing. Every voice that participates in the common wave testifies, by this action, to its adhesion to the constituted collective body.

Sociologically, or on a related acoustic register, modulations of religious chants, often amplified by the reverberation of surrounding spaces, create a wave effect also resulting from a collective expression. Psalmodies of Gregorian chant, Koranic verses, and Buddhist ceremonies all develop a sinusoidal rhythm rooted in breathing, slowly creating the sedimentation of a vision of the world with each new sound phrase. The wave effect is then clearly a collusion effect.[5] By analogy, certain everyday experiences of fragmentation are related to this effect. These are cases in which a sound source is similar in terms of permanence and rhythm to the wave effect; laments and tears are two examples. In their diverse expressions (moans, murmurs, sobbing, screams), these attitudes evoke both a fluctuation linked to fundamental human breathing, and a potential submersion by suffering. We can submerge ourselves in moans and let ourselves be covered by our own sound expression. Also, the aquatic metaphor directly connects teardrops and the sea. In this case the perspective changes and the wave effect expresses a rupture with the group.[6]

MUSICAL AESTHETICS

By allowing the repetition of sound motifs over a short period, composers of contemporary music, particularly with electroacoustics, may create low "impulses" built on a mode analogous to a wave effect. This pattern often involves one or a number of low frequencies adopting a non-regular sinusoidal form, like heartbeats that are almost connected together. Cinema often uses this type of accompaniment to generate suspense and anguish.[7] An impulse, acting as a sound infrastructure likely to be forgotten because of its repetition, often borrows from the wave effect its bewitching character and its reference to the archetypal nature of low sounds: frequency takes precedence over timbre, and listening involves the vibration of the ribcage as much as the ear.[8]

In contemporary music, religious psalmody, or in some types of traditional music (such as Balinese), the use of the wave effect reinforces the hypnotizing character of a sound message. By channeling breath in the logic of its curve, the wave imposes a time that slowly becomes integrated by the listener. By moving from frequencies of rest to agitation, music can directly act on the perceptive equilibrium in a semiconscious way.[9]

By extension, we may list here a series of electroacoustic effects used in both classical and popular electrophonic music: flange, phasing, chorus, and vibrato (which is like an accelerated wave effect). These additives either allow a cyclical variation of intensity or frequency of notes, or they introduce a phase shift with the original source, producing a stereophonic effect with movement that, when slow enough, can be similar to waves. These techniques are most evident in the phase effect.

TEXTUAL AND MEDIA EXPRESSIONS

Poets have always been sensitive to the ageless harmony of the sea. One of the first, Homer, provides us with a good example of imitative harmony.[10] The human voice also uses a wave effect, notably when a single person talking to the public tries to persuade. Sports commentators on radio and television offer good examples of amplitude modulations of the voice according to the movements of the action. Vocal waves reflect dramatization and the progression of the stakes. A similar technique is also practiced in marketing and selling fields to obtain a strategic effect: the voice must soothe, calm, and wake up. Ancient rhetoric developed with the *inventio* and the *dispositio* – concerning argumentation and construction – and the *elocutio*, by choice of words, their order, their periodic recurrence, and their imitative effects exploited the sound possibilities of oratory art. Thus repetition, symmetry, alliteration, assonance, paronomasid, all include the periodical return of similar sound phenomena.

RELATED EFFECT	masking
OPPOSITE EFFECT	niche

An electroacoustic effect that intervenes in the filtration of a sound and allows successive subtraction or reinforcement of diverse frequencies, notably higher ones. Wha-wha was commonly used by rock guitarists in the 1970. Stimulated by means of an additional pedal plugged between an electric guitar and an amplifier, this effect is named after a simple phonetic analogy.

Wha-Wha

Wobble

An electroacoustic effect of analog tape recorders that characterizes the deformation produced during playback due to an incorrect alignment between the magnetic tape and the playback head. The shaping effect gives the impression of a "slobbering" sound with blurred contours.

Wow

An effect characterizing variations in the pitch of a sound message caused by the irregular rotation of a turntable deck or the maladjusted or broken mechanism of an analog magnetic tape recorder. The wow effect is particularly audible when it affects held sound; the analogy with tears (the French term for wow is *pleurage*) can be clearly heard.

Notes

TRANSLATOR'S NOTE

1 B. Hellström. "Noise design: Architectural modelling and the aesthetics of urban acoustic space."

2 Murray Schafer, R. "A review of À l'écoute de l'environnement: Répertoire des effets sonores."

INTRODUCTION

1 The calls of the hunters in New Caledonian forests are "musical" only in our interpretation. For the Pygmies, a sound is considered as music only if it can be danced. See Shima Arom, p. 50, in J.-F. Augoyard, "Séminaire environnement sonore et société."

2 The compositions and performances of John Cage that incorporate noise in music constitute an important moment in the twentieth-century aesthetic. Cage's thinking remains preponderant; it has made an essential change in listening culture.

3 H. Torgue et al., "L'oreille active."

4 This transformation propels the surprising sound utopia proposed by Athanase Kircher in the seventeenth century. Among his writings, see in particular, *Musurgia universalis sive ars magna consoni et dissoni* (Rome, 1650) and *Phonurgua nova sive Conjugium mechanico-physicum artis et naturae* (Kempten, 1673).

5 The concert hall shaped like a guitar body in Palladio's Villa Contarini is a remarkable illustration of an extreme form of this analogy: see J. Dalmais, "La résonance."

6 Following this approach, Denis Muzet recorded the sound of the Place Sainte-Catherine, Paris, over a year: see D. Muzet, "Approche typo-morpho-sociologique du paysage sonore."

7 We could include all the enterprises inspired by the methodology of R. Murray Schafer (see note 8 below). In France, since 1980, important research has been done by the Centre de recherche sur l'espace sonore et l'environnement urbain (CRESSON), and more recently, by researchers such as Alain Léobon and Philippe Wolosczyn, inspired by the thinking of Abraham Moles.

8 See J.-F. Augoyard, "L'objet sonore ou l'environnement suspendu." See also further interesting, contemporary comments in the collection *Ouir, écouter, entendre, comprendre après Schaeffer*.

9 A critical point was proposed in 1976 by François Delalande, one of the disciples of Pierre Schaeffer. Delalande noticed that while the phenomenological perception of the sound object (our second sense) does not imply the notion of scale, the Gestalt sense (our third sense) implies a division based on an articulation and the delimitation of basic perceptual elements: F. Delalande, "Le traité des objets musicaux, dix ans après."

10 While reading Schafer's numerous publications, it is indispensable to listen to the international soundscape recordings, edited by Schafer and the World Soundscape team (Arcana, Vancouver and Bancroft Editions). The ideal is still to attend one of the exceptional outdoor concerts where the environment becomes a full-fledged instrumentalist.

11 CRESSON is a thirty-five-member team in the Centre national de la recherche scientifique (CNRS) laboratory "Ambiances architecturales et urbaines" at the École nationale supérieure d'architecture de Grenoble.

12 J.-F. Augoyard, "Les pratiques d'habiter à travers les phénomènes sonores"; J.-F. Augoyard, P. Amphoux, and O Balaÿ, "Environnement sonore et communication interpersonnelle"; O. Balaÿ and G. Chelkoff, "La dimension sonore d'un quartier."

13 G., Chelkoff et al., "Entendre les espaces publics"; P. Amphoux et al., "Le bruit, la plainte et le voisin"; J.-P. Thibaud and J.-P. Odion, "Culture sonore en chantier."

14 Psychoacoustics research is concerned with contextual sound phenomena. Georges Canévet and his team worked on an interesting effect of time-shift where virtual sources take over real sources in perceptive localization (Laboratoire d'acoustique et de mécanique appliquée of the CNRS, Marseille).

15 The interesting concept of an "internal soundscape," particularly affecting psychological and physiological approaches, was proposed by Manuel Perianez in "Testologie du paysage sonore interne."

16 This relation between event and effect is perfectly demonstrated by Gilles Deleuze in *The Logic of Sense*. More recently, in an apparently very different sphere, R. Casati and J. Doxic deal with sound and the orientation of the receptive sound field: *La philosophie du son*. While this is a complex

and difficult work, persistent readers will find an inspiring and original approach underlying a rich body of theory.

17 We use the term "environment" in its most common meaning. In a more detailed analysis, it would be necessary to distinguish between the terms "environment," "milieu," and "soundscape" (*paysage*), as proposed by Pascal Amphoux in "L'identité sonore des villes européennes, guide méthodologique." This distinction respects three points of view – the given, the interactive, and the aesthetic – that can be applied to any constructed space.

18 J.-F. Augoyard, P. Amphoux, and O. Balaÿ, "Environnement sonore et communication interpersonnelle"; J.-P. Thibaud, "Le baladeur dans l'espace public"; O. Balaÿ, *L'espace sonore de la ville aux XIX siècle*; J.-L. Bardyn, "L'appel du port"; P. Amphoux, "L'identité sonore des villes européennes, guide méthodologique."

19 See Cécile Regnault's universal survey, "Les représentations visuelles des phénomènes sonores."

20 The Beaubourg effect can be seen as a combination of cocktail and metamorphosis effects. The square of the Pompidou Centre in Paris, often occupied by passersby, tumblers, musicians, and homeless people, presents a mixture typical of these two effects.

21 See the extensive use of sonic effects in Björg Hellström, *Noise Design, Architectural Modelling, and the Aesthetics of Urban Acoustic Space*.

22 For example, when learning a foreign "language." See Colette Augoyard, "L'espace sensible, outil pédagogique en classe de langue."

23 The music/environment interaction that we propose here is brilliantly demonstrated by the enlightening work of François-Bernard Mâche, *Music, Myth and Nature, or The Dolphins of Arion*. For the Doppler effect, listen to the trumpet *glissandi* in the first movement of Gustav Mahler's Symphony no. 2 or the first movement of his Symphony no. 6.

24 Since 1998, Adolfo Conrado, a professor at the Academy of Music of Torino and the Italian translator of this repertoire, has been systematically exploiting sonic effects in his teaching. He also uses sonic effects extensively in his compositions, including operas for children. "Learning to use the 'repertory of sonic effects' in daily life helps us to better understand the soundscape in which we live, and therefore, to look for its transformation. It helps us to listen more closely to music and to find the music we need. It allows us to learn how to play music if we have no one to play it for us." Adolfo Conrado and Stefania Barbieri, *Effetti sonori nella composizione e nell'ascolto della musica: Guida al repertorio degli effetti sonori di J.F. Augoyard – Henry Torgue*.

25 We acknowledge the important and knowledgeable help of librarian Claire Becaud and Jean-Claude Foulon, director of studies, at the Conservatoire de Grenoble.

26 See Balaÿ's analysis of sonic effects in Balzac, Stendhal, Proust, and Zola in *L'espace sonore de la ville aux XIX siècle*.

27　For examples from world music culture, we have provided specific references to easily accessible discographies and scores. Numerous recordings of sequences and soundscapes made since 1980 can be found at CRESSON, Grenoble. CRESSON has also produced a number of geographic or thematic K7 and CDs, including soundscapes of European harbours and railway stations (Jean-Luc Bardyn, "L'appel du port" and "La portée ferroviaire"). Examples of thematic works include: Pascal Amphoux, "Paysage sonore urbain. Introduction aux écoutes de la ville"; J.F. Augoyard and Martine Leroux, "Les faiseurs de bruit"; Nicolas Rémy and Björn Hellström: "Espaces, musiques et environnement sonore"; Nicolas Tixier et al., "Effet de métabole."

ANAMNESIS

1　See the works of Edith Lecourt, particularly "The musical envelope."

2　A woman has recently lost her husband. In the following week, at a friend's house, the telephone rings. Being alone, the woman answers the phone and is disconcerted because she thinks she recognizes the voice of her husband. This example illustrates the importance of the present context, which favours a projection of identity that is still close to the surface of memory, but that will probably gain perspective as time goes by. See also the account of Alfred Tomatis (*The Conscious Ear*), who presented to a young child the voice of his mother, filtered so that it sounded more like his intra-uterine perception.

3　One of the most beautiful examples of therapy is Mélanie Klein's description of "the child with the train." This child presented deep perturbations in the learning of letters and numbers. Clinical work was undertaken and researchers soon realized the child associated numbers with the sound of a train. Gradually, they understood the link between the train and the phantasm of parental coitus that had probably been heard. By associating a sound inductor to a psychological block, the child was also preserving one of the ways to the anamnesis and its psychic release: Mélanie Klein, *Essais de Psychanalyse*, 59 and 125.

4　Sound diffusion devices play a large role in the recording stage of a situation that could possibly be evoked later on: the sound of a television, a theatre, the way in which our memory records voices of the speakers and actors, all mark situations and time in an inescapable chronology.

5　We have already mentioned anamnesis as a psychotherapeutic method; it is also used as a survey tool in sociological research, in the form of "reactivated listening." Researchers make sound recordings in a familiar environment for a particular test group while asking them to comment on the recordings. This survey technique is an excellent tool to decode sounds of everyday life, notably in their territorial character. This method was developed in 1983 and has been used at CRESSON, Grenoble, ever since.

6　This personalization of sound can also be illustrated by the tradition of symphonic poems (for example, *The Sorcerer's Apprentice* by Paul Dukas, or *Peter and the Wolf* by Sergei Prokofiev), although the effect is then closer to repetition than to anamnesis in its strict sense. In Marcel Proust's *In Search of Lost Time*, the short section of the sonata of Vinteuil, inspired by César Franck, illuminates Swann's love for Odette: "And before Swann had had time to understand what was happening, to think: 'It is the little phrase from Vinteuil's sonata. I mustn't listen!,' all his memories of the days when Odette had been in love with him, which he had succeeded, up till that evening, in keeping invisible in the depths of his being, deceived by this sudden reflection of a season of love, whose sun, they supposed, had dawned again, had awakened from their slumber, had taken wing and risen to sing maddeningly in his ears, without pity for his present desolation, the forgotten strains of happiness." Marcel Proust, *Swann's Way*, 496.

7　Milan Kundera, *The Unbearable Lightness of Being*, 51.

8　See O. Balaÿ and G. Chelkoff, "Conception et usage de l'habitat."

9　In a work by German choreographer Pina Bausch, twenty dancers sit, facing the audience. They all speak each in their native language, relating a personal story. Slowly, the leader passes a microphone in front of each of them, and for a short moment, a voice, a language, a dramatic expression (comic or tragic) fills up the sound space through amplification. For many members of the audience, the series of words from the dancers provokes a series of anamneses, referring to the countries evoked by their language, to the situations we can guess based on understood fragments and the timbre of the voice. In such a situation, the process of evocation works perfectly, the spectators become involved as soon as they understand the rule. Anamnesis is expected – rather than fortuitous, as in everyday life – in a register clearly defined but flexible enough for everyone to be able to project their own memories.

10　Blaise Cendras, *Moravagine*, 150.

ANTICIPATION

1　See H.R. Jauss, *Toward an Aesthetic of Reception*.

ASYNDETON

1　See J.-F. Augoyard, "Répons pour voix discrètes et trois silences."

COCKTAIL

1　E. Cherry, "Some experiments on the recognition of speech, with one and two ears." See also R. Plomp, "Acoustical aspects of cocktail parties."

2 G. Canévet. "Audition binaurale et localisation auditive," 107.

CUT OUT

1 Most evidence illustrating this effect comes from leading research at the CRESSON laboratory. The following quotations are excerpts from interviews about real-life situations: "When we come here, we really feel like being in another world. I stayed two hours, and then I left. As soon as I crossed the buildings, I found the street, cars. I forgot that it existed." G. Chelkoff et al., "Entendre les espaces publics," 50.

2 "It's true that we usually get out of a noisy place and come here. I think that we are immediately more attentive. Our attitudes change. It's fairly silent. The noise you make while walking will be audible. At least you'll hear it. Maybe others won't hear it but you'll hear yourself walking. You know that you cross a specific place, you locate yourself. It is noisy because the flagstones click a little bit, it's like a reconnaissance sound, you are the one who's passing through." G. Chelkoff et al., "Entendre les espaces publics," 50.

3 "At a certain moment, everybody wondered what was happening. We were quietly chatting in the living room with some friends. Something quite distressing happened. We couldn't tell exactly what it was. I realized, while talking, that everyone was becoming distracted, as if something was broken. Then someone said 'Hey! The fan stopped!' That was it!" (J.-F. Augoyard, P. Amphoux, and O Balaÿ, "Environnement sonore et communication interpersonnelle," anecdote 22).

4 An inhabitant of Grenoble described the moment when he entered the courtyard of an older district (Barnave street): "The cut, the change is very abrupt, because I move from the city where I'm very sensitive to sounds; then, all of a sudden, I find myself in a deep silence where the only sounds are that of the baker, the pork butcher, some doors, and my footsteps." An inhabitant of Paris said: "It is very noisy in Wagram Avenue, but then we cross the carriage entrance and ... nothing. Nothing, as soon as we cross the gateway. There is no noise inside; we're somewhere else ... But we also get used to that" (G. Chelkoff and O. Balaÿ, "Conceptions et usages de l'habitat").

5 See the work of Alfred Tomatis (particularly *L'oreille et le langage*), who presents the notion of "éblouissement auditif," and his hypothesis on the plasticity of the response curve of the ear and its conditioning to listening to the environment.

6 The anecdote about broken glass perfectly illustrates this adaptation of behaviour to a cut out effect: "Suspended for a moment, the murmurs of the hall resume. The timbre and rhythm change. People come back to their stories. We can feel the warmth of the place rising again. A consensus has been found again, as if cards had been re-dealt" (J.-F. Augoyard,

P. Amphoux, and O Balaÿ, "Environnement sonore et communication interpersonnelle," anecdote 37).

7 "Three people are conversing in a living room. The telephone rings, and discussion stops. Someone answers the phone, talks for a moment and hangs up; the two others do not talk. Is it to avoid hearing, to avoid disturbing? Once the telephone call has ended, the discussion resumes where it had left off" (J.-F. Augoyard, P. Amphoux, and O Balaÿ, "Environnement sonore et communication interpersonnelle," anecdote 35).

8 "In a calm rural environment, two people are talking and proceed to get into a car. The doors slam, and the car starts. The driver stops talking to listen to the sound of the motor for a moment and to verify that it is functioning properly. Then, the passenger starts speaking again, repeating what he said at the moment of ignition. Neither of them realize that there had been a repetition" (J.-F. Augoyard, P. Amphoux, and O Balaÿ. "Environnement sonore et communication interpersonnelle," anecdote 36).

9 "The sound level has peaked in a classroom where students are using machines. To restore order, the teacher uses an even louder machine to emit a sound that brutally cuts through the racket and provokes silence" (J.-F. Augoyard, P. Amphoux, and O Balaÿ, "Environnement sonore et communication interpersonnelle," anecdote 106).

10 These well-known compositions provide good illustrations of a variety of cut out effects.
  – Intensity cut: Ludwig van Beethoven: Symphony no. 2, second movement (*Scherzo*), mm. 145–60 and mm. 380–90; Igor Stravinsky: *The Rite of Spring*, "Introduction" and "Augurs of Spring," rehearsal nos. 12–22 and the end of "Spring Rounds".
  – Cut out linked to abrupt ending of a phrase: Claudio Monteverdi, *Altri canti di marte*, in "Gira'l nemico insidioso," eighth book of madrigals.
  – Tonality cut out: Albert Roussel, *Bacchus et Ariane*; Arthur Honegger, *Symphonie pour cordes* (Symphony no. 2, 1940–41).

11 See Pierre Schaeffer, *Traité des objets musicaux*.

12 See Marc Fumaroli, *L'âge de l'éloquence*.

13 See Gillo Dorflès, *L'intervalle perdu*.

DEBURAU

1 The Deburau effect was named by Michel Chion and is described in *The Voice in Cinema*, 102–6.

DRONE

1 Constant sounds such as mechanical ventilation systems, fluorescent tubes, and the humming of motors are all woven into the everyday envi-

ronment in layers. Cathode ray tube (CRT) screens produce a continuous drone at about 15,000 Hz. The hum of ventilation systems in computers, another drone that has recently appeared in everyday, occupies an omnipresent place in the workplace.

2 "Un bruit sourd et continu" J. Dubois, *Lexis, Dictionnaire de la langue française* (Paris: Larousse, 1975).

3 Among natural elements, the sea (or more precisely storms at sea that we can hear far inland), a torrent in the middle of a mountain village, and the wind all produce drone effects that receive a positive or negative appreciation. In the animal world, the sound of a swarm or the gallop of a herd are the most characteristic forms of drones. The insect bearing the same name as this sound ("bourdon" is the French word for a bumblebee) refers to an image of a type of uselessness linked to a frightening buzzing. The *bourdon* is not associated with the hive (as is the sound of many bees) as much as with the relative solitude that marks the appearance of the drone of a single bee in human activities. As a clear warning of its presence and movements, it emits a shriller and more annoying tone than the sound derivative that bears its name.

4 R. Murray Schafer, *The Tuning of the World*, 76–7.

5 See. J.-P. Thibaud and J.-P. Odion, *Culture sonore en chantier*.

6 In correlation, the sound background that an inhabitant diffuses in his or her residence improves the soundproofing in relation to the outside or to a noisy neighbourhood, because of the principles developed in masking. Here is a simple example: if the sound background created by an inhabitant in one residence is at 45 dB (A), the person in the neighbouring apartment can produce noises of about 45 dB (A) + 51 dB (A) – corresponding to regulations regarding sound insulation between apartments according to the standards in effect – for a total of 96 dB (A) without being perceived too obviously.

7 Until recently, sound insulation was relatively neglected in most means of transportation, including cars, trains, and planes. Since sound levels often exceeded 80 dB (A), operators subjected to these high intensities could lose a large portion of their mental aptitude.

8 The Françoise-Marguerite bell – also called "la Savoyarde" after its founder (Paccard installations, Annecy) – installed at Sacré-Cœur in Montmartre, weighs 19 tons. Opposite to a drone but sharing the same constancy of sound, we can also mention the chanterelle, an additional string added to some instruments that vibrates in sympathy when the principal strings are plucked or bowed. The role of the chanterelle is to boost the harmonics and resonance of the instrument by keeping a constant pitch in the high frequency range.

9 One example of a harmonic pedal is the third movement of Antonio Vivaldi's *L'inverno*, op. 8, no. 4. Pachelbel's well-known Canon in D minor is constructed over an eight-note bass line (a ground bass) that is repeated over and over throughout the entire work. Later examples of a ground

bass include the bass line of George Bizet's *L'Arlésienne* and the left hand of Chopin's *Marche funèbre*.

10 G. Rouget, *Music and Trance: A Theory of the Relations between Music and Possession*; see also the CD *Flûtes du Rajasthan* (Le chant du monde, CD LDX274 645, 1989).

11 C. Gregory, *Encyclopedia Universalis* (Paris, 1973), vol. 11, 470.

12 Ibid., vol. 12, 103.

13 In *Music for Airports*, Brian Eno, a British composer, superimposes many sustained bass notes that slowly evolve, continuously modifying the drone effect. By multiplying saxophone lines at different pitches while basing their parts on repetitive sequences, the group *Urban Sax* has developed a musical style based on a constant sound from which melodic bursts arise. The sound is produced by a number of saxophones playing repetitive sequences at different pitches. This group often performs in the heart of cities, filling streets and squares with a musical flow.

14 The expression "soniferous garden" was coined by R. Murray Schafer in *The Tuning of the World*. The French term *jardin sonifère* was first used by Bernard Lassus around 1980. Soniferous gardens are made up of "instruments" stimulated by natural elements (rain, wind) or by passersby and walkers (the footbridge-xylophone). Only the wind creates drones (modeled the Aeolian harp). The soniferous garden Les Glycines in Evry, Essonne (France), was conceived by architect Alain Sarfati and the Swiss composer Pierre Mariétan.

ECHO

1 E. Lecourt, *L'expérience musicale: résonances psychanalytiques.*

FILTRATION

1 See E. Leipp, *Acoustique et musique*: "The anatomical human ear: Ear bones protect the hearing system, while serving a similar function to the iris in the eye. Figure 58 shows the ear as seen from above. For clarity, tendons and passive organs used only to maintain the ear bones have been deleted, but the two muscles and active organs that allow us to understand the mechanisms involved have been retained. The schematic outline of the ear (Figure 59) shows the general layout, including the pinna, ear bones, and cochlea, where sensitive cells transform sound signals into electrical impulses. The cochlea is a complex hydrodynamic system, a sort of liquid oscillating piston comprising two membranes (oval and round windows), the function of which still remains largely hypothetical" (E. Leipp, *Acoustique et musique*, 105).

In *La machine à écouter*, Leipp discusses modification of the sensitivity of the ear with age. "According to the researchers who produced this diagram [Figure 60], all musical faculties seem to decrease with age,

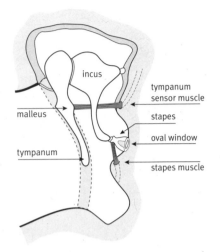

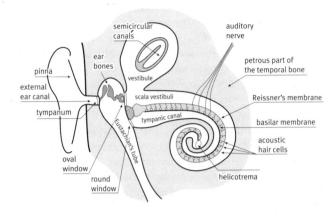

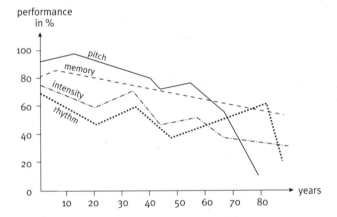

Figure 58 (above left)
E. Leipp, *Acoustique et musique* (Paris, Masson, 1984), 105.

Figure 59 (above right)
E. Leipp, *Acoustique et musique* (Paris, Masson, 1984), 105.

Figure 60 (bottom right)
Decrease of musical faculties with age.
E. Leipp, *La machine à écouter* (Paris: Masson, 1977), 146.

except for the perception of rhythm! Of course these are simplifications and generalizations!" (146)

2　See J.-F. Augoyard, P. Amphoux, and O Balaÿ, "Environnement sonore et communication interpersonnelle," vol. 2. This research is illustrated with many anecdotes linked to the sound environment that describe situations of adaptive sound imagination.

3　Effects of hygrometry on this attenuation are analyzed in *REEF*, vol. 2, *Science du bâtiment*, 101.

4　Example cited in Pierce, *Science of Musical Sound*, 144.

5　See G. Chelkoff and O. Balaÿ, "Conception et usage de l'habitat," 49.

6　See O. Balaÿ and G. Chelkoff, "La dimension sonore d'un quartier."

7　L. Hamayon and C. Michel, *Guide d'acoustique pour la conception des bâtiments d'habitation*, 62.

8 E. Viollet-Le-Duc, *Discourses on Architecture*, vol. 2, 266.

9 César Daly, *L'architecture privée sous Napoléon III*, 15–16.

10 This mechanism is very practical, as Honoré de Balzac describes: "'If you will come into this room with me, we shall be more conveniently placed for talking business than we are in this room,' said Madame Hulot, going to an adjoining room, which, as the apartment was arranged, served as a card-room. It was divided by a slight partition from a boudoir looking out on the garden, and Madame Hulot left her visitor to himself for a minute, for she thought it wise to shut the window and door of the boudoir, so that no one should get in and listen. She even took the precaution of shutting the glass door of the drawing-room, smiling on her daughter and her cousin whom she saw seated in an old summer-house at the end of the garden. As she came back she left the card-room door open so as to hear if any one should open that of the drawing-room to come in." Honoré de Balzac, *Cousin Bette*, 6–7.

11 B. Céleste, F. Delalande, and E. Dumaurier. *L'enfant, du sonore au musical* (Paris: Butchet-Chastel, 1982).

12 A. Tomatis, *L'oreille et le langage*, 120. The period during which a baby can produce sounds in all frequency ranges is very shortly after birth. The specific frequency concentration for French is around 800 to 1800 Hz, while that for English is between 2000 and 12000 Hz.

13 Sound recording and reproduction devices (microphones, recorders, phonographs, players, etc.) also act as filters. The electrophonic chain is a succession of filters: some are inherent in the function of the material used (for example, a microphone); others are conceived to optimize quality of reproduction (noise reduction systems, Dolby, DBX). These techniques consist mainly of an artificial amplification of specific frequencies of the signal before the recording, so as to increase their level in relation to background noise. The recorded message is first coded by a noise-reduction device, and then decoded during reading before it is returned to its normal course of diffusion.

14 See Gérard Blanchard, *Image de la musique de cinéma*.

15 Pierre Schaeffer, *Traité des objets musicaux*, 190, 191, and 236.

16 J.-P. Vian. "Rapport annuel des travaux du CSTB" (Grenoble, 1978), 259. This observation was only made for statutory insulation of 51 dB (A). It appears that in conditions of identical background noise and conversation, "the recognition of pronounced words in a neighbouring apartment can vary from 0 percent to around 60 percent, depending on the type of material used in the partition." This means that, in terms of intelligibility of everyday language, conversations will be either totally unintelligible, or totally intelligible with partitions that nevertheless offer the same insulation rating in dB (A).

17 M. Proust, *Swann's Way*.

18 O. Balaÿ, *L'espace sonore de la ville aux XIX siècle*.

19 In Stendhal's *The Charterhouse of Parma* (which is set in 1820) the narrator compares how the sound from a party is perceived from two different locations. The first location is on top of a steeple; "When the Blessed Sacrament approaches, the trail of powder is ignited, and then begins a running fire of successive explosions that are irregular and absurd; the women are entranced." From a second location farther away from the party, it seems to the narrator that "Nothing is so gay as the noise of these *mortaretti* heard from across the lake, softened by the lapping of the waves" (161).

20 Cousin Pons will be introduced in Mrs. Camusot's living room: "'Madame, here is your Monsieur Pons – still wearing his spencer!' Madeleine came and told the Présidente … From her bedroom, Madame Camusor hears a man's footsteps and throws her daughter a glance, shrugging her shoulders. 'You're always so clever at giving me warning, Madeleine,' said the Présidente, 'that I never have time to decide what to do' … Then, as she caught the woebegone expression on her poor pet's face, she added: 'Look, hadn't we better get rid of him once and for all?' 'Oh, the poor man!' replied Mademoiselle Camusot. 'Do him out of a dinner?' A simulated cough resounded in the ante-room – that of a man trying to indicate that he was within earshot. 'Oh well, let him come in!' said Madame Camusot de Marville with a shrug." Honoré de Balzac, *Cousin Pons*, 45–6.

21 "And scarcely had I tapped before I heard three others, different from mine, stamped with a calm authority, repeated twice over so that there should be no mistake, and saying to me plainly: 'Don't get agitated; I've heard you; I shall be with you in a minute!' and shortly afterwards my grandmother would appear. I would explain to her that I had been afraid she would not hear me, or might think that it was someone in the room beyond who was tapping; at which she would smile: 'Mistake my poor pet's knocking for anyone else's Why, Granny could tell it a mile away!" Marcel Proust, *In Search of Lost Time*, volume 2, *Within a Budding Grove*, 285.

22 Michel Foucault, *The Use of Pleasure*.

IMITATION

1 "What is more extolled by poets than the bewitchingly beautiful song of the nightingale, in a lonely stand of bushes, on a still summer evening, under the gentle light of the moon? Yet there have been examples in which no such songbird is to be found, and some jolly landlord has tricked the guests staying with him by hiding a mischievous lad who knew how to imitate this song … just like nature in a nearby bush. As soon as one becomes aware that it is a trick, no one would endure listening to this song, previously taken to be so charming. The same is true with every other songbird. It must be nature, or taken to be nature, for us

to be able to take such an immediate interest in the beautiful. This feeling is heightened by the fact that we expect others to appreciate this beauty; and they do. For we consider those who have no feeling for the beauty of nature to be coarse and ignoble ... they confine themselves to the enjoyment of mere sensory sensations at table or from a bottle." E. Kant, *Critique of the Power of Judgment*, § 42.

2 See the notion of imitation in the *Poetics* of Aristotle, vol. 2, 216–338. See also the notion of simulacra in Plato's *Sophist*.

3 Examples include *The Four Seasons* by Antonio Vivaldi, *La bataille de Marignan* by Clément Janequin, and Arthur Honegger's *Pacific 231* (which is associated with a famous American train of the same name). During the seventeenth and eighteenth centuries, music was filled with numerous and frequent forms of imitation, and even stereotypes. Composers of the Baroque period used phrasing and style to create musical "imitations" of natural elements such as wind, calm, storms, and earthquakes, as well as expressions of human feeling. Good examples can be found in the works of Giacomo Carissimi, Claudio Monteverdi, Jean-Baptiste Lully, and Henry Purcell.

4 For instance, the size and arrangement of the orchestra required for performances of works by Hector Berlioz or Richard Wagner; see the comments of O. Splenger in *The Decline of the West*.

5 R. Murray Schafer, *The Tuning of the World*, 116–17.

6 Trân Van Khê, "Musique traditionnelle et évolution culturelle."

7 Louis Matabon, "La mémoire de l'oreille."

8 "Sometimes nature seems to take risks for the sake of music. Three species of American *Mimidae* (*Toxostoma rufum*, *Dumetella cariolinensis*, and *Himus polyglottos*) imitate one another, yet their rate of individual variation is very high. This pushes the freedom of invention so far that it has still not been understood how they themselves can recognize one another." J.-B. Mâche. *Music, Myth and Nature*, 159.

9 "A long time ago, people from Su'upanra created bamboo music. They were living up there, in a place called Rokera, over a bay where they used to go fishing. In these times, nobody knew about bamboo music; it was ignored by everyone, everywhere ... It is the porare bird that inspired this music. Necessity was the mother of invention as they made a flute, which they called bamboo of the porare bird, used to draw the bird's attention. This bird was pillaging their domestic garbage. When they played this instrument, the bird believed it heard one of its friends coughing, and flew toward the sound. The flute players waited nearby and as the bird approached, they aimed at it with a bow and killed it," Related by Irispan in Daniel de Coppet and Hugo Zemp, *'Aré 'Aré: Un peuple mélanésien et sa culture.*

10 In the sequence of bells and brass band in *Decoration Day*, the third movement of *A Symphony: New England Holidays* by Charles Ives, urban space suddenly appears as a symphonic statement.

Figure 61
Luigi Russolo, *The Art of Noises* (New York: Pendragon Press, 1986), 44.

11 In contemporary stringed-instrument instrument making, imitation is based on timbre, and the semiotic effect produced inevitably refers to the original instrument. The fascination that accompanied the use of synthesizers and the logic of their first phase of marketing was linked to their ability to imitate existing instruments. The instruction manuals are organized like instrumental catalogues rather than sound catalogues: flute, clarinet, oboe, harpsichord, piano, percussion, etc. Although it is true that digital synthesis and sampling of real sounds allow an extremely faithful reproduction (in the case of sampling, the timbre is elaborated directly from a traditional instrument), this imitative aspect of the synthesizer is less fascinating than its extraordinary capacity to explore new sound spaces.

12 F.-B. Mâche and C. Poché, *La voix, maintenant et ailleurs.*

13 "I can reproduce this imitation. There is nothing to add; it is perfect. After the second *ten*, (the bell), the child prolongs the *en* and gradually raises the pitch. He interrupts the enharmonic scale for two more *ten tens* and resumes the interrupted scale until reaching a high point, from which he descends rapidly but enharmonically to end with two or three *shiiou shiiou* (the valves of the compressed-air brakes!) [see Figure 61]." Luigi Russolo, *The Art of Noises*, 44.

14 François Delalande (INA-GRM) made a careful study of the semiology of vocal imitation. "Cyril moves a toy on the ground (by rolling or sliding it), over a short distance (around 30–40 cm). He accompanies this slow movement with a long varied tonic sound, ascending and descending, covering about an octave. Here, movement and sound are not homologous. The displacement is not at all spectacular: there is a machine moving slowly and then stopping, while the sound could easily evoke a fighter plane in a vertical dive, followed by an ascent. In fact, the sound possesses details related to the gesture. The downward section of the sound probably represents the slowing down of the vehicle, and the ascent, brake noise. We thus have a double representation: that of the movement (iconic) and that of the real sound (indicative)." F. Delalande, in B. Céleste, F. Delalande, and E. Dumaurier, *L'enfant du sonore au musical*, 137–8.

15 "During a walk in a silent area, one of us starts imitating television sounds, particularly programs that present voices with modified timbres. Then, everyone starts to imitate the timbres of the voices of this show." J.-F. Augoyard, P. Amphoux, and O Balaÿ, "Environnement sonore et communication interpersonnelle," anecdote no. 69.

16 M.-F. Koulumdjian and R. Busato, *L'empreinte des médias dans le langage des adolescents.*

17 "Before anything else, the child imitates an adult's melodic line rather than the differentiated words. Even if we can identify some words or syllables that would stand out in the verbal stream, we mostly recognize intonations: the order, the question, the call." Annie Moch, *Le son de l'oreille.*

18 B. Boysson-Bardies, "La production de la parole."

19 "Aude, five months old, is in a cradle placed near a door that creaks every time the mother's helper enters ... that is to say, about a hundred times a day! In a recording, we find the striking presence of this high-pitched sound in Aude's tears and babbles – a perfect example of osmosis between reception and emission on the level of sensation." Anne Bustarret, *L'oreille tendre,* 51. The effect plays between reception of a sound coming from outside and emission; the immediacy of this relation allows the baby to adjust her sound production to that of her environment.

20 A. Tomatis, *The Conscious Ear* and *L'oreille et le langage.*

21 A celebrity such as General de Gaulle marked a whole epoch with his elocution, and many other orators adopted his way of speaking. Sometimes, it is not the sign of the times that is used as a semiotic effect, but rather the sign of belonging to a particular political group. With a little bit of attention, it is easy to observe the stylistic auras that surround political leaders and their propagation to close collaborators.

22 Bernard Lassus, "Le jardin de l'antérieur."

23 Experiments by Bernard Delage provide good examples: "Metro-bird-creek. The intervention on a moving walkway transports us: a bird perches on a shoulder, a beam of light precedes you in an obscure environment. Stimulation of sensitive cells combine to create random sound events. Sounds from the moving walkway are like sounds of a liana bridge in the trees. One can also walk: contact flagstones transform the sounds of footsteps." Bernard Delage, "Huit propositions d'intervention sonore en milieu urbain."

24 "This exhibition of antiques in their original location is quite conclusive, in the same way as the contemporary cleaning of Notre-Dame de Paris, suggested by Quatramère de Quincy. Museographers freeze monuments in a native and abstract purity. In the process, they exchange assignation to the past with an overbearing presence that is often turbulent." Michel Vernes, "Paysage de la mémoire," in *Traverses* (Paris), no. 36, "L'archive," CCI, 1986.

25 See Jean-Sylvain Liénard, "Machines: il faut ar-ti-cu-ler!," in *Science et avenir* (Paris), no. 79 (October–November 1990).

INTRUSION

1 E. Lecourt, *L'expérience musicale,* 31 ff.

MASK

1 The mask effect is discussed in several works on acoustics and acoustic psychology. An analysis and a more specialized bibliography can be found in E. Zwicker and R. Feldtkeller, *The Ear as a Communication Receiver*.

2 The "beep-beep" of watches can be heard each hour on the hour, even in situations such as concerts and movie theatres, cutting through already high levels. Emitted in a precise frequency, this sound can be distinguished even in a very intense context. The same is true for the beeping of trucks and construction vehicles in reverse: because they are usually diffused in a noisy environment, their sound signal can be better perceived through a specialization of timbre than an increase in volume.

3 For example, staff at the Western Michigan University Library voluntarily modified the vanes of the mechanical ventilation system to create a mask that seemed necessary for readers' concentration.

4 Surveys indicate that people working in open-concept offices want a sound background that is as continuous as possible, at around 50 dB (A). Such a mask generally allows for normal conversation at a distance of one metre.

5 "Japanese manufacturers of sanitary equipment observed that many users developed the habit of flushing the toilet while they were in the washroom to mask their own sounds. This lead to a waste of water and significant exploitation cost overrun. They proposed up-market products which, apart from their robotic cleaning system, water jets, and urine control, are equipped with a device that, when activated, produces the sound of a waterfall. A Japanese bank that installed these toilets in 1,600 branches has saved eighty million yen in water consumption." *Dictionnaire de domotique*, under the direction of Witold Zaniewicki (Paris: Eyrolles, 1990), 312.

6 In restaurants, people can discreetly fix their attention on voices coming from neighbouring tables, despite a mask background that may be quite loud (brouhaha or music). This ability to listen selectively is called the cocktail effect. However, comprehension of the same simultaneous conversations recorded on tape would be impossible.

7 Complaints about neighbourhood noise can arise after the construction of an acoustic screen, since before its installation these sounds were masked by the loud murmur of traffic. Another variable is the importance accorded to sounds of devices in an apartment (ventilation, water circulation) between day and night or week and week-end.

8 Ethnology has particularly emphasized the symbolic richness of masks and their role in the ritualization of collective life: see J. Cazeneuve, *Les rites et la condition humaine*; J. Cazeneuve, *L'ethnologie*; M. Griaule, *Masques Dogons*.

9 Particularly with sound examples, Gilles Dorflès developed the notion of *adiasthénie* – that is, the loss of the interval and the sonic pause; see *L'intervalle perdu*.

10 For example, annual sound rituals (calendar traditions, change of seasons) or exceptional celebrations (wedding, parties) in Claudie Marcel-Dubois, "Signaux sonores des petits métiers," 20.

11 See Jacques Attali, *Noise*.

12 In a more innocuous form, some inhabitants prefer to open their windows to urban noise, rather than put up with the "savage music" of their neighbours; see O. Balaÿ, "La proxémie acoustique dans l'habitat."

13 In any society, certain more or less incongruous sounds are declared as intolerable. Sometimes their creators have no other solution than sound mask. In this respect, surveys show that sounds of a sexual origin are less easily tolerated by neighbours, and that when acoustic insulation is deficient, only sound masking may make this type of situation acceptable.

14 The personal stereo is an efficient individual mask. The following excerpt is taken from a discussion with a fourteen-year-old: "I was listening to my walkman while walking with my friend. It was cold so the music was warming me up. I was singing and saw my friend burst into laughter. When I asked her why she was laughing, she shouted at me: 'You talk so loud!' as if I wasn't hearing her!" (J.-F. Augoyard, P. Amphoux, and O. Balaÿ, "Environnement sonore et communication interpersonnelle"). See J.-P. Thibaud, "Le baladeur dans l'espace public urbain."

15 In the film by Paolo and Vittorio Taviani, *Le soleil même la nuit* (*Sunshine even by Night*, 1990), a young hermit is fleeing from the world's temptations. He is joined by someone he loved previously, and finds himself in a cell facing a woman who speaks tenderly to him while undressing herself. Outside, it starts to rain, and the pattering becomes progressively as loud as the words that trouble him. Believing that this sound mask is a divine aid to avoid his collapse, he implores: "Lord, make me hear the rain!"

16 See J.-F. Augoyard. "Réflexions autour de la notion de parasite sonore."

17 Numerous examples of masked keys can be found in Albert Roussel's *Bacchus et Ariane*. Concerning timbre alliances, a new timbre sometimes results from the temporary fusion of two others (notably in the orchestration styles of Hector Berlioz or Franz Schubert).

18 Charles Ives used masking extensively, particularly to create atmospheres characteristic to the urban milieu or public scene. We can listen to his symphony entitled *New England Holidays* with this perspective. But masking was also a process of writing for this American composer, as illustrated by the hide-and-seek interplay between the continuum and emerging phrasings in *Decoration Day*, the second movement of this work.

19 The role of the conductor appears clearly here: she or he determines not only the quality of performance but also the balance between different

sections, managing all possible masks commanded by the score. It is the individual way of emphasizing specific sound layers that creates the style and identity of great conductors. An orchestra is not a stable sound element; discreet and fragile sounds can easily be covered by deeper and louder instruments. The role of the conductor is to ensure the clarity of the musical text and the fair and subjective mixing of all components of the sound. See J.-F. Pierce, *The Science of Musical Sound*.

20 See, for example, the music of Karlheinz Stockhausen; analyses of his works can be found in J.-J. Nattiez, *Music and Discourse*.

21 "Each pretends to pass; one appears, the other swears; Mules' ringing adds to the murmur; … We can only hear confused shouts: to be heard, God would really need to thunder." Nicolas Boileau, "Les embarras de Paris," from *Les Satires* (1660–1711), V I, 21–70.

22 "In the country more so than the city, the sonorousness of floors should be avoided. In the city, incessant street noises prevent the ear from distinguishing sounds in the house itself; it is the opposite in the country, where we repair to find quiet and the least sound is audible." E.-E. Viollet-le-Duc, *Discourses on Architecture*, vol. 2, 352.

METAMORPHOSIS

1 "The perceptual 'something' is always in the middle of something else, it always forms part of a 'field'. A really homogeneous area offering nothing to perception cannot be given to any perception." M. Merleau-Ponty, *Phenomenology of Perception*, 4.

2 Does sonic simultaneity require the perception of a figure/background distinction? How can we listen to two sounds at the same time – for instance, two different radio shows simultaneously? Either both sounds form a whole, which will be difficult to understand, or discrimination favours one of the two and the other is pushed into the background. In visual perception, the figure/background relations are better known: "Shapes always relate to the field they are part of, which constitutes the background. Rubin (1921) has defined what distinguishes a figure from the background. The background is relatively undifferentiated, as it seems to extend under the figure over the outline that limits it, or a section of it. This illusion happens even when it is contradicted by knowledge." R. Francès, *Psychologie de l'esthétique*, 56.

3 The spatial aspect linked to Western history of the two notions, and their contemporary foundation in a visual experimentation (Gestalt theory), makes the terms "figure" and "background" suspicious. J.-F. Augoyard suggests replacing them with the "event/duration" pairing, which is closer to the fundamental nature of sound; see "La vue est-elle souveraine dans l'esthétique paysagère?"

4 On a visual level, the background acts on the figure in many ways; for instance by modifying its aspect until it becomes unrecognizable, as in

certain optical illusions. In the sound domain, the figure/background relation also mutually acts on sound identification and recognition. The cry of a seagull emerging from white noise (artificial noise composed of the totality of frequencies) will cause the white noise to be perceived as a sea sound, whereas the sound of a car braking over the same white noise will make it appear as traffic noise (a didactic exercise realized at CRESSON).

5 Yannis Xenakis explains the origin of his inspiration for the work *Metastasis* (a Greek word meaning transformation): "Athens ... An anti-Nazi demonstration ... hundreds of thousands of people reciting a slogan repeated rhythmically. Then, the battle against the enemy begins. The rhythm bursts into an enormous chaos of high-pitched sounds; whizzing of bullets; sputtering of machine guns. Rifles progressively become more isolated. Slowly, silence comes back over the city. When strictly considered from a listening point of view and detached from any other reference, these sound events, formed by a large number of particular sounds, cannot be perceived separately; but bring them together again, and a new sound is created that can be heard in its integrity. It is the same for the sound of cicadas, hail and rain, the breaking of waves on shingles." Xenakis analyzed these complex sonorities in the hope of detecting particular characteristics of the event. He concluded that it was not the intrinsic characteristics of the sounds, such as the low or high-pitched screams of the crowd, the firing of machine guns or rhythmic psalmody, but the characteristic distribution of a large number of events (including movement in space), which, by continuously modifying its mixes and proportions, produced a single, composite sound. From these observations, the author identifies the internal logic, which is based on the calculation of probabilities, and from this deduces a practical cognitive plan: the notion of "field"(*champ*). Sound fields are created by varying the quantities and directions of forces including dynamics, frequency, intensity, and duration. See Y. Xenakis, *Musique, architecture*, 26 ff. and 67 ff. on the role of metamorphosis in the theory of sieves.

6 The metamorphosis effect created by a meeting of mixed voices is due to the fact that these sounds are located in a small range of intensity and their spectrums overlap. In turn, some of these voices emerge from the background into which they plunge again. By concentrating, the listener will be able to follow one voice or another, but only for a short period of time. "This phenomenon, known as the 'cocktail effect' (Cherry, 1953), is facilitated by factors such as directive listening, visual information, differences of timbre, voice accent, and the probabilities of transitions between sounds ... We now have experimental data concerning the 'cocktail effect' at our disposal, which tends to show that the hearing system can model two simultaneous streams at a fair level of treatment (Weintraub, 1987)." C. Sorin, "Perception de la parole continue," 125 and 129.

7 The French norm NF S 31-010 defines background noise as "the average minimal level of acoustic pressure at the moment of listening or measurement ... In a given space, ambient sound is what results from all the sounds with a near-stationary character during the duration of listening, due to the influence of all considered sound sources." From the point of view of acoustic theory, the background is thus distinguished by a criterion of stability, being opposed to what emerges in discontinuity.

8 "When a set of persons are on familiar terms and feel that they need not stand on ceremony with one another, inattentiveness and interruptions are likely to become rife, and talk may degenerate into a happy babble of disorganized sounds." E. Goffman, *Interaction Ritual*, 40.

9 An inhabitant's description of what he hears in the Beaubourg square: "There is a general tone, a more or less diffuse noise of brouhaha, in which a burst of laughter or some other distinguishable sound appears. It is the same in meetings: it is calm for a moment, and then suddenly a shout or a conversation will get through the general noise." In G. Chelkoff, "Entendre les espaces publics," 85.

10 In music, a major triad demonstrates this oscillation of the scale between a group of notes perceived globally and each single note perceived individually. See Pierre Schaeffer, *Traité des objets musicaux*, 268 ff. The physical manifestation of a tonic or dominant major chord does not separate the three notes and their intervals (a major 3rd and a perfect 5th). Only cultural listening can accomplish this discrimination.

11 See R. Francès, *Psychologie de l'esthétique*, 54 ff.

12 *Métaboles*, a symphonic work by Henri Dutilleux composed in 1964, is based on a particular concept of variation. This score presents many ideas in a different order, under different aspects, until, after many successive steps, they undergo a profound change of nature.

NICHE

1 "Guests arrive at the entrance door and they hear the sound of an electric saw coming from the inside of the house. They wait until the sound stops before knocking, supposing that it would cover their own signal." J.-F. Augoyard, P. Amphoux, and O Balaÿ, "Environnement sonore et communication interpersonnelle," anecdote 31.

2 "A new-born baby lies in a cradle. When sound intensity increases, and the background sound is mostly in the higher frequencies (a background produced by the street has a different spectrum), the baby falls silent. This is because babbles, songs, and sounds of games are particularly rich in high frequencies. The baby thus waits for quieter moments to produce her or his noises (moments of waking up and falling asleep, in the laundry room or toilet)." See A. Bustarret, *L'oreille tendre*, 47.

3 Good musical examples of timbre niche are found in *The Sorcerer's Apprentice* by Paul Dukas and *Bolero* by Maurice Ravel. Repetitive music

also uses this effect frequently. Because it is based on harmonic and rhythmic stability, the play of timbres remains a large field of evolution and renewal for this musical genre.

4 "I was once drilling a hole when the neighbour's dog started to bark ... I stopped because I felt that it was annoying the dog, and my neighbour at the same time, so I started again and stopped; it was quite a game ... all of this to simply drill four holes. It took me four hours because I tried to space it out!" Augoyard, Amphoux, and Balaÿ, "Environnement sonore et communication interpersonnelle," anecdote 15.

5 F.-B. Mâche, *Music, Myth and Nature.*

6 See F. Busnel, "Siffler pour communiquer," 84–5, and F.-B. Mâche and C. Poche, *La voix, maintenant et ailleurs.*

7 On a construction site, workers are attentive to the rhythm created by pounding and the noise of their machinery. Thus it is possible for workers to listen to a recording made on-site and note that: "This is a site that works well, we can feel that workers are coordinated and competent," or "This is not an efficient site, we can hear how disorganized it is." See J.-P. Thibaud and J.-P. Odion, *Culture sonore en chantier.*

8 The composer is not subjected to the sound environment, since it is part of the composition. However, musical writing, paradigmatically, voluntarily emphasizes niche effects, as if oppositions and dialectical relations between the milieu and the event were natural. In Maurice Ravel's *Rhapsodie espagnole*, see "Prélude à la nuit," from rehearsal no. 4 to the end, the two clarinet cadences followed by the bassoon. In Igor Stravinsky's *The Rite of Spring* see "Procession of the Sage," "The Adoration of the Earth," and "Dance of the Earth" (rehearsal number 54 to the end of part 1).

9 There is an excellent example of pitch and timbre niches in a chorus played by tenor saxophonists Sonny Stitt and Sonny Rollins (playing instruments of the same range) in "On the Sunny Side of the Street" (Verve Records, 1958).

10 See Marc Touché's study, *Connaissance de l'environnement sonore urbain.*

PHONOMNESIS

1 See Manuel Perianez, "Testologie du paysage sonore interne."

REMANENCE

1 "When the hallucinatory component is not totally created by the disease, but results from the distortion of authentic sensorial data ... we are facing a sensorial illusion, a phenomenon very close to a hallucination with a similar semiologic value." A. Prot, *Manuel alphabétique de psychiatrie,* 293.

2 "The sonic stimulation provoked by the buzzing of a mosquito awakes a sleeper only because of the presentiment of a possible sting. Sound sensations to which an individual is constantly subjected during his or her entire life bear affective factors and generate emotions more than any other sensation." Paul Besson, "Physiologie de l'homme face au bruit."

3 "He was called Louis. Originally a Southerner, he had to exile himself in the East as a simple railway worker and was refereeing rugby games only for pleasure. It is not always easy to pronounce decisions disadvantageous to the local team – these decisions provoked booing from the crowd. Louis refereed with such concentration that he did not hear the hostile hissing. He would nevertheless memorize these sounds, since the sonic storms to which he had been literally deaf during a game would later return to his ears. It surprised as much as it amazed me, because we always perceive more or less consciously what later comes back to our memory. In Louis's case, these sound were not vague reminiscence but strong sensations, as if it took a certain time before they would strike him. Then something even more wonderful happened. The crowd from Lorraine ... used to applaud him at the end of the games for his "no fault" (he was an irreproachable referee) ... Still, because his modesty was real and because his attention had been fully mobilized by his refereeing, he did not listen to the cheers addressed to him at the time. One or two days later, he would hear them for the first time. He came to realize that he did not forget them. Then came the time for his retirement: he would no longer wear his black costume for ninety minutes while the game was played. He went through this applause in his mind ... He had acquired the ability to leaf through his sound archive, just as others in a more ordinary way might open the family photograph album. It was his real treasure – a treasure of hearing." P. Sansot, *Le rugby est une fête*, 176–7 (Le trésor de Louis).

4 R. Murray Schafer, "Entrance to the Harbour," from *The Vancouver Soundscape* (2 audio cassettes, Vancouver: Arc Publications, 1979).

5 See, for example, "Rituel de la vénérable Yoghini de diamant," *Tibet, Musiques sacrées* (Ocora CD, 1987, the two first sequences), or the sequence "Les divinités paisibles" from Pierre Henry, *Le voyage* (1962).

6 "In very noisy districts of the Grands Boulevards, the hall that allows one to 'turn one's back to the boulevard,' to quickly forget it, announces a clearly domestic space; it even anticipates it: 'we feel at home.' Even the staircase or the elevators whose mechanical hum seem here insignificant, extend a similar atmosphere. In the apartment, everything changes again, noise reappears. We can nonetheless understand that the apartment, although noisy, remains marked by its strong qualitative difference from the places that punctuate its access. There is probably a prolonged remanence of this cut out effect and of its perception every time we enter a building." J.-F. Augoyard, "Les pratiques d'habiter à travers les phénomènes sonores."

7 In music, the indication *morendo* ("dying away") refers to the suspension that leads from the end of the music into silence. This same intention is expressed in the well-known laudatory phrase, "the silence that follows is still Mozart's!"

8 "So deeply does the quivering of her tacit temple / Conspire with the spacious silence of this scene ... Branchage, you rustle it! O rending / Rumour, and plaint to faceless breaths ..." Paul Valéry, "Fragments of the Narcissus," [1938], in *Poems*, 142 and 246.

REPETITION

1 Every musical system selects and develops units of reproduction from which cycles and self-references are organized. Through the history of music, one or more of tonality, theme, leitmotiv, musical note, have served as (re-usable) units of temporal arrangement.

2 It seems initially that music, the intentional activity of sound production and listening, develops the active pole primarily while the environment develops the passive pole. However, we must not categorize these two poles too strictly, even if their use facilitates the observation and analysis of the two facets embedded in any repetition effect. The two poles between which repetition oscillates can be found in every domain of reference. It would thus be wrong to simply bind positivity with reprise. In everyday life, we may find repetition to be positive.

3 In music, one of the indications of the reprise is *D.C.* or *Da Capo* (meaning "from the beginning," or literally, "from the head"). The reprise in music may be considered a sub-effect of the repetition effect. The two poles of repetition, including the mechanical part, also exist in the musical domain.

4 Depending on the repetition effects observed, we may perceive them as closer or farther from one pole or the other. The situation of the listener and his or her range of intervention are fundamental to this bipolarity: whether one is a passive witness of a composition effect or, on the contrary, a vector directly acting on the sound has a radical effect on both perception and feeling. An effect that depends on oneself cannot be experienced in the same way as an effect listened to passively, even with positive attention.

5 Redundancy may be both a generic process of a form and a process of indetermination. In information theory, redundancy may be what destroys meaning, but in other cases, it is closer to the idea of potential self-organization – that is to say the constitution of a form through repetition. In the theory of contextual communication, redundancy is absolutely necessary. We still find here the two polarities: loss of formal recognition and morphogenesis effect.

6 Linked to the dragging effect, repetition may move in the direction of an accumulative progression, valorized by the context. We then witness

a series of sporadic exclamations, as in the case of players who mark the progression of a game with shouts or ordered soundmarks. These reprises are established in a rhythm that gives a framework to the sonic progression of the particular social time experienced at that moment. Also, multiple repetitions (of sound, pitch, meaning) at diverse intervals can cross each other, composing a reference soundscape that is at the same time familiar and singular. Comedy based on repetition proposes exceeding, through laughter, the stressful dimension on which it is often based, through a paradoxical perception of the mechanical aspect hidden in life.

7 "In a residential building, every morning someone emptied coffee grounds by hitting the receptacle against the garbage chute. A neighbour heard this sound and, for fun, answered by also hitting the chute. The first time the person perceived this response, he became conscious that this habit was stimulating a repetition effect; he could not hit anymore, and tried to empty the receptacle with subtle knocks, as if he was paralyzed in this gesture that had always been automatic. The echo, which testified both to the presence of the other and his capacity to copy the movement, totally modified his behaviour." J.-F. Augoyard, P. Amphoux, and O Balaÿ, "Environnement sonore et communication interpersonnelle," anecdote 62.

8 All intervals exist in sound repetition, whether they relate to the domain of consciousness or of memory: the fire station siren tested at noon on the first Wednesday of each month partakes of this rhythmic organization of the sound universe. This analysis of the establishment of social order through isochronic repetitions, particularly sonic, has been largely developed by Lewis Mumford in his well-known *Technics and Civilization.*

9 Metronome speeds for music are closely related to heartbeats and act directly on the listener: slow tempos for the resting heart (50 to 70 beats per minute), and progressively faster tempos to produce an "out of breath" sound, even if the listener makes no physical effort while listening. Some music educators suggest adjusting the speed of the beat (often about 60 beats per minute) according to the age of students; 80, for instance, would be appropriate for children.

10 For people confronted with noisy environments, perception often finds a way of taming sonic aggressiveness by establishing marks and recomposing them. All mechanical phenomena that confine one to a sound obsession because of their repetition (machines, trains) can be tamed through selective listening, which creates its own path through the sonic potential, playing with the different gestalts in presence.

11 See the chapter on bird song in Gilles Deleuze and Félix Guattari, *A Thousand Plateaus.*

12 A structuralist trend in music analysis that has developed since the 1970s analyzes musical works according to the number of repetitions of dif-

ferent notes and their frequency of appearance. The analysis of style may then identify certain recurrent traits "put into series" (J.-J. Nattiez), whose pertinence may be validated through a comparison with a counter-corpus. In the same way, a statistical analysis also allows one to "compose" works (see Henry Barraud's string quartet, composed in 1940). See the many thematic issues of the magazine *Analyse musicale* (Paris), particularly nos. 28 and 32.

13 A whole part of the development of music in the twentieth century took place as a reaction on the one hand against the use of reprises ("never do what a copier could do in your place," said Arnold Schoenberg to his students), and on the other hand against the hierarchy of repetitions organized by the tonal system, which privileges the pivot notes – tonic and dominant. Dodecaphony established a principle that uses each of the twelve semitones of the scale equally in a musical work. This succession of twelve sounds is called a series: a sound reappears only after the appearance of the eleven others. Serial music generalizes the use of the series to the four properties of the sound phenomenon: pitch, duration (and therefore rhythm), intensity, and timbre. See Henry Barraud, *Pour comprendre les musiques d'aujourd'hui.*

14 Jazz is constructed precisely around this particular mode of musical repetition and variation: what every musician follows when replaying a theme is no longer the fixed alignment of a written phrasing, but a structural weave, the organizing scheme of the piece. While this unfolds silently as a landmark in each interpreter's mind, the players improvise around it, making only certain notes audible, adding others, moving away more or less from the thread that still connects them together. This abstract frame, which remains once we remove all the sounds from a piece, is the irreducible watermark that allows the recognition and identification of the theme by the listener. Such a dialogue between absence and presence would not work without the effect of mental repetition that is implied and that allows us to measure the degrees of remoteness and freedom taken and presented by the interpreters.

15 Beethoven's *Thirty-three Variations on a Waltz by Diabelli*, op. 120, fully illustrates the integration of the dimension of repetition in the evolution of a work. Each part combines the reprise of a chorus with the sensation of discovery. The second variation is not only the second part but also the first plus the second; the third is the first plus the second plus the third, and so on, up to the thirty-third and final part. This sedimentation at the scale of a work supposes that the theme still exists, always remembered, a unifying thread never lost, around which are joined the successive surges of its own drifting developments. In such cases, repetition is sublimated into a permanent resurrection.

16 The principal composers of repetitive music include La Monte Young, Terry Riley, Steve Reich, and Philip Glass. Works of repetitive music have been widely used in contemporary dance; experience has shown

that dancers, and other listeners confronted by frequent listening to the same musical piece, would whistle a melody that was only part of the sound structure. In this particular example of the move from polyphony to monophony, it is as if the listeners isolated certain notes that actually exist, but which are also superimposed with other notes in the piece. A sorting takes place. Through listening, melodies are chosen within the structure. As an involuntary consequence, once the melody is memorized, it becomes impossible to hear the piece in another way.

17 "Echo is an automatic, dehumanized response, which breaks any relation. We will emphasize three points:
   - in the first version (of the myth), it is a conviction concerning wrong use of speech (padding speech, and deceitful speech);
   - it is an involuntary, automatic repetition which escapes any form of control and any meaning, it is limitless (it continues even after death);
   - it leads to a radical isolation, an absolute solitude.
   These legends seem to express the anguish of human beings facing this natural acoustic phenomenon that transforms them into automatons and alienates them. The interpretation that is given presents echo as a punishment, a conviction which, through speech, reaches the true essence of human beings, making it meaningless. Elusive, inaccessible, Echo is everywhere, it haunts us." Edith Lecourt, "Le sonore et les limites du soi," 577–82.

18 "Human time does not turn in a circle; it runs ahead in a straight line. That is why man cannot be happy: happiness is the longing for repetition." Milan Kundera, *The Unbearable Lightness of Being*, 298.

19 Until the appearance of the compact disc (CD), there was an audible hierarchy between the original master and its reproductions; technical quality even allowed one to measure the wear and age of recordings. The advent of CDs transformed this chain by proposing an access to originals on the market, since the difference between the master and its digital copies is almost non-existent. The auditor listens not to a "reproduction," but truly to the original.

20 In some cases, sound motifs of the environment can offer, by mere chance, the perception of a soundscape that appears as particularly "composed." When R. Murray Schafer presents the entrance into the Vancouver harbour, boat horns, buoys, and bells exchange melodic, rhythmic, and harmonic elements that seem almost musically organized. Here is an effect of the environment which, although it is not deliberate, gives a feeling of intentionality. When everyday sounds adopt, even fleetingly, the form of musical language – for example, when boat horns play a major chord – the located structure of organization projects an intention, while there is only random circumstance in the game of repetitions.

21 See P. Amphoux et al., "Le bruit, la plainte et le voisin."

22 When magnetic tape was the best recording medium, reverberation and echo were required in the world of additional effects. With digitization

– that is to say, the possibility of reproduction without an initial signal distortion – the field opened to very short delays that not only create a new space of diffusion, but also intervene directly in the nature of the original sound itself. The effect does not seem to be added, but rather integrates with the source.

RESONANCE

1 In the case of a mechanical oscillator, mass-spring system, the periodic movement described by the mass (M) put into motion, considering that loss is nil, is characterized by the particular frequency of the system, which depends only on M and K (stiffness of the spring):

$$f_0 = \frac{1}{2\pi}\sqrt{\frac{K}{M}}$$

2 The catastrophe of the suspension bridge at Basse-Chaîne, Angers, on 16 April 1850, is described in *Le Journal du Maine-et-Loire*, 17 April 1850.

3 Helmholtz used hollow glass spheres, equipped with two short tubular necks diametrically opposed. The opening of one neck was placed at the ear, while the other opening was pointed toward a source emitting a periodic sound. When the sound contained a harmonic frequency equal to the resonance frequency of the resonator's cavity, it amplified the harmonic, which could then be heard separately. The sound in the resonator persisted after the sudden cessation of the periodic sound source.

4 RT60: the duration of the reverberation is equivalent, for a given frequency in a given location, to the duration corresponding to a decrease of 60 dB in amplitude while the decrease rate is almost constant. The reverberation effect is probably the most similar to resonance, since it corresponds to the decrease of all characteristic modes of the resonating chamber. More specifically, reverberation describes the behaviour of a wave hitting a surface.

5 Early decay time (EDT) is a short RT calculated on the decrease of the first ten decibels, and plotted at 60 dB of decrease. EDT reveals the balance between early energy and total energy. The more energy that is concentrated in the beginning of the response (useful sound), the stronger the slope will be, thus resulting in a short EDT.

6 Ratios given in the Bolt diagrams. Among the most well-known, we cite 3 x 4 x 5 or:

H	W	L
1	1.2	1.43
1	1.4	1.86

7 An article on the propagation of sound in prehistoric caves describes characteristic frequencies of certain caves that acted as acoustic pipes. They were put into resonance by people standing at particular locations,

Figure 62
Regio Theatre, Turin

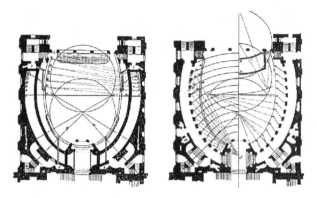

marked by wall paintings. I. Reznikoff and M. Dauvois, "La dimension sonore des grottes ornées."

8 "Bronze vases are to be made in mathematical ratios corresponding to the size of the theatre. They are to be so made that, when they are touched, they can make a sound from one to another of a fourth, a fifth and so on to the second octave. Then compartments are made among the seats of the theatre, and the vases are to be so placed there that they do not touch the wall, and have an empty space around them and above. They are to be placed upside down. On the side looking towards the stage, they are to have wedges put under them not less than half a foot-high ... The voice, spreading from the stage as from a center and striking by its contact the hollows of the several vases, will arouse an increased clearness of sound, and by concord, a consonance harmonizing with itself." Vitruvius Pollio, *De theatri vasis*, in *On Architecture*, vol. 1: 277 and 179.

9 See the research by R. Floriot: "Contribution à l'étude des vases acoustiques du Moyen-Age" and "Les vases acoustiques du Moyen-Age."

10 In France, the most important concentrations of buildings with acoustic vases are in Haute-Normandie, Lower Brittany, and in the region of Nantes and the Rhône valley.

11 The Villa Contarini in Piazzola sul Brenta, Italy, is famous for its "reverse-guitar" hall, a unique arrangement of two adjoining rooms; see J. Dalmais, "La Résonance," vol. 1: "Villa Contarini." Theatres of the Galli-Bibiena family are well-known for their bell-shaped plan. Similarly, "direct-sound" halls, such as the Pleyel Hall in Paris, have the profile of a phonograph.

12 In the Regio Theatre, Turin, (see Figure 62) sound holes allowed communication between the pit and the hall. In the Teatro Argentina in Rome, an artificial lake located under the hall acted as a sound reflector. In the Besançon Theatre (See figure 63), Claude-Nicholas Ledoux, designed a pit for the orchestra so that the audience would have an unobstructed

view. He also placed a half cylinder of wood in the bottom of the pit to enhance the depth and clarity of sound.

13 See A. Tomatis above; M.-L. Aucher, *L'homme sonore* and *En corps chante*.

14 See P. Le Rouzic, "La résonance des prénoms," in *Un prénom pour la vie*. Here are some examples: Marie, 120,000 vibrations per second; André, Charles, Jean, Michael, Pierre, 114,000; Joseph, Hélène, 110,000; Marguerite, 102,000; Alphonse, 96,000; Étienne, 94,000; Gérard, 92,000; Thérèse, 64,000; Léon, 62,000; Félix, 58,000; Barnabé, 48,000.

15 "At six o'clock it had stopped raining, and outside the Rue Raynouard was noisy with the song of birds and the din of playing children; it was like the garden of a boarding school" (Colette, *The Last of Chéri*, 101). "Au pied de la montagne, le matin, les voix résonnent comme dans un corridor" [At the foot of the mountain, in the morning, voices resonate as in a corridor], (Max Jacob, *Le cornet à dés*, I: "Le coq et la perle").

16 "And so we were able to measure the resonance being aroused in the depths of the people by our refusal to accept the defeat" (Charles De Gaulle, *War Memoirs: The Call to Honour*, 101). "For a sensitive reader each word changes its quality and its resonance and perhaps its meaning according to whether it is used by a poet or a prose-writer, a master or an apprentice, a shy man or an aggressive one, a soft-hearted man or a hard one" (G. Duhamel, *In Defence of Letters* II, xvii, 190).

17 Composers of every era have adapted their works to the spaces in which they were to be performed, but this tendency was particularly prevalent in the fourteenth century and during the Romantic period (for example, symphonies by Beethoven and Mahler).

18 Inspired by the concept of the harmony of the spheres, Gustav Holst (1874–1934) composed a symphonic suite entitled *The Planets*.

REVERBERATION

1 J. Jacques and A.-M. Ondet. "Acoustique prévisionnelle intérieure."

2 Sound energy, like many other forms of energy, is transformed into heat by absorption. However, the weak amount of energy involved in sound phenomena does not increase the temperature of a concert hall.

3 See Edith Lecourt, "Le sonore et les limites du soi."

4 L. Beraneck. *Music, Acoustics and Architecture.*

5 For example, the theatre constructed in Bayreuth for Richard Wagner by Louis II of Bavaria; see "L'acoustique des lieux d'écoute," in *L'oreille oubliée*. Some composers exploit the reverberation effect at the level of the composition itself. For instance, at the entrance of the Mandarin in *The Miraculous Mandarin* by Béla Bartók, many instruments relay the sound back and forth, maintaining the same pitches, to produce a halo typical of natural reverberation.

6 See M. Griaule, *Dieux d'eau.*

7 In terms of decoration, the interior of cathedrals was sometimes totally covered with hangings, statues, and curtains. The evolution of rituals, adaptation to reforms, and occasional fires lead to the disappearance of these ornaments. Also, during the middle ages, the church floors were frequently used as bedding for pilgrims and destitutes, and were thus often covered with straw, a material that would absorb the reverberation of flagstones.

SHARAWADJI

1 William Temple, "Upon the Gardens of Epicurus," (1685), quoted by L. Marin, in "L'effet sharawadji," 114.

2 "The creeping plant, parasite of the tree; the garden, parasite of the domain; the letter XI, parasite of the novel of Saint-Preux and of Julie, marginality at every level – so is my discourse, my own reading, in relation with Rousseau's text." Marin, "L'effet sharawadji," 124.

3 "Effects of beauty obtained through the anamorphosis of the geometric representation, if and only if calculated distortions do not appear: so is the sharawadji effect." Marin, "L'effet sharawadji," 119.

4 "There was the Chinese book of oracles, the I Ching. But before the I Ching, I worked with the magic square ... Instead of numbers, I put sounds, groups of sounds, in the square. That's how I wrote *Sixteen Dances*, as well as the *Concerto for Prepared Piano*." John Cage, *For the Birds*, 43.

5 In an anecdote, an inhabitant of Grenoble speaks of the sudden beauty of a "kind of prayer" sung once or twice by her upstairs neighbour. This "incantation" was quite surprising since the neighbourhood was used to unpleasant sounds of this notorious alcoholic. It was even "admirable": "This guy ... who we didn't think about because his sounds were quali-

fied only as annoying ... then, suddenly he ... well, he was on our side and straight away it was as if his sound was being sublimated, as if it was ... more beautiful than ours, more worthy ... thus, suddenly he became a feature as well." J.-F. Augoyard, P. Amphoux, and O Balaÿ, "Environnement sonore et communication interpersonnelle," anecdote 32.

6   "The unlimited withdraws when delimited. It does not consist by itself in a delimitation, which would be negative, since the latter would still be, precisely, a delimitation, and the unlimited would end up having its characteristic form – let's say the form of an infinite ... It is not exactly the infinite in the unlimited which touches the feeling of the sublime. The infinite would only be the 'digital concept', as Kant would say, of the unlimited whose 'presentation' would be involved in the infinite. That is to say, the gesture by which any finite form disappears in the absence of form." J.-L. Nancy. "L'offrande sublime," 52.

7   "The beautiful in nature concerns the form of the object, which consists in limitation; the sublime, by contrast, is to be found in a formless object insofar as limitlessness is represented in it or at its instance, and yet it is also thought of as a totality." The feeling of the sublime "is a pleasure that arises only indirectly, being generated, namely, by the feeling of a momentary inhibition of the vital powers and the immediately following and all the more powerful outpouring of them." "That is sublime which pleases immediately through its resistance to the interest of the senses." E. Kant, *Critique of the Power of Judgment*, 128–9, 150.

8   Luigi Russolo exalted the beauty of noises, which he judged as richer than musical sounds: "The street is an infinite mine of noises: the rhythmic strides of the various trots or paces of horses, contrasting with the enharmonic scales of trams and automobiles ... and over all these noises, the continuous, very strange and marvelous hubbub of the crowd, of which only the few voices that arrive clear and distinct can be distinguished from the others, so anonymous and confused ... As everyone knows, the electric motor produces a beautiful and characteristic hum, which is musically very close to a fifth held by a harmonium." L. Russolo, *The Art of Noises*, 45–6.

9   "The wind is an element that grasps the ear forcefully. The sensation is tactile as well as aural. How curious and almost supernatural is it to hear the wind in the distance without feeling it, as one does on a calm day in the Swiss Alps, where the faint, soft whistling of the wind over a glacier miles away can be heard across the intervening stillness of the valleys." R. Murray Schafer, *The Tuning of the World*, 22.

10 "The abject is edged with the sublime. It is not the same moment on the journey, but the same subject and speech bring them into being. For the sublime has no object either. When the starry sky, a vista of open seas or a stained glass window shedding purple beams fascinate me, there is a cluster of meaning, of colors, of words, of caresses, there are light touches, scents, sighs, cadences that arise, shroud me, carry me away, and

sweep me beyond the things that I see, hear or think. The 'sublime' object dissolves in the raptures of a bottomless memory. It is such a memory, which, from stopping point to stopping point, remembrance to remembrance, love to love, transfers that object to the refulgent point of the dazzlement in which I stray in order to be. As soon as I perceive it, as soon as I name it, the sublime stimulates – it has always stimulated – a spree of perceptions and words that expand memory boundlessly. I then forget the point of departure and find myself removed to a secondary universe, set off from the one where 'I' am – delight and loss. Not at all short but always with and through perception and words, the sublime is a something added that expands us, overstrains us, and causes us to be both here, as dejects, and there, as other and sparkling. A divergence, an impossible bounding. Everything missed, joy – fascination." J. Kristeva, *Powers of Horror*, 11–12.

11 "The self-sound interval therefore covers the relations of individual sound identity with the present environment. It is located on many axes: inside/outside, subjective/objective, near/far, in the relation to the object ... The extent of this interval depends on perceptive and sensorial capacities (perception of vibrations for instance), and their mode of use. On a deeper level, this sound interval clearly seems to depend on the integration of paranoid anguish." E. Lecourt, "Le sonore et les limites du soi," 570.

12 "Testing limits is the second point that I would like to raise here. Limits of intensity, or of the sonorous, for example, is our everyday lot. Musical research during these last fifty years has constantly modified and pushed back the boundaries between noise/silence/music by introducing more and more noise into music: the development of percussion in the classical orchestra, works such as those of Pierre Henry (Les variations pour une porte et un soupir, 1963, and all that followed), or J. Cage (starting with his piano préparé, 1938), and many others, are illustrative. This may be a way of seeking to reinforce and stretch this sonorous envelope." Edith Lecourt, "The musical envelope," 229.

13 On these ideas, see D. Anzieu, "L'enveloppe sonore du soi."

14 "Using a computer, Shepard created in 1964 a series of twelve sounds forming a chromatic scale that seem to go up indefinitely when they are repeated. By dissociating the variations of the fundamental frequency and the spectral envelope for sounds composed of octaves, we obtained sounds that seem to go down indefinitely. The paradoxes may be interpreted in terms of a composite conception of the pitch attribute – this conception is confirmed by studies on the perception of presented sounds" (J.-C. Risset, "Paradoxes de hauteur").

SYNCHRONIZATION

1 See J.-P. Thibaud, "Temporalités sonores et interaction sociale" and W.S. Condon, "Une analyse de l'organisation comportementale."

1 Asyndeton and synecdoche are fundamentally complementary; see J.-F. Augoyard, *Step by Step*. The asyndeton effect characterizes the suppression of the perception or memory of one or many sound elements in an audible ensemble.

2 Three domains of research, in particular, use synecdoche as a rhetorical effect: the study of mobile practices (see Augoyard, *Step by Step*); the analysis of the structure of the imaginary (see G. Durand, *Les structures anthropologiques de l'imaginaire*); and psychoanalysis in order to understand the mechanisms of the unconscious. According to Roman Jakobson, the notion of synecdoche is comparable to the notion of condensation developed by Sigmund Freud; see Jakobson, *Essais de linguistique générale*.

3 See A. Moles, *Information Theory and Esthetic Perception*, 60.

4 A. Tomatis develops the notion of "visée" (sighting) in *Vers l'écoute humaine*.

5 See Pierre Schaeffer, *Traité des objets musicaux*.

6 "Since the goal of the enemy is to go round the guard or to get behind him, an alert guard must suspect any sound behind him, any pebbles or rustling leaves, to such an extent that he will begin to imagine them, being afraid that the sound he hears will be the last. He listens intensively to precisely those sounds that no one cares about – unimportant murmurs, background sounds. Such a concern can keep him very active." E. Goffman, *La mise en scène de la vie quotidienne*, vol. 2 (Paris: Minuit, 1973).

7 "Perceived duration is thus a characteristic of the organization of succession. It is only possible in an existing organization, and always at the limits of the latter. This can be proved experimentally. When the organization of succession is difficult, the duration is perceived with some uncertainty." P. Fraisse, *La Perception*.

8 "Nervous regulation acts on sensations and hearing perception, but we don't yet know its role; it is perhaps, notably, to facilitate the identification of sound signals from a background sound (understanding speech through noise, for instance), in other words, to allow us to turn our attention to certain sounds rather than others. Whatever precice role is played by the subsidiary hearing nervous system, we do not hear with our ear in isolation; rather, the ear functions in the overall psychophysiological context of the organism." A. Gribenski, *L'audition*, 116.

9 See the cases of Verner and Felix, and the importance of sounds with strong symbolic value in M. Klein, *Essais de psychanalyse*, 142–65.

10 J.-P. Thibaud and J.-P. Odion, "Culture sonore en chantier."

11 See D. Aubrée, "La perception des sons."

12 Sonic symbols may be defined in these terms: "one or two sounds tend to have value for the ensemble of the soundscape to which they "give the tuning." But this selection by synecdoche has great expressive strength

and gives to miniatures and sound symbols a symbolic unity. One will notice that every district seems to have preferential sonic symbols, either being constantly heard with a minimal degree of discretion (which allows inhabitants to discriminate them from the background), or else inhabitants find them particularly useful to stimulate their imaginary." J.-F. Augoyard, "Les pratiques d'habiter à travers les phénomènes sonores," 161–2.

13 In *The Tuning of the World* R. Murray Schafer describes some soundmarks that he finds original: "the scraping of the heavy metal chairs on the tile floor of Parisian coffee-houses; the brilliant slam of the doors of the old carriages of the Paris Métro, followed by a sharp click, as the latch falls to the locked position (the effect can now, 1976, be heard only on the Marie d'Issy-Port de la Chapelle line); the sound of the leather straps on the trams in Melbourne, Australia – when they are tugged they twist around the long horizontal support poles and make rich squeaking noises; the virtuoso drumming of the Austrian bureaucrats with their handled rubber stamps: ta-te-te-daaa-ta-te-te-daaa; the high-pitched brilliant bells of the horse-drawn taxis in Konya, the last to be heard in any major town in Turkey; or in London, the memorable voice on the recording at certain suburban stations that says (or used to say), 'Stand clear of the doors!'" (240).

14 Pierre Schaeffer, "L'oreille primitive."

15 "The mark of practical listening is precisely the disappearance of banal significations, for the benefit of the intention of a specific activity" (Pierre Schaeffer, *Traité des objets musicaux*, 123).

16 "The musician also often ignores the extent to which his or her practical listening operates as a displacement and a selection of signification, by creating a reserved domain of objects considered as musical. Outside of this domain are found, rejected, the non-values, called noises. Having a tendency, similar to the physician, to connect his or her activity to some abstract and absolute aim, the musician will easily forget the mechanical contingencies, the energetic origin of objects, cultural practice, and will forget that there were indeed vibrating resonant bodies, familiar to everyday listening, long before the creation of the first musical instrument. There lie the great difficulties encountered, at all times, by musicians trying to introduce into musical practice new objects that were only perceived as 'sonic,' and were rejected with precisely the same pretext: that they were not 'musical'" (Schaeffer, *Traité des objets musicaux*, 124).

17 The components of process music include "sounds / melodies heard inside melodic motifs repeated, stereophonic effects due to the location of the listener, slight irregularities of performance, harmonics, differences between tones" (Steve Reich, "Pendulum Music," in VH 101 (Paris), no. 4 (1970), quoted in D. Avron, *L'appareil musical*, 129).

18 "In face of the inextricable diversity of sounds, the problem is to select those that best describe the scene and the commentary or the dialog which accompanies it. I propose in this way what we call "three-plan

sonic effects." Even if it may first appear somewhat restrictive, this method in fact helps in imposing practical limits to the number of sonic effects included in any scene, and also helps to determine the degree of preeminence of each one of them." Alan Edward Bebey, "Sound Effects on Tapes," *Tape Recording Magazine* (London), 1966, 12. [Translators' note: The quotation presented here is a direct translation of Augoyard's French translation in the French edition of the Repertoire; the original English source was unavailable.]

19 H. Torgue et al., "L'oreille active," 50.

20 In this respect, William Faulkner's *The Sound and the Fury* is a rich source – particularly the shouts of Benjy (an idiot for whom nothing exists outside of sensations), which punctuate the entire first section of the novel and impose themselves as essential elements of the atmosphere.

21 See J.-P. Thibaud, "Le baladeur dans l'espace urbain, essai sur l'instrumentation sensorielle de l'interaction sociale."

TARTINI

1 This effect was added to the English translation of the Repertoire; it is not in the original French edition. See: Giuseppe Tartini, *Trattato di musica seconda la vera la dell'armonia* (Padova, 1754); Frederick Neumann, *Ornamentation in Baroque and Post-Baroque Music with Special Emphasis on J.S. Bach*; Pierre Liénard, *Petite histoire de l'acoustique: Bruit, sons et musique*; Gary Eastwood, "L'air qui engendre un son parfait." Internet sources include Jacques Prost, "Physical approach of biological problems," 2001, HTML version: http://www.curie.fr/recherche/themes/detail_equipe.cfm/lang/_gb/id_equipe/66.htm and P.C. Angelo, "Analisi armonica del suono," 2002, HTML version: http://pcangelo.eng.unipr.it/dispense01/messetti131774/messetti131774.doc

2 See Jean-Jacques Rousseau, *Dictionnaire de musique* (Paris, 1768); Sigmund Freud and J. Crick, *The Interpretation of Dreams*, chapter 7.

3 Elwood Norris is located at the American Technology Corporation in Poway, California; Peter Fryer is a research director at B&W Loudspeakers in Steyning, Sussex, England.

UBIQUITY

1 As Michel Chion demonstrates, the notion of "location" of a sound is quite confusing: "In cases in which the source is punctual (the shock of a ball on a wall), this location of the sound could be described as a sphere with a central core and diffused contours. The core is where we locate the maximum of sound presence and intensity, where it is 'born' … Inevitably, this leads us to confuse the act of 'localization of the sound' … and the "localization of the source" – a confusion that is tied, in everyday experience, to the words we use to express it ('I hear footsteps')" (*Le son au cinéma*, 29–30).

2 These three categories are dear to certain ethologists (for instance, Henri Laborit).

3 Grand-Palais, Paris. Glass and metal architecture from the 1970s. All day long the annual festival of sound emits a "demonstrative" cacophony of high-intensity hi-fi emissions. Three students working in the southwest wing start tapping, using pebbles, on a lateral metallic column of the structure. In a few seconds, the whole building starts to vibrate and is transformed into a sonic vault, which completely masks the loudest electroacoustic emissions coming from the stands. Despite the urgency of the situation, the director of the exposition takes more than a quarter of an hour to identify and locate the source.

4 "He went down a narrow winding stair cut out of the heart of the ramparts and his footsteps resounded above and below him as if there were others there" (Dino Buzzati, *The Tartar Steppe*, 45).

5 The relationship between the ubiquity effect and verticality is underlined by G. Chelkoff and O. Balaÿ in "Conceptions et usages de l'habitat."

6 One example is the architecture of jails and prisons. See also Leibniz's description of a "palace of marvels": "These buildings will be constructed in such a way that the master of the house will be able to hear and see everything that is said and done without himself being perceived, by means of mirrors and pipes, which will be a most important thing for the State, and a kind of political confessional." Quoted by J. Attali in *Noise*, 7.

7 See the examples of solid transmission in collective housings mentioned above. See also the difficulties of apprehension of sound distances underwater (for example, whale songs).

16 What is the relation between the ubiquity effect and the hygrometric degree of air? Does the expression "to be in a fog" have an acoustic reality? Is there sound diffraction as there is with light? Or is it only a perceptive effect due to the acousmatic context and the "disappearance" of visual aids?

9 See "Architecture and Urbanism" above.

10 A. Gribensky, *L'audition*.

11 The following three experiences emphasize the role of synesthesia in processes of sound localization.
(a) In a conference room equipped with a stereo P.A. system, a listener located on the right side of the room follows with his eyes a speaker who moves to one side, then comes back to the other side while speaking into a Lavalier microphone. When the speaker is on the same side as the listener, the listener will localize the acoustic information transmitted to him on the lips of the speaker; but when the speaker, walking in the opposite direction (the left), reaches a certain point, the listener will suddenly turn to the nearest speaker (the one on the right). From a perceptive point of view, there is a threshold limit over which visual decentring in relation to stereophony leads to a paradoxical feeling of inadequacy between the eye and the ear.

(b) A subject is facing a square wall on which loudspeakers are mounted in each of the four corners. When the sound alternates up and down between the two speakers on one side (either the right or the left) or side to side (between either the two top speakers or the two bottom loud), the subject will identify the source and the movement of the sound accurately. However, if the sound alternates on the diagonal (between upper right and lower left, or vice versa) the subject will usually be unable to identify the diagonal path. However, if a fifth speaker (which looks similar to the others but does not emit any sound) is placed in the centre of the wall, the subject will be able to accurately identify any source and movement of the sound. Although this situation is purely experimental, it emphasizes the major role of synesthesia in the process of localization. (c) A subject and a single sound source placed laterally (on the side of the left or the right ear) are located on a moveable platform. The platform, the listener, and the lateral sound source form an integral ensemble. If this ensemble is rotated, the subject will have the impression that the sound is moving above him, hanging over his head.

We thank Y. and F. de Ribeaupierre, of the Institut de physiologie at the Faculté de médecine in Lausanne for their description of these three experiments.

12 A superb cinematographic example is found in Jacques Tati's film *Trafic*. M. Hulot is in an embarrassing situation, pressed against a wall, his head down and his feet tangled in the ivy, and he is powerlessness in the face of the seduction attempt of his rival for Maria. "Then from Hulot's pockets, who is head down, papers start to fall down silently, then coins and keys jingling on the cement in front of the house. Pierre (the rival) is worried – he hears these sounds but cannot locate them: his behavior is troubled, his awkward gestures in trying to reach his pockets show that he wonders if he is losing these objects himself. His discomfort contributes to the failure of his attempt and Maria, freeing herself from his embrace, can leave in her small car." Described by M. Chion in *Le son au cinéma*, 22.

13 Allongées / dilatées / triomphantes vibrations / des sons / des nids de sons / des sons / où tout s'engloutit / des coulées / de sons / des couloirs de sons / des sons qui refluent de partout / l'espace en espaces se déplace." [Long / dilated / triumphant vibrations / sounds / nests of sounds / sounds / in which all disappears / flows / of sounds / channels of sounds / sounds coming from everywhere / space moves by spaces]. H. Michaux, *Face à ce qui se dérobe* (Paris: Gallimard, 1975).

14 See the figure of the sonic paranoiac outlined in J.-F. Augoyard, P. Amphoux, G. Chelkoff, "La production de l'environnement sonore."

15 An inhabitant said of his own sound production: "Since there are neighbours under, I feel like I am trapped; there is only one side I don't hear" (Augoyard, Amphoux, and Chelkoff, "La production de l'environnement sonore").

16 "We hear telephones so clearly, we never know if it is ringing here or in the neighbour's ... When we're outside, everyone runs in to pick up

the phone" (J.-F. Augoyard, O. Balaÿ, and P. Amphoux, "Environnement sonore et communication interpersonnelle," anecdote 55).

17 In the category of "Mimicry," Roger Caillois places all play in which "the subject makes believe or makes others believe that he is someone else than himself." In the category "Ilynx," Caillois includes play "which is based on the pursuit of vertigo and which consists of an attempt to momentarily destroy the stability of perception and inflict a kind of voluptuous panic upon an otherwise lucid mind" (23). In both cases, the sound environment and sound production can contribute through very diverse modalities. It is not by coincidence that Callois calls the societies in which these two forms of play seem to be dominant, "Dyonisian" societies (*Man, Play and Games*, 19, 23, 87ff).

18 A Chinese story relates that in a region where harvests had been decimated by bird colonies, town inhabitants took turns to make a continuous uproar during three days and three nights to prevent birds from landing and to exhaust them to death; birds fell from the sky, dead because of fatigue. According to the story, these birds totally disappeared from the region, which was then invaded by equally voracious insects, freed from the predators that regulated their population.

19 The voice of God is a voice with no place and no name – ubiquitous and anonymous. Ubiquity is a primary attribute of God, who is present everywhere at the same time. In fact, many cosmogonies begin in the great noise of the primordial chaos, a ubiquitous sound by principle since it is the creator of the world and space.

20 Concerning the voice of the father, see, for instance, the account of President Schreber in S. Freud, "The case of Schreber," *The Complete Psychological Works of Sigmund Freud*, vol. 12.

21 See the principle of "inspection" in the presentation of Bentham's panopticon: "Here is the principle, to establish and maintain order; but an inspection of a new kind, which strikes the imaginary instead of the senses, which brings hundreds of men under the control of a single person, giving to this man a sort of universal dependence within his domain." Quoted by T. Gaudin in *Pouvoirs du rêve*, 84. This principle of inspection has always been presented as a principle of observation, but it must also be understood as a principle of listening.

22 See the arguments of Jacques Attali on power, which on the one hand imposes its own noise, and on the other hand, reduces others to silence (J. Attali, *Noise*).

23 "Who among us is free of the feeling that this process, taken to an extreme, is turning the modern state into a gigantic, monopolizing noise emitter, and at the same time, a generalized eavesdropping device" (Attali, *Noise*, 7). We know, for instance, about the police use of loudspeakers as microphones.

24 See Louis Quéré, *Des miroirs équivoques*, 166.

25 See, for example, the discussions about the Integrated Services Digital Network.

26 Ubiquity even becomes a frequent argument for sales and promotion, as illustrated by a recent speech about home automation, communication, and the conviviality of the "interactive home" See P. Amphoux, "L'intelligence de l'habitat," or an advertisement campaign of Télécom in France that read "J'ai le don d'ubiquité" (I have a gift for ubiquity), or even a business offering fast translation named "Ubique."

27 Quéré, *Des miroirs équivoques*, 155–6.

28 This is the paradox presented by Dominique Wolton between diffusion and participation in television communication: "The diffusion dimension refers to the idea of choice and liberty, while the participation dimension manifests itself through the adhesion to values and norms conveyed by television. If we increase too much the capacity of diffusion, it risks ... reducing the dimension of participation, and even provoking a phenomenon of rejection ... The explosion of mass media raises again the question of their mission as social links since too much opening to the world risks, by reaction and difference, producing a disengagement, and even a temptation to fold in on oneself." (D. Wolton, "La prospective de l'audiovisuel est-elle une question technique?")

29 For example, the appearance, diffusion, and growing banality of stereophony, the attempts to introduce a quadraphonic system (abandoned for reasons of standards), and even polyphonic systems on the market. See also the appearance of spherical omnidirectional loudspeakers. We must also mention, in the experimental domain, all the realizations based on a will to create a totally ubiquitous sound matrix: the "Audiosphère" of the Atelier Espaces nouveaux (Louis Dandrel), the "Acousmonium" of the Maison de la radio in Paris, and the "Acoustigloo" of the Groupe de Recherches Musicales of Lyon.

30 Charles Ives's Symphony no. 4, scored for orchestra, piano, and optional chorus, and composed between 1912 and 1925, illustrates two ideas for which this composer was an amazing precursor: "spatial music" and "simultaneous music." The orchestra is in fact divided into groups, and the number of musicians in each group varies from one movement to the next; each group has rhythmic and often tonal autonomy. This collage of sections produces an impression that is sometimes kaleidoscopic, with sometimes disparate or even dissonant sound levels, evoking in a striking way the sound ubiquity of ordinary or festive urban spaces. You might also listen to several movements of Ives's Symphony no. 5 (subtitled *New England Holidays*). *La fête des belles eaux* by Olivier Messiaen, premiered in 1937 in Paris at the festival of sound, water, and light, is an electronic work composed of six sextets of ondes Martenot retransmitted on the Seine by loudspeakers placed on surrounding buildings.

31 For instance the ritual of Morgenstreich at the Bâle Carnival: at four o'clock in the morning, processions of fifes and drums start in every corner of the city, moving toward and converging in one of the central squares where crowds are gathered.

32 See J.-P. Dupuy. "Randonnées carnavalesques," in *Temps libre* (Paris), no. 1 (1980).

33 Writing for several choirs was a Venetian fashion during the Baroque era, notably at San Marco: examples include Claudio Monteverdi's *Vespers* (1610) and works by Andrea and Giovanni Gabrieli. The opening chorus of Johann Sebastian Bach's *St Matthew Passion* also uses three choirs (with the children's choir singing a chorale melody in the relative major key).

34 In the act 1 finale of Wolfgang Amadeus Mozart's opera, *Don Giovanni*, the scene of the masks and the minuet, musicians climb on the stage to echo back into the pit.

35 Examples include the play of echoes and hunting scenes in music by Handel (see *Music for the Royal Fireworks* and *Water Music*).

36 H. Barraud, "Harmonie," in *Encyclopedia universalis* (Paris, 1968).

37 Numerous ritual musics refer to such logic of a lack of differentiation (for example, certain oriental music and Buddhist rituals); it is obtained by the use of sounds that are monotonous to the Occidental ear: repetitive and sometimes haunting, often low-pitched, and eventually looping. The bull roarer (an instrument made of a wood strip attached to a rope that is swung rapidly in a circle) produces a roaring sound that is linked to magic powers since it opens a way to the voices of ancestors; see: Claude Levi-Strauss, *Tristes tropiques*; Marcel Griaule, *Dieux d'eau*.

38 See musical developments based on the cumulative reprise of the same theme, such as Ravel's *Bolero*, the *crescendo* of which seems endless, or the paradoxical synthesized sound that gives the impression of constantly rising; Jean-Claude Risset, "Paradoxes de hauteur."

39 See the *Musical Offering* by J.S. Bach and the *Kleines harmonisches Labyrinth*, BWV 591 (formerly attributed to Bach but now believed to be the work of J.D. Heinichen). "The Little Harmonic Labyrinth is a piece by Bach in which he tries to lose you in a labyrinth of quick key changes. Pretty soon you are so disoriented that you don't have any sense of direction left – you don't know where the true tonic is." D. Hofstadter, *Gödel, Escher, Bach: An Eternal Golden Braid*, 130.

40 Chion, *Le son au cinéma*, 32.

41 Ibid.

42 One example is the role of the voice-over in films of Marguerite Duras that seems to refer to a voice without body.

43 The voice-over has entered the conventions of cinema, and it is often used precisely so as not to produce any particular effect. "A sonic effect, when it reaches its goal, will rarely be noticed as such, and the complementary or contradictory value that it brings to the scene is rarely attributed to its action, but more to the character with which it merges." Chion, *Le son au cinéma*, 85. We find here a distinction between the perception effect and the semiotic effect.

44 Such is the comical use made of this effect by Jacques Tati in most of his films. He invites the spectator to interrogate himself about the origin of

a sound, and leaves the answer visible on the screen just long enough for the spectator to realize it before he moves to another sequence (Chion, *Le son au cinéma*, 13–24). See for instance the diversion of Father François by bicycle through the subtle cracking of the mast that he goes round in *Jour de fête*.

45 "An entire image, an entire story, an entire film can thus hang on the epiphany of the acousmêtre. Everything can boil down to a quest to bring the acousmêtre into the light. In this description, we can recognize *Mabuse* and *Psycho*, but also numerous mystery, gangster, and fantasy films that are all about "defusing" the acousmêtre, who is the hidden monster, or the Big Boss, or the evil genius, or on rare occasions a wise man." And the prime power of acousmêtre is precisely ubiquity: "The acousmêtre is everywhere, its voice comes from an immaterial and non-localized body, and it seems that no obstacle can stop it. Media such as the telephone and radio, which send acousmatic voices travelling and which enable them to be here and there at once, often serve as vehicles of this ubiquity. In *2001*, Hal, the talking computer, inhabits the entire space ship." Chion, *The Voice in Cinema*, 23–4.

46 For example, sounds that are both inside and outside, "stacked sounds" in a hierarchy of double recordings; see the testament of doctor Mabuse, analyzed by Chion in *The Voice in Cinema*.

47 Translator's note: The derealization effect was proposed by Augoyard to express perceptual distortions linked to the physical arrangement of an urban space. See Augoyard, *Pas à pas*, 113.

WAVE

1 "The sea is the keynote sound of all maritime civilizations. It is also a fertile sonic archetype. All roads lead back to water. We shall return to the sea" (R. Murray Schafer, *The Tuning of the World*, 18)

2 In the urban environment, sounds or groups of sounds that partake of a wave effect often belong to the world of machines, notably moving in cyclic patterns. One of the most striking examples is car traffic punctuated by traffic lights. At regular intervals, the sound wave of cars rises at the beginning, reaches a maximal point, and decreases to idling while the wave of the other road takes the relay. Often this urban wave effect, as unconsciously perceived as the sound of the sea for the seaside resident, imposes itself on the listener when it reaches the threshold of discomfort: for example, when two people converse on the sidewalk of a boulevard, understanding each other only in the hollow moments of the passing of cars, or at night, when a sound wave with a greater amplitude awakens the inhabitants at a crossroads. Any vehicle with a rotation pattern can illustrate this effect: for example at small aerodromes, the circling of student pilots in flight school who learn to land by barely touching the ground with their wheels each time they pass before immediately taking off again.

3　"The crowd grew more and more restless, owing to the smallness of the church, and, since the greater part of it had been forced to remain outside, from inside you could hear a noise like the ebb and flow of the tide." Aldo Palazzeschi, *The Sisters Materassi*, 275.

4　In July 1988, Pink Floyd gave a concert on one of the seven hills in Rome. The power of amplification and the natural propagation made the music audible on the other hills, even though they were far away. On one hill, the intensity of the wave effect was continuously present, developing over large movements. But with more concentrated listening, it was clear that the lows and the highs each seemed to have their own evolutionary rhythm: the low frequencies adopted a long period that never seemed to completely disappear, while the highs were more subjugated to the variations of wind and could only be perceived intermittently.

5　In China, traffic at crossroads is directly controlled by an agent at the lights. While the growing number of bicycles facing a red light are waiting for the light to turn to green, the bicycle bells are activated, creating a rising wave. The change to a green light brusquely and almost magically interrupts this *crescendo* of bells until the light changes, the next crowd gathers, and the ringing starts again. The agent is totally submerged in the sonic mass, but has the power to reduce it to silence, at least for a moment.

6　"In the afternoon, sometimes, a sound of distress emerges from the small yard below my window. Where does it come from? I cannot know, maybe somewhere above. Who is moaning? I cannot know – there are only two floors above and I know all the women in this building. What does the voice say? I cannot know; it is not exactly a moaning, but a wail with no destination, expressing all the distress of this world, rising and falling; it begins subtly and increases like a restrained voice that finally succumbs and is submerged, drawn through successive waves; it is a life that collapses. Suffering in the deepest part of being." P. Amphoux, "Le bruit, la plainte et le voisin," vol. 2, 190.

7　See, for example, *Eraser Head* by David Lynch.

8　See Henry Torgue and Serge Houppin, *Les Louves* (Spalax discs, CD 14251, 1987).

9　Compare with Tibetan rituals: there are many examples in *Tibet: Musiques sacrées* (Ocora discs, CD 559011). In orchestral works that evoke the sea, the music does not strictly translate wave effects. In such works, the composer combines song and counterpoint in an arrangement that suggests rather than illustrates the ocean; see *La mer* by Claude Debussy.

10　"*Para thina polyphloisboio thalassès*, says Homer (*Iliad*, I, 34), catching onomatopoeically the splendid armies of waves on the sea beach and their recession." Schafer, *The Tuning of the World*, 16.

Thematic Reading List

Full bibliographic details for these publications are given in the Bibliography (pp. 203–16).

ACOUSTICS

Alexandre, Ariel, and Jean-Philippe Barde. *Le temps du bruit.* (1973)

Augoyard, Jean-François. "Du bruit à l'environnement sonore urbain: Evolution de la recherche française depuis 1970." (2000)

Bar, Pascal, and Brigitte Loye. *Bruit et formes urbaines.* (1981)

Beranek, Léo L. *Music, Acoustics and Architecture.* (1962, 1979)

Canac, François. *Acoustique musicale.* (1959)

Chocholle, René. *Le bruit.* (1960, 1964)

Dalmais, Jean. "La résonance." 2 vols. (1990)

Hamayon, Loïc, and C. Michel. *Guide d'acoustique pour la conception des bâtiments d'habitation.* (1982)

Jacques, Jean, and Anne-Marie Ondet. "Acoustique prévisionnelle intérieure." (1984)

Jouhaneau, Jacques. *Acoustique des salles et sonorisation.* (1997)

Leipp, Émile. *La machine à écouter.* (1977)

– *Acoustique et musique.* (1984)

Liénard, Pierre. *Petite histoire de l'acoustique: Bruit, sons et musique.* (2001)

Maekawa, Z., and P. Lord. *Environmental and Architectural Acoustics.* (1994)

Matras, Jean-Jacques. *Le son.* (1967, 1990)

– *L'acoustique appliquée.* (1977)

Mercier, Daniel, ed. *Le livre des techniques du son.* (1987)

Migneron, Jean-Gabriel. *Acoustique urbaine.* (1980)

Pierce, John Robinson. *The Science of Musical Sound.* (1983)

Plack, Christopher J. *The Sense of Hearing.* (1999)
Pujolle, Joseph. *La pratique de l'isolation acoustique des bâtiments.* (1978)
Radau, Rodolphe. *L'acoustique ou les phénomènes du son.* (1867, 1880)
Risset, Jean-Claude. "Paradoxes de hauteur." (1978)
– *Les instruments de l'orchestre.*
Valcic, J. *Le bruit et ses effets nocifs.* (1980)

LISTENING TO THE SONIC WORLD

Aucher, Marie-Louise. *En corps chante.* (1987)
Augoyard, Jean-François. "L'objet sonore ou l'environnement suspendu."
   (1999)
Bayer, Francis. *De Schönberg à Cage: essai sur la notion d'espace sonore dans
   la musique contemporaine.* (1981)
Blanchard, Gérard. *Images de la musique de cinéma.* (1984)
Bull, Michael, and Les Back, eds. *The Auditory Culture Reader.* (2003)
Cage, John. *For the Birds: John Cage in Conversation with Daniel Charles.*
   (1981)
Chion, Michel. *Le son.* (1998)
Chocholle, René. *Les bruits: effets, réduction (isolation), prévention, mesure et
   détection.* (1973)
Dallet, Sylvie, and Anne Veitl, eds. *Du sonore au musical: cinquante années
   de recherches concrètes, 1948–1998.* (2001)
Delalande, François. "Le traité des objets musicaux, dix ans après." (1976)
Dumaurier, Elisabeth, ed. *Le pouvoir des sons.* (1978).
Fortier, Denis. *Les mondes sonores.* (1992)
Francès, Robert. *The Perception of Music.* (1988)
Gutton, Jean-Pierre. *Bruits et sons dans notre histoire.* (2000)
Handel, Stephen. *Listening: An Introduction of the Perception of Auditory
   Events.* (1989)
Leroy, Yveline. *L'univers sonore animal.* (1979)
Mâche, François-Bernard, and Christian Poche. *La voix: maintenant et
   ailleurs.* (1985)
Mariétan, Pierre. *L'environnement sonore: approche sensible, concepts, modes
   de représentation.* (2005)
McAdams, Stephan, and Emmanuel Bigand, eds. *Thinking in Sound: The
   Cognitive Psychology of Human Audition.* (1993)
Molino, Jean "La musique et le geste: prolègomènes à une anthropologie de
   la musique." (1988)
Oreille oubliée, L'. Exhibition report. (1982)
Ouïr, écouter, entendre, comprendre après Schaeffer. (1999)
Russolo, Luigi. *The Art of Noises.* (1913, 1986)
Schaeffer, Pierre. *Traité des objets musicaux.* (1966)
Szendy, Peter. *Écoute: une histoire de nos oreilles.* (2001)
Torgue, Henry. *La pop-music.* (1975)

Torgue, Henry, et al. "L'oreille active: Les relations à l'environnement sonore dans la vie quotidienne." (1985)

Truax, Barry. *Acoustic Communication.* (2000)

La voix, l'écoute. Traverses, no. 20 (1980)

Xenakis, Yannis. *Musique, architecture.* (1971)

Zemp, Hugo. *Les voix du monde.* (1996)

Zwicker, Eberhart, and Paul Feldtkeller. *The Ear as a Communication Receiver.* (1999)

SOUNDSCAPE, SOUND OBJECT, SONIC EFFECT

Augoyard, Jean-François. "Contribution à une théorie générale de l'expérience sonore: le concept d'effet sonore." (1989)

Augoyard, Jean-François. "La vue est-elle souveraine dans l'esthétique paysagère?" (1995)

Balaÿ, Olivier. *L'espace sonore de la ville aux XIX siècle.* (2003)

Bardyn, Jean-Luc. "L'appel du port." (1993)

Bebey, A. E. "Sound Effects on Tapes." (1966)

Bosseur, Jean-Yves. *Le sonore et le visuel: Intersection musique/arts plastiques aujourd'hui.* (1993)

Chion, Michel. *Guide des objets sonores: Pierre Schaeffer et la recherche musicale.* (1983)

Conrado, Adolfo, and Stefania Barbieri, trans. and ed. *Effetti sonori nella composizione e nell'ascolto della musica: Guida al Repertorio degli effetti sonori di J.F.Augoyard, Henry Torgue.* (2004)

Corbin, Alain. *Les cloches de la terre: paysage sonore et culture sensible dans les campagnes au XIXe siècle.* (1994)

Dallet, Sylvie, and Anne Veitl, eds. *Du sonore au musical: cinquante années de recherches concrètes, 1948–1998.* (2001)

Delage, Berbard. *Approche exploratoire du paysage sonore.* (1979)

Delalande, François. "Le traité des objets musicaux, dix ans après." (1976).

Fortier, Denis. *Les mondes sonores.* (1992)

Järviluoma, Helmi, and Greg Wagstaff, eds. *Soundscape Studies and Methods.* (2002)

Léobon, Alain. *Paysage sonore urbain.* (1983)

Mariétan, Pierre. *Musique paysage.* (1979)

McLuhan, Marshall. *D'œil à oreille.* (1977)

Moles, Abraham. *Phonographie et paysages sonores.* (1979)

Muzet, Denis. "Approche typo-morpho-sociologique du paysage sonore." (1983)

Odion, Jean-Pierre, and Grégoire Chelkoff. "Testologie architecturale des effets sonores." (1995)

Ouïr, écouter, entendre, comprendre après Schaeffer. (1999) .

Paysage sonore urbain: deux journées d'exposition d'écoute et de communications. (1981)

Schafer, R. Murray. *The Tuning of the World.* (1977)

Schafer, R. Murray, ed. *Five Village Soundscapes.* (1977)

Schaeffer, Pierre. *Traité des objets musicaux.* (1966)

Soundscape: The Journal of Acoustic Ecology. (2000–)

Tomatis, Alfred. *The Conscious Ear: My Life of Transformation through Listening.* (1991)

Thompson, Emily. *The Soundscape of Modernity: Architectural Acoustics and the Culture of Listening in America, 1900–1933.* (2002)

Westerkamp, Hildegard. "Listening and Soundmaking: A Study of Music-as-Environment." (1988)

Zemp, Hugo. *Les voix du monde.* (1996)

SOUND AND PLACE

Amphoux, Pascal. "Aux écoutes de la ville." (1992)

– "L'identité sonore des villes européennes: guide méthodologique."(1993)

Argan, Giulio Carlo. *L'histoire de l'art et la ville.* (1995)

Aubrée, Dominique. "La perception des sons." (1985)

Augoyard, Jean-François. *Step by Step.* (1979, 2005)

– "La sonorizacion antropologica del lugar." (1995)

Augoyard, Jean-François, ed. *La qualité sonore des espaces habités/Sonic quality in living spaces.* (1992)

Balaÿ, Olivier. *L'espace sonore de la ville aux XIX siècle.* (2003)

– "La proxémie acoustique dans l'habitat." (1986)

Balaÿ, Olivier, and G. Chelkoff. "La dimension sonore d'un quartier." (1985)

Balaÿ, Olivier, et al. "La conception sonore des espaces habités." (1994)

Belmans, Jacques. *La ville dans le cinéma: de Fritz Lang à Alain Resnais.* (1977)

Chelkoff, Grégoire. "Ambiances en banlieue, imaginaire et expérience sonore." (1995)

Chelkoff, Grégoire, and Olivier Balaÿ. "Conception et usage de l'habitat: proxémies sonores comparées." (1988)

Chelkoff, Grégoire, et al. "Entendre les espaces publics." (1991)

Chion, Michel. *Le promeneur écoutant: essai d'acoulogie.* (1993)

Crunelle, Marc. *Étonnantes acoustiques des bâtiments anciens. Connaissances sensibles de l'espace.* (1999)

Hellström, Bjorn. *Noise Design: Architectural Modelling and the Aesthetics of Urban Acoustic Space.* (2003)

"Musique, les sons et la ville, la." (1976)

Paquette, David. "Describing the contemporary sound environment: An analysis of three approaches, their synthesis and a case study of Commercial Drive, Vancouver, BC." (2004)

La qualification sonore des espaces urbains. (1991)

La qualité sonore des espaces habités / Sonic Quality in Housing and Living Environments. (1991)

Southworh, M. "The Sonic Environment of Cities." (1969)

Thompson, Emily. *The Soundscape of Modernity: Architectural Acoustics and the Culture of Listening in America, 1900–1933.* (2002)

Touche, Marc. "Connaissance de l'environnement sonore urbain: L'exemple des lieux de répétition: faiseurs de bruit, faiseurs de sons?" (1994)

Xenakis, Yannis. *Musique, architecture.* (1971)

SOUND AND TIME

Time permeates every aspect of sound, and therefore constitutes a primary component of the various themes listed. The following list includes publications concerned with psychological and aesthetic expressions of time.

Avron, Dominique. *L'appareil musical.* (1978)

Bebey, A.E. "Sound Effects on Tapes." (1966)

Daniélou, Alain. *Traité de musicologie comparée.* (1959)

Deleuze, Gilles. *Cinéma 1: l'image-mouvement.* (1983)

– *Cinéma 2: l'image-temps.* (1985)

Fraisse, Paul. *Les structures rythmiques: étude psychologique.* (1956)

– *Psychologie du rythme.* (1974)

– *The Psychology of Time.* (1975)

Hall, Edward Twitchell. *The Dance of Life: The Other Dimension of Time.* (1983)

Imberty, Michel. *Les écritures du temps: sémantique psychologique de la musique.* (1981)

Lacombe, Alain, and Claude Rocle. *La musique de film.* (1979)

Leroi-Gourhan, A. *Gesture and Speech. vol. 2: Memory and Rhythms.* (1993)

SOUND AND THE SELF

Anzieu, Didier. "L'enveloppe sonore du soi." (1976)

Aucher, Marie-Louise. *En corps chante.* (1987)

Augoyard, Jean-François. "Les qualités sonores de la territorialité humaine." (1991)

Barbaras, Renaud. *La perception: essai sur le sensible.* (1994)

Blacking, John. *How Musical Is Man?* (1976)

Botte, Marie-Claire, et. al. *Psychoacoustique et perception auditive.* (1989)

Bregman, Albert S. *Auditory Scene Analysis: The Perceptual Organization of Sound.* (1990)

Bustarret, Anne. *L'oreille tendre.* (1982)

Céleste, Bernadette, François Delalande, and Eizabeth Dumaurier. *L'enfant du sonore au musical.* (1982)

Feld, Steven. *Sound and Sentiment: Birds, Weeping, Poetics, and Song in Kaluli Expression.* (1982)

Fonagy, Ivan. *La vive voix: essais de psycho-phonétique.* (1983)

Fraisse, Paul. *Perception*. vol. 6 of *Experimental Psychology: Its Scope and Method*, ed Paul Fraisse and J. Piaget. (1968–69)

Francès, Robert. *Le développement perceptif*. (1962)

– *The Perception of Music*. (1988)

Gribenski, André. *L'audition*. (1975)

Handel, Stephen. *Listening: An Introduction of the Perception of Auditory Events*. (1989)

Lecourt, Edith. "Le sonore et les limites du soi." (1983)

Lecourt, Edith. *L'expérience musicale: résonances psychanalytiques*. (1994)

– *Freud et l'univers sonore: le tic-tac du désir*. (1992)

– "The Musical Envelope." (1990)

McAdams, Stephan, and Emmanuel Bigand, eds. *Thinking in Sound: The Cognitive Psychology of Human Audition*. (1993)

Perianez, Manuel. "Testologie du paysage sonore interne." (1981)

"Psychanalyse musique." (1972)

Szendy, Peter. *Écoute: une histoire de nos oreilles*. (2001)

Tomatis, Alfred. *The Conscious Ear: My Life of Transformation through Listening*. (1991)

– *L'écoute et la vie*. (1980)

– *L'oreille et le langage*. (1963, 1978)

– *Vers l'écoute humaine*. (1974)

Zenatti, Alfred. *Psychologie de la musique*. (1994)

Zwicker, Eberhart, and Paul Feldtkeller. *The Ear as a Communication Receiver*. (1999)

SOUND AND THE OTHER

Alexandre, Ariel, and Jean-Philippe Barde. *Le temps du bruit*. (1973)

Attali, Jacques. *Noise: The Political Economy of Music*. (1985)

Amphoux, Pascal, et al. "Le bruit, la plainte et le voisin." (1989)

Augoyard, Jean-François, Pascal Amphoux, and Olivier Balaÿ. "Environnement sonore et communication interpersonnelle." (1985)

Cosnier, Jacques, and Alain Brossard, eds. *La communication non verbale*. (1984)

De Coppet, Daniel, and Hugo Zemp. *'Aré'Aré: un peuple mélanésien et sa culture*. (1978)

Deleuze, Gilles, and Felix Guattari. *A Thousand Plateaus: Capitalism and Schizophrenia*. (1987)

Drobnick, J., ed. *Aural Cultures*. (2004)

Fumaroli, Marc. *L'âge de l'éloquence*. (1980)

Goffman, Erving. *Forms of Talk*. (1981)

Gombrich, Ernst. *Écologie des formes*. (1989)

Grosjean, Michelle. "Les musiques de l'interaction: contribution à une recherche sur les fonctions de la voix dans l'interaction." (1991)

Kalekin-Fisherman, D. "From the Perspective of Sound towards an Explication of the Social Construction of Meaning." (1986)

Kouloumdjian, Marie-France, and Luiz Busato. *L'empreinte des médias dans le langage des adolescents: le facteur sonore.* (1985)

Lecourt, Edith "La musique, le groupe et l'inconscient: Une écoute analytique entre parole et musique." 2 vols. (1985)

Leroux, Martine, et al. "Les faiseurs de bruit." (1989)

Leroy, Yveline. *L'univers sonore animal.* (1979)

Mumford, Lewis. *Technics and Civilization.* (1963)

Quéré, Louis. *Des miroirs équivoques: aux origines de la communication moderne.* (1982)

Rouget, Gilbert. *Music and Trance: A Theory of the Relations between Music and Possession.* (1980, 1985)

Thibaud, Jean-Paul. "Le baladeur dans l'espace public: essai sur l'instrumentation sensorielle de l'interaction sociale." (1992)

Thibaud, Jean-Paul, and Jean-Pierre Odion. "Culture sonore en chantier." (1987)

Thibaud, Jean-Paul, et al. *À l'écoute du chantier: des productions sonores aux modes de prévention.* (1989)

Trân Van Khê. "Musique traditionnelle et évolution culturelle." (1973)

Truax, Barry. *Acoustic Communication.* (2000)

SOUND AND SEMIOTICS

Ackerman, D. *Le livre des sens.* (1991)

Adorno, Theodor. *Philosophy of Modern Music.* (1984)

Andréani, Eveline. *Antitraité d'harmonie.* (1979)

Arom, Shima. *Polyphonies et polyrythmies instrumentales d'Afrique centrale: structure et méthodologie.* (1985)

Barraud, Henry. *Pour comprendre les musiques d'aujourd'hui.* (1968)

Berthoz, Alain. *The Brain's Sense of Movement.* (2000)

Blacking, John. *How Musical Is Man?* (1973, 1976)

Bosseur, Jean-Yves. *Le sonore et le visuel: Intersection musique/arts plastiques aujourd'hui.* (1993)

Casati, Roberto, and Jérôme Doxic. *La philosophie du son.* (1994)

Chion, Michel. *Un art sonore, le cinema.* (2003)

– *Audio-vision: Sound on Screen.* (1994)

– *Le son au cinéma.* (1985)

– *La toile trouée: la parole au cinéma.* (1989)

– *The Voice in Cinema.* (1982, 1999)

Daniélou, Alain. *Sémantique musicale: essai de psycho-physiologie auditive.* (1978)

Deleuze, Gilles. *The Logic of Sense.* (1990)

Dorflès, Gilles. *L'intervalle perdu.* (1987)

Dufrenne, Mikel. *L'œil et l'oreille.* (1991)

Dumaurier, Elizabeth, ed. *Le pouvoir des sons.* (1978)

Dumézil, Georges. *Apollon sonore et autres essais: esquisses de mythologie.* (1982)

Eisler, Hanns, and Theodor Adorno. *Composing for the Films.* (1994)

Francès, Robert. *Psychologie de l'esthétique.* (1968)

Imberty, Michel. *Entendre la musique, sémantique psychologique de la musique.* (1979)

Jakobson, Roman. *Six Lectures on Sound and Meaning.* (1976, 1978)

Jankélévitch, Vladimir. *Music and the Ineffable.* (1961, 2003)

Kahn, Douglas. *Noise, Water, Meat: A History of Sound in the Arts.* (1999)

Kalekin-Fisherman, D. "From the Perspective of Sound towards an Explication of the Social Construction of Meaning." (1986)

Litwin, Mario. *Le film et sa musique.* (1992)

Mâche, François-Bernard. *Music, Myth and Nature, or The Dolphins of Arion.* (1983, 1992)

McLuhan, Marshall. *D'œil à oreille.* (1977)

Merleau-Ponty, Maurice. *Phenomenology of Perception.* (1962)

Merriam, Alan P. *The Anthropology of Music.* (1964)

Moles, Abraham. *Information Theory and Esthetic Perception.* (1958, 1966)

Nattiez, Jean-Jacques. *Music and Discourse: Toward a Semiology of Music.* (1987, 1990)

Ninio, Jacques. *L'empreinte des sens.* (1989)

Porcile, François. *La musique à l'écran.* (1969)

Pousseur, Henry. *Musique, sémantique, société.* (1972)

Regnault, Cécile. "Les representations visuelles des phénomènes sonores." (2001)

Serres, Michel. *Les cinq sens.* (1985)

Strauss, Ervin. *Du sens des sens.* (1988)

Tinoco, Carlos. *La sensation.* (1997)

Zuckerkandl, Viktor. *Sound and Symbol.* (1969, 1976)

BIBLIOGRAPHY

Ackerman, D. *Le livre des sens*. Trans. Alexandre Kalda. Paris: Grasset, 1991.
First published in English as *A Natural History of the Senses*.

Adorno, Theodor. *Philosophy of Modern Music*. New York: Continuum, 1984.

Alexandre, Ariel, and Jean-Philippe Barde. *Le temps du bruit*. Paris: Flammarion, 1973.

Amphoux, Pascal. "Aux écoutes de la ville." Research report, IREC-EPFL; CRESSON, 1992.

– "L'identité sonore des villes européennes: guide méthodologique." Research report, IREC-EPFL; CRESSON, 1993.

– "L'intelligence de l'habitat." Communication. Paris, Congrès domotique, 1988.

Amphoux, Pascal, et al. "Le bruit, la plainte et le voisin." 2 vols. Research report, CRESSON, 1989.

Andréani, Eveline. *Antitraité d'harmonie*. 10–18. Paris: Union Générale d'éditions, 1979.

Angelo, P.C. "Analisi armonica del suono." 2002. HTML version:
http://pcfarina.eng.unipr.it/Dispense01/messetti131774/messetti131774.doc

Anzieu, Didier. "L'enveloppe sonore du soi." *Nouvelle revue de psychanalyse*, no. 13 (1976), 161–79.

Argan, Giulio Carlo. *L'histoire de l'art et la ville*. Trans. Claire Fargeot. Paris: Éditions de la passion, 1995. First published in Italian as *Storia dell'arte come storia della città*.

Aristotele. *Poetics*. Trans. S.H. Butcher. New York: Hill & Wang, 1962.

Arom, Shima. *Polyphonies et polyrythmies instrumentales d'Afrique centrale: structure et méthodologie*. Paris: SELAF, 1985.

Attali, Jacques. *Noise: The Political Economy of Music*. Trans. Brian Massumi. Minnesota: University of Minnesota Press, 1985.

Aubrée, Dominique. "La perception des sons." *Urbanisme*, no. 206 (1985).

Aucher, Marie-Louise. *En corps chante*. Paris: Hommes et Groupes Éditeurs, 1987.

– *L'homme sonore*. New ed. Paris: Epi, 1983.

Augoyard, Colette. "L'espace sensible, outil pédagogique en classe de langue." Research report. Grenoble: CRESSON, Ecole supérieure d'architecture, 1993.

Augoyard, Jean-François. "Contribution à une théorie générale de l'expérience sonore: le concept d'effet sonore." *Revue de musicothérapie*, vol. 9, no. 3 (1989), 18–36.

– "Du bruit à l'environnement sonore urbain: évolution de la recherche française depuis 1970." In *Données urbaines*, no. 3, ed. Denise Pumain and Marie-Flore Mattei, 397–409. Paris: Anthropos, 2000.

– "L'objet sonore ou l'environnement suspendu," In *Ouïr, écouter, entendre, comprendre après Schaeffer*, 83–106. Paris: Buchet-Chastel, 1999.

– "Les pratiques d'habiter à travers les phénomènes sonores." Research report. ESA / Plan Construction, Paris, 1978.

– "Les qualités sonores de la territorialité humaine." In *Architecture and Behaviour / Architecture et comportement*, vol. 7, no 1: La qualification des espaces urbains (1991), 13–23.

– "Réflexions autour de la notion de parasite sonore." In *Urbanité sonore*, ed. I. Joseph and M. Grosjean. Paris: RATP, 1989.

– "Répons pour voix discrètes et trois silences." In *Traverses no 20: La voix, l'écoute* (novembre 1980), 134–41. Japanese translation in *Traverses no. 20: La voix, l'écoute*. Tokyo: Libro-Prot, 1988.

– "Seminaire environnement sonore et société." Research report. Grenoble: CNRS, 1987.

– "Une sociabilité à entendre." *Espaces et sociétés. no 115:* Ambiances et espaces sonores. (4, 2004). Ed. L'Harmattan, 25–42.

– *Step by Step*. Trans. David Curtis. Minneapolis: Minnesota University Press, forthcoming 2005. First published in French as *Pas à pas*. Paris: Seuil, 1979.

– "La sonorizacion antropologica del lugar." Trans. José Luis Carles. In Mari Jose Amerlinck, ed. *Hacia una antropologia arquitectonica*. Jalisco, Mexico: Ed. Universidad de Guadalajara, Colleccion Jornadas Academicas, 1995.

– "La vue est-elle souveraine dans l'esthétique paysagère?" *Le débat* no. 65 (May–August 1991), 51–9. Republished in Alain Roger, ed. *La théorie du paysage en France (1974–1994)*. Seyssel: Champ-Vallon, 1995, 334–45.

Augoyard, Jean-François, ed. *La qualité sonore des espaces habités/Sonic quality in living spaces*. Symposium proceedings, 20–22 March 1991, Centre de recherche sur l'espace sonore et l'environnement urbain, Grenoble. Grenoble: CRESSON, 1992.

Augoyard, Jean-François, Pascal Amphoux, and Olivier Balaÿ. "Environnement sonore et communication interpersonnelle." 2 vols, includes cassette. Research report, CRESSON; CNRS; CNET, 1985.

Augoyard, Jean-François, Pascal Amphoux, and Grégoire Chelkoff, "La production de l'environnement sonore." Research report. CRESSON, 1985, Grenoble.

Avron, Dominique. *L'appareil musical.* Paris: Union générale d'éditions, 1978.

Balaÿ, Olivier. *L'expérience sonore de la ville aux XIXe siècle: une face cachée de l'art de bâtir.* Ambiances, ambiance. Bernin: Éditions à la croisée, 2003.

– "La proxémie acoustique dans l'habitat." Research report, CRESSON, 1986.

Balaÿ, Olivier, and G. Chelkoff. "La dimension sonore d'un quartier." Research report, CRESSON, 1985.

Balaÿ, Olivier, et al. "La conception sonore des espaces habités." Research report, CRESSON, 1994.

Balzac, Honoré de. *Cousin Bette.* Trans. James Waring. New York: Alfred A. Knopf, 1991. First published 1847.

– *Cousin Pons.* Trans. Herbert J. Hunt. Baltimore: Penguin Books, 1968. First published 1848.

Bar, Pascal, and Brigitte Loye. *Bruit et formes urbaines.* Paris: Cetur, 1981.

Barbaras, Renaud. *La perception: essai sur le sensible.* Paris: Hatier, 1994.

Bardyn, Jean-Luc. "L'appel du port." Research report with CD, CRESSON, 1993.

Barraud, Henry. *Pour comprendre les musiques d'aujourd'hui.* Paris: Seuil, 1968.

Bayer, Francis. *De Schönberg à Cage: Essai sur la notion d'espace sonore dans la musique contemporaine.* Paris: Klincksieck, 1981.

Bebey, A.E. "Sound Effects on Tapes." *Tape Recording Magazine* (London), 1966.

Belmans, Jacques. *La ville dans le cinéma: de Fritz Lang à Alain Resnais.* Bruxelles: A. de Boeck, 1977.

Beranek, Léo L. *Music, Acoustics and Architecture.* New York: Huntington Krieger, 1979. First published New York: Wiley, 1962.

Berthoz, Alain. *The Brain's Sense of Movement.* Trans. Giselle Weiss. Cambridge: Harvard University Press, 2000.

Besson, Paul. "Physiologie de l'homme face au bruit." Excerpt from the abstract of the colloquium Noise and the City, Toulouse, 12–13 March 1981.

Blacking, John. *How Musical Is Man?* Seattle: University of Washington Press, 1973; London: Faber & Faber, 1976.

Blaise Cendras. *Moravagine.* London: Peter Owen, 1968. First published 1926.

Blanchard, Gérard. *Images de la musique de cinéma.* Paris: Edilig, 1984.

Boileau, Nicolas. "Les embarras de Paris." In *Les Satires* (1660–1711), I, 21–70.

Bosseur, Jean-Yves. *Le sonore et le visuel: Intersection musique/arts plastiques aujourd'hui.* Paris: Dis-Voir, 1993.

Botte, Marie-Claire, et. al. *Psychoacoustique et perception auditive.* Paris: INSERM, 1989.

Boysson-Bardies, Bénédicte de. "La production de la parole." *Science et vie* (Paris), no. 185 (1983).

Bregman, Albert S. *Auditory Scene Analysis: The Perceptual Organization of Sound*. Cambridge: MIT Press, 1990.

Bull, Michael, and Les Back, eds. *The Auditory Culture Reader*. Sensory Function Series. Oxford: Berg, 2003.

Busnel, François. "Siffler pour communiquer." In *L'oreille oubliée*. Paris: Centre Georges Pompidou, 1982.

Bustarret, Anne. *L'oreille tendre*. Paris: Éditions ouvrières, 1982.

Buzzati, Dino. *The Tartar Steppe*. Trans. Stuart C. Hood. New York: Farrar, Strauss and Young, 1952.

Cage, John. *For the Birds: John Cage in Conversation with Daniel Charles*. London, Boston: Marion Boyars, 1981

Caillois, Roger. *Man, Play and Games*. Trans. Meyer Barash. New York: Free Press of Glencoe, 1961.

Canac, François. *Acoustique musicale*. Paris: Éditions du CNRS, 1959.

Canévet, G. "Audition binaurale et localisation auditive." In Marie-Claire Botte et al., *Psychoacoustique et perception auditive*. Paris: INSERM, 1989.

Casati, Roberto, and Jérôme Doxic. *La philosophie du son*. Arles: Jacqueline Chambon, 1994.

Cazeneuve, Jean. *L'ethnologie*. Paris: Larousse; Livre de poche, 1967.

– *Les rites et la condition humaine, d'après des documents ethnographiques*. Paris: Presses universitaires de France, 1958.

Céleste, Bernadette, François Delalande, and Eizabeth Dumaurier. *L'enfant du sonore au musical*. Paris: Buchet-Chastel, 1982.

Chelkoff, Grégoire, et al. "Entendre les espaces publics." Research report, CRESSON, 1991.

– "Ambiances en banlieue, imaginaire et expérience sonore." *Cahiers de la recherche architecturale*, no. 38 (1995).

Chelkoff, Grégoire, and Olivier Balaÿ. "Conception et usage de l'habitat: proxémies sonores comparées." Research report, CRESSON, 1988.

Cherry, E. "Some experiments on the recognition of speech, with one and two ears." *Journal of the American Acoustic Society*, no. 25 (1953), 975–79.

Chion, Michel. *Un art sonore, le cinema: histoire, esthetique, poetique*. Paris: Cahiers du Cinéma, 2003.

– *Audio-vision: Sound on Screen*. Ed. and trans. Claudia Gorbman. New York: Columbia University Press, 1994.

– *Guide des objets sonores: Pierre Schaeffer et la recherche musicale*. Paris: Buchet-Chastel, 1983.

– *Le promeneur écoutant: essai d'acoulogie*. Paris: Éditions Plume, 1993.

– *Le son*. Paris: Nathan, 1998.

– *Le son au cinéma*. Paris: Cahiers du cinéma / Éditions de l'Étoile, 1985.

– *La toile trouée: la parole au cinéma*. Paris: Seuil, 1989

– *The Voice in Cinema*. Trans. Claudia Gorbman. New York: Columbia University Press, 1999. First published as *La voix au cinéma*, Paris: Éditions de l'Étoile in 1982.

Chocholle, René. *Le bruit.* Paris: Presses universitaires de France, 1960; 2nd edition, 1964.

– *Les bruits: effets, réduction (isolation), prévention, mesure et détection.* Paris: Guy Le Prat, 1973.

Colette. *The Last of Chéri.* New York: Putnam, 1932. First published 1926.

Condon, W.S. "Une analyse de l'organisation comportementale." In *La communication non verbale*, ed. J. Cosnier and A. Brossard. Paris and Neuchatel: Delachaux et Niestlé, 1984, 31–70.

Conrado, Adolfo, and Stefania Barbieri, trans. and ed. *Effetti sonori nella composizione e nell'ascolto della musica: Guida al Repertorio degli effetti sonori di J.F. Augoyard, Henry Torgue.* Torino: Agamus, 2004.

Corbin, Alain. *Les cloches de la terre: paysage sonore et culture sensible dans les campagnes au XIXe siècle.* Paris: Albin Michel, 1994.

Cosnier, Jacques, and Alain Brossard, eds. *La communication non verbale.* Paris and Neuchatel: Delachaux et Niestlé, 1984.

Crunelle, Marc. *L'architecture et nos sens.* Bruxelles: Presses universitaires de Bruxelles, 1996.

– *Étonnantes acoustiques des bâtiments anciens. Connaissances sensibles de l'espace.* Bruxelles: Presses universitaires de Bruxelles, 1999.

Dallet, Sylvie, and Anne Veitl, eds. *Du sonore au musical: cinquante années de recherches concrètes, 1948–1998.* Paris: L'Harmattan, 2001.

Dalmais, Jean. "La résonance." 2 vols. DEA diss. École d'architecture, Grenoble, 1990.

Daly, César. *L'architecture privée sous Napoléon III.* Paris: A. Morel, 1864.

Daniélou, Alain. *Sémantique musicale: essai de phsyco-physiologie auditive.* Paris, Hermann, 1978. First published 1967.

– *Traité de musicologie comparée.* Paris: Hermann, 1959.

De Coppet, Daniel, and Hugo Zemp. *'Aré 'aré: un peuple mélanésien et sa culture.* Paris: Seuil, 1978.

De Gaulle, Charles. *The Call to Honour, 1940–1942.* Trans. J. Griffin. Vol. 1 of *War Memoirs.* 5 vols. New York: Viking, 1955.

Delage, Bernard. *Approche exploratoire du paysage sonore.* Paris: Plan Construction, 1979.

– "Huit propositions d'intervention sonore en milieu urbain." In *Alain Léobon, Paysage sonore urbain.* Paris: Plan Construction, 1980.

Delalande, François. "Le traité des objets musicaux, dix ans après." *Cahiers Recherche Musique*, no. 2 (1976).

Deleuze, Gilles. *Cinéma 1: l'image-mouvement.* Paris: Minuit, 1983.

– *Cinéma 2: l'image-temps.* Paris: Minuit, 1985.

– *The Logic of Sense.* Trans. Mark Lester and Charles Stivale. New York: Columbia University Press, 1990.

Deleuze, Gilles, and Felix Guattari. *A Thousand Plateaus: Capitalism and Schizophrenia.* Trans. Brian Massumi. Minneapolis: University of Minnesota Press, 1987.

Dorflès, Gilles. *L'intervalle perdu.* Paris: Librairie des Méridiens, 1987.

Drobnick, J., ed. *Aural Cultures*. Includes cassette. Toronto: YYZ Books, 2004.

Dufrenne, Mikel. *L'œil et l'oreille*. Paris: Jean-Michel Place, 1991.

Duhamel, Georges. *In Defence of Letters*. Trans. E.F. Bozman. Port Washington: Kennikat, 1968.

Dumaurier, Elisabeth, ed. *Le pouvoir des sons*. Cahiers recherche musique 6. Paris: Institut national de l'audiovisuel, Groupe de recherches musicales, 1978.

Dumézil, Georges. *Apollon sonore et autres essais: esquisses de mythologie*. Paris: Gallimard, 1982.

Dupuy, Jean-Pierre. "Randonnées carnavalesques." *Temps libre* (Paris), no. 1 (1980).

Durand, Gilbert. *Les structures anthropologiques de l'imaginaire: introduction à l'archétypologie générale*. Paris: Presses universitaires de France, 1963.

Eastwood, Gary "L'air qui engendre un son parfait." *New Scientist*, 7 Sept. 1996.

Eisler, Hanns, and Theodor Adorno. *Composing for the Films*. London: Athlone Press, 1994. [First published under Eisler's name alone: New York: Oxford University Press, 1947.]

Feld, Steven. *Sound and Sentiment: Birds, Weeping, Poetics, and Song in Kaluli Expression*. Philadelphia: University of Pennsylvania Press, 1982.

Floriot, René "Contribution à l'étude des vases acoustiques du Moyen-Age." Doctoral thesis. Faculty of Sciences, Université d'Aix-Marseilles, 1964.

– "Les vases acoustiques du Moyen-Age." *GAM newsletter*, no. 98 (June 1978).

Fonagy, Ivan. *La vive voix: essais de psycho-phonétique*. Paris: Payot, 1983.

Fortier, Denis. *Les mondes sonores*. Paris: Presses Pocket, 1992.

Foucault, Michel. *The Use of Pleasure*. Vol. 2 of *The History of Sexuality*. Trans. Robert Hurley. London: Penguin Books, 1992.

Fraisse, Paul. *La perception*. Vol. 6 of *Traité de psychologie expérimentale*. Paris: Presses universitaires de France, 1963. English translation, *Perception*. Vol. 6 of *Experimental Psychology: Its Scope and Method*, ed Paul Fraisse and J. Piaget. New York: Basic Books, 1968–69.

– *Psychologie du rythme*. Paris: Presses universitaires de France, 1974.

– *Psychologie du temps*, Paris: Presses universitaires de France, 1957. English translation, *The Psychology of Time*. Trans. Jennifer Leith. Westport, Conn.: Greenwood Press, 1975.

– *Les structures rythmiques: étude psychologique*. Paris: Presses universitaires de France, 1956.

Francès, Robert. *Le développement perceptif*. Paris: Presses universitaires de France, 1962.

– *The Perception of Music*. Trans. W. Jay Dowling. Hillsdale, N.J.: L. Erlbaum, 1988.

– *Psychologie de l'esthétique*. Paris: Presses universitaires de France, 1968.

Freud, Sigmund. *The Standard Edition of the Complete Psychological Works of Sigmund Freud*. Trans. James Strachey. 24 vols. London: Hogarth Press, 1958.

- *The Interpretation of Dreams.* Trans. Joyce Crick. Oxford: Oxford University Press, 1999.

Fumaroli, Marc. *L'âge de l'éloquence.* Paris: Albin Michel, 1980.

Gaudin, Thierry. *Pouvoirs du rêve.* Paris: Centre de recherche sur la culture technique, 1984.

Gingras, Nicole, ed. *Le son dans l'art contemporain canadien / Sound in Contemporary Canadian Art.* Montreal: Editions Artexte, 2003.

Goffman, Erving. *Forms of Talk.* Oxford: Blackwell, 1981.

- *Frame Analysis: An Essay on the Organization of Experience.* Cambridge: Harvard University Press, 1974.

- *Interaction Ritual: Essays on Face-to-Face Behavior.* Chicago: Aldine, 1967.

- *The Presentation of Self in Everyday Life.* Harmondsworth: Penguin, 1971.

Gombrich, Ernst. *Écologie des formes.* Paris: Flammarion, 1989.

Griaule, Marcel. *Dieux d'eau.* Paris: Le Chêne, 1948.

- *Masques Dogons.* Paris: Institut d'ethnologie, 1938.

Gribenski, André. *L'audition.* Paris: Presses universitaires de France, 1975.

Grosjean, Michelle. "Les musiques de l'interaction: contribution à une recherche sur les fonctions de la voix dans l'interaction." Thesis, Université Lumière, Lyon, 1991.

Gutton, Jean-Pierre. *Bruits et sons dans notre histoire.* Paris: Presses universitaires de France, 2000.

Hall, Edward Twitchell. *The Dance of Life: The Other Dimension of Time.* Garden City, New York: Doubleday, 1983.

Hamayon, Loïc, and C. Michel. *Guide d'acoustique pour la conception des bâtiments d'habitation.* Sous la direction du RAUC. Paris: Moniteur, 1982.

Handel, Stephen. *Listening: An Introduction of the Perception of Auditory Events.* Cambridge: MIT Press, 1989.

Hellström, Bjorn. *Noise Design: Architectural Modelling and the Aesthetics of Urban Acoustic Space.* Göteborg: Bo Ejeby Förlag, 2003.

Hofstadter, Douglas R. *Gödel, Escher, Bach: An Eternal Golden Braid.* New York: Basic Books, 1979.

Imberty, Michel. *Les écritures du temps: sémantique psychologique de la musique.* 2 vols. Paris: Dunod, 1981.

- *Entendre la musique, sémantique psychologique de la musique.* Paris: Dunod, 1979.

Jacob, Max. *Le cornet à dés,* I: *Le coq et la perle.* Paris: Gallimard, 1967.

Jacques, Jean, and Anne-Marie Ondet. "Acoustique prévisionnelle intérieure," *Les notes scientifiques et techniques de l'INRS,* 56 (1984).

Jakobson, Roman. *Essais de linguistique générale.* Paris: Minuit, 1963.

- *Six Lectures on Sound and Meaning.* Trans. John Mepham. Cambridge: MIT Press, 1978. First published in French as *Six leçons sur le son et le sens.* Paris: Éditions de Minuit, 1976.

Jankélévitch, Vladimir. *Music and the Ineffable.* Trans. Carolyn Abbate. Princeton: Princeton University Press, 2003. First published in French as *La Musique et l'ineffable.* Paris: A. Colin, 1961.

Järviluoma, Helmi, and Greg Wagstaff, eds. *Soundscape Studies and Methods.* Helsinki: Finnish Society for Ethnomusicology; Turku: Dept. of Arts, Literature and Music, University of Turku, 2002.

Jauss, Hans Robert. *Toward an Aesthetic of Reception.* Trans. from German by Timothy Bahti. Minneapolis: University of Minnesota Press, 1982.

Jouhaneau, Jacques. *Acoustique des salles et sonorisation.* Paris: Lavoisier-Technique et documentation, 1997.

Kahn, Douglas. *Noise, Water, Meat: A History of Sound in the Arts.* Cambridge, Mass.: MIT Press, 1999.

Kalekin-Fisherman, D. "From the Perspective of Sound towards an Explication of the Social Construction of Meaning." *Sociologica internationalis,* vol. 24, no. 2 (1986), 171–95.

Kant, Immanuel. *Critique of the Power of Judgment.* Trans. Paul Guyer and Eric Matthews Cambridge: Cambridge University Press, 2000. First published in German as *Kritik der Urteilskraft,* 1790.

Klein, Melanie. *Essais de psychanalyse.* Paris: Payot, 1972.

Kouloumdjian, Marie-France, and Luiz Busato. *L'empreinte des médias dans le langage des adolescents: le facteur sonore.* Lyon: IRPEACS / CNRS, Édition du Centurion, 1985.

Kristeva, Julia. *Powers of Horror: An Essay on Abjection.* Trans. Leon S. Roudiez. New York: Columbia University Press, 1982.

Kundera, Milan. *The Unbearable Lightness of Being.* New York: Harper & Row, 1984.

Lacombe, Alain, and Claude Rocle. *La musique de film.* Paris: Van de Velde, 1979.

Lassus, Bernard. "Le jardin de l'antérieur." *Traverses* no. 5–6: "Jardins contre nature" (1983).

Lecourt, Edith. *L'expérience musicale: résonances psychanalytiques.* Paris: L'Harmattan, 1994.

– *Freud et l'univers sonore: le tic-tac du désir.* Paris: L'Harmattan, 1992.

– "The Musical Envelope." In D. Anzieu, ed., *Psychic envelopes.* Trans. Daphne Briggs. London: Karnac, 1990.

– "La musique, le groupe et l'inconscient: une écoute analytique entre parole et musique." 2 vols. PhD diss., Université de Lyon 2, 1985.

– "Le sonore et les limites du soi." *Bulletin de psychologie,* 36, no. 360 (1983), 577–82.

Le Rouzic, Pierre. *Un prénom pour la vie: choix, rôle, influence du prénom.* Paris: Albin Michel, 1978.

Leroux, Martine, et al. "Les faiseurs de bruit." Research report. Grenoble: Cresson / SRETIE, 1989.

Leipp, Émile. *Acoustique et musique.* Paris: Masson, 1984.

– *La machine à écouter.* Paris: Masson, 1977.

Leroi-Gourhan, André. *Gesture and Speech.* Trans. Anna Bostock Berger. Cambridge: MIT Press, 1993. First published in French as *Le geste et la parole.* 2 vols. Paris: A. Michel, 1964–65.

Leroy, Yveline. *L'univers sonore animal*. Paris: Gauthier-Villard, 1979.

Léobon, Alain. *Paysage sonore urbain*. Paris: Plan Construction, 1983.

Levi-Strauss, Claude. *Tristes tropiques*. Trans. John and Doreen Weightman. New York: Penguin, 1992.

Liénard, Jean-Sylvain. "Machines: il faut ar-ti-cu-ler!" *Science et avenir*, no. 79 (octobre–novembre 1990).

Liénard, Pierre. *Petite histoire de l'acoustique: Bruit, sons et musique, Sciences et techniques*. Paris: Éditions Hermès, 2001.

Litwin, Mario. *Le film et sa musique*. Paris: Romillat, 1992.

Mâche, François-Bernard. *Music, Myth and Nature, or The Dolphins of Arion*. Trans. Susan Delaney. Philadelphia: Harwood Academic Publishers, 1992. First published in French as *Musique, mythe, nature ou les Dauphins d'Arion*. Paris: Klincksieck, 1983.

Mâche, François-Bernard, and Christian Poché. *La voix: maintenant et ailleurs*. Exposition de la Bibliothèque publique d'information du Centre Georges Pompidou. Paris: Fondations Royaumont, Centre Georges Pompidou, 1985.

Maekawa, Z., and P. Lord. *Environmental and Architectural Acoustics*. London: E & FN Spon, 1994.

Marcel-Dubois, Claudie. "Signaux sonores des petits métiers." In *L'oreille oubliée*. Paris: Centre Georges Pompidou, 1982.

Mariétan, Pierre. *L'environnement sonore: approche sensible, concepts, modes de représentation*. Nimes: Champ social, 2005.

– *Musique paysage*. Paris: Pro Helvetia, 1979.

Marin, L. "L'effet sharawadji, ou le jardin de Julie." *Traverses* (Paris) no. 4–5 (1979).

Matabon, Louis. "La mémoire de l'oreille." In *L'oreille oubliée*. Paris: Centre Georges Pompidou, 1982.

Matras, Jean-Jacques. *L'acoustique appliquée*. Paris: Presses universitaires de France, 1977.

– *Le son*. Paris: Presses universitaires de France, 1967; 9th ed., Paris, Presses universitaires de France, 1990.

McAdams, Stephan, and Emmanuel Bigand, eds. *Thinking in Sound: The Cognitive Psychology of Human Audition*. Oxford: Clarendon Press, 1993.

McCartney, Andra. "Soundscape works, listening and the touch of sound." In *Aural Cultures*, ed. Jim Drobnick, 179–85. Toronto: YYZ, 2004.

– "Circumscribed journeys through soundscape composition," editorial. *Organised Sound: An International Journal of Music Technology* (2002): 1–3.

– "Alien intimacies: hearing science fiction narratives in Hildegard Westerkamp's Cricket Voice (or 'I don't like the country, the crickets make me nervous')." *An International Journal of Music Technology* (2002): 45–50.

– "Soundscape composition and the subversion of electroacoustic norms." *Journal SEAMUS* 14, 2 (2000): 6–24. Published electronically in *CEC: EContact! Electroacoustic Histories*. Reprinted in *The Radio Art Companion*, eds.

Darren Copeland and Nadene Thériault, 14–22. Toronto: New Adventures in Sound Art, 2002.

McLuhan, Marshall. *D'œil à oreille*. Trans. Derrick de Kerckhove. Paris: Denoël-Gonthier, 1977.

Mercier, Daniel, ed. *Le livre des techniques du son*. Paris: Eyrolles, 1987.

Merleau-Ponty, Maurice. *Phenomenology of Perception*. Trans. Colin Smith. London: Routledge and Kegan Paul, 1962.

Merriam, Alan P. *The Anthropology of Music*. Evanston, Illinois: Northwestern University Press, 1964.

Migneron, Jean-Gabriel. *Acoustique urbaine*. Paris: Masson; Québec: Presses de l'université Laval, 1980.

Moch, Annie. *Le son de l'oreille*. Toulouse: Privat, 1985.

Moles, Abraham. *Information Theory and Esthetic Perception*. Trans. Joel F. Cohen. Urbana: University of Illinois Press, 1966. First published in French as *Théorie de l'information et perception esthètique*. Paril: Flammarion, 1958.

– *Phonographie et paysages sonores*. Paris: Fréquences, 1979.

Molino, Jean "La musique et le geste: Prolègomènes à une anthropologie de la musique." *Analyse musicale*, no. 10 (January 1988).

Mumford, Lewis. *Technics and Civilization*. New York: Harcourt, Brace & World, 1963.

"Musique, les sons et la ville, la." *Musique en jeu*, no. 24 (1976).

Muzet, Denis. "Approche typo-morpho-sociologique du paysage sonore." Research report. Paris: SRETIE, 1983.

Nancy, Jean-Luc. "L'offrande sublime." In Jean-François Courtine et al., *Du sublime. L'extrême contemporain*. Paris: Belin, 1988.

Nattiez, Jean-Jacques. *Music and Discourse: Toward a Semiology of Music*. Trans. Carol Abbate. Princeton: Princeton University Press, 1990. First published in French as *Musicologie générale et sémiologie*. Paris: C. Bourgeois, 1987.

Neumann, Frederick. *Ornamentation in Baroque and Post-Baroque Music with Special Emphasis on J.S. Bach*. Princeton, N.J.: Princeton University Press, 1978.

Ninio, Jacques. *L'empreinte des sens*. Paris: Odile Jacob, 1989.

Odion, Jean-Pierre, and Grégoire Chelkoff. "Testologie architecturale des effets sonores." Research report. CRESSON, 1995.

Oreille oubliée, L'. Catalogue of exhibition at Galerie du CCI, Paris, 28 October 1982 – 3 January 1983. Centre Georges Pompidou, 1982.

Ouïr, écouter, entendre, comprendre après Schaeffer. Paris: Buchet-Chastel; Bry-sur-Marne: Institut national de l'audiovisuel, 1999. Ouvrage issu d'un colloque, Perpignan, Auditorium John Cage, 19–21 novembre 1996.

Palazzeschi, Aldo. *The Sisters Materassi*. Trans. Augus Davidson. Garden City: Doubleday, 1953.

Paquette, David. "Describing the contemporary sound environment: An analysis of three approaches, their synthesis and a case study of Commercial

Drive, Vancouver, BC." Master's thesis. School of Communication, Simon Fraser University, Burnaby, British Columbia, 2004.

Paysage sonore urbain: deux journées d'exposition d'écoute et de communications. Paris, 30 et 31 mai 1980. Includes cassette. Paris: Plan Construction, 1981.

Perianez, Manuel. "Testologie du paysage sonore interne." Research report. Paris: CSTB, 1981.

Pierce, John Robinson. *The Science of Musical Sound.* New York: Scientific American Library, 1983.

Plack, Christopher J. *The Sense of Hearing.* Mahwah, N.J.: Lawrence Erlbaum, 2005.

Plato. *Sophist.* Trans. Seth Bernardete. Chicago: University of Chicago Press, 1986.

Plomp, R. "Acoustical aspects of cocktail parties," *Acoustica,* no. 38 (1977), 186–91.

Porcile, François. *La musique à l'écran.* Paris: Éditions du Cerf, 1969.

Pousseur, Henri. *Musique, sémantique, société.* Paris: Casterman, 1972.

Prost, Jacques. "Physical approach of biological problems." 2001, HTML version: http://www.curie.fr/recherche/themes/detail_equipe.cfm/lang/_gb/id_equipe/66.htm.

Prot, A. *Manuel alphabétique de psychiatrie clinique et thérapeutique.* Paris: Presses universitaires de France, 1975. First published 1952.

Proust, Marcel. *In Search of Lost Time,* vol. 1. *Swann's Way.* Trans. C. K. Scott Moncrieff. New York: Modern Library, 1928.

– *In Search of Lost Time,* vol. 2: *Within a Budding Grove.* London: Chatto & Windus, 1981.

"Psychanalyse musique." *Musique en jeu,* no. 9 (1972).

Pujolle, Joseph. *La pratique de l'isolation acoustique des bâtiments.* Paris: Moniteur, 1978.

La qualification sonore des espaces urbains. Special edition of *Architecture et comportement,* 7, no. 1 (1991).

La qualité sonore des espaces habités / Sonic Quality in Housing and Living Environments. Proceedings from the international colloquium. Grenoble: Cresson 1991.

Quéré, Louis. *Des miroirs équivoques: aux origines de la communication moderne.* Paris: Aubier Montaigne, 1982.

Radau, Rodolphe. *L'acoustique ou les phénomènes du son.* Paris: Hachette, 1880. First published 1867.

REEF, vol. 2. *Science du bâtiment.* Paris: CSTB, 1984.

Regnault, Cécile. "Les representations visuelles des phénomènes sonores." 2 vols. PhD diss. École Nationale Supérieur d'Architecture, Grenoble, 2001.

Reich, Steve. "Pendulum Music." *VH 101* (Paris), no. 4 (1970).

Reznikoff, Iégor, and M. Dauvois, "La dimension sonore des grottes ornées." *Bulletin de la Société préhistorique française,* vol. 85, no. 8 (1988).

Risset, Jean-Claude. "Paradoxes de hauteur." Texte d'une communication présentée au Symposium IRCAM sur la psychoacoustique musicale, juillet 1977. Paris: Institut de recherche et coordination acoustique-musique, 1978.

– *Les instruments de l'orchestre.* Bibliothèque pour la science. Paris: Belin, 1977.

Rouget, Gilbert. *Music and Trance: A Theory of the Relations between Music and Possession.* Trans. Brunhilde Biebuyck. Chicago: University of Chicago Press, 1985. First published in French as *La musique et la transe: esquisse d'une théorie générale des relations de la musique et de la possession.* Paris: Gallimard, 1980.

Rousseau, Jean-Jacques. *Dictionnaire de musique.* Paris, 1768.

Russolo, Luigi. *The Art of Noises.* Trans. Barclay Brown. New York: Pendragon Press, 1986. Futurist manifesto first published in Italian as *Arti dei rumori* (1913).

Sansot, Pierre. *Le rugby est une fête.* Paris: Plon, 1991.

Schaeffer, Pierre. *La musique concrète.* Paris: Presses universitaires de France, 1973. First published 1967.

– "L'oreille primitive." In *L'oreille oubliée.* Paris: Centre Georges Pompidou, 1982.

– *Traité des objets musicaux.* Paris: Éditions du Seuil, 1966.

Schafer, R. Murray, ed. *Five Village Soundscapes.* Vancouver: A.R.C. Publications, 1977.

– "A review of *À l'écoute de l'environnement: Répertoire des effets sonores,* eds. Jean-Francois Augoyard and Henry Torgue." *Yearbook of Soundscape Studies* I (1988): 158–63

– *The Tuning of the World,* Toronto: McClelland & Stewart, 1977.

– *The Vancouver Soundscape.* 2 audio cassettes. Vancouver: Arc Publications, 1979.

Sorin, C. "Perception de la parole continue." In Marie-Claire Botte et al. *Psychoacoustique et perception auditive.* Paris: INSERM, 1989.

Serres, Michel. *Les cinq sens.* Paris: Grasset, 1985.

Soundscape: The Journal of Acoustic Ecology. Published by the World Forum for Acoustic Ecology, 2000– .

Southworh, M. "The Sonic Environment of Cities." *Environment and Behaviour,* 1, no. 1 (June 1969), 49–70.

Splenger, Oswald. *The Decline of the West.* Trans. Charles Francis Atkinson. New York: A.A. Knopf, 1934.

Stendhal. *The Charterhouse of Parma.* Trans. Richard Howard. New York: Modern Library, 1999. First published 1839.

Strauss, Ervin. *Du sens des sens.* Grenoble: Jérôme Million, 1988. First published in 1935.

Szendy, Peter. *Écoute: une histoire de nos oreilles.* Paris: Minuit, 2001.

Tartini, Giuseppe. *Trattato di musica seconda la vera la dell'armonia.* Padova, 1754.

Temple, William. "Upon the Gardens of Epicurus." (1685).

Thibaud, Jean-Paul. "Le baladeur dans l'espace public: Essai sur l'instrumentation sensorielle de de l'interaction sociale." PhD. diss., Institut d'urbanisme de Grenoble, Université Pierre Mendès, France, Grenoble, 1992.

– "Temporalités sonores et interaction sociale," *Architecture et comportement* (Lausanne), 7, no. 1 (1991), 63–74.

Thibaud, Jean-Paul, and Jean-Pierre Odion, "Culture sonore en chantier." Research report. Paris: Plan Construction, 1987.

Thibaud, Jean-Paul, et al. *À l'écoute du chantier: des productions sonores aux modes de prévention*. Grenoble: CRESSON, Plan Construction, 1989.

Thompson, Emily. *The Soundscape of Modernity: Architectural Acoustics and the Culture of Listening in America, 1900–1933*. Massachusetts: MIT Press, 2002.

Tinoco, Carlos. *La sensation*. Paris: Flammarion, 1997.

Tomatis, Alfred. *The Conscious Ear: My Life of Transformation through Listening*. Trans. Stephen Lushington and Billie M. Thompson. Barrytown, N.Y.: Station Hill Press, 1991. First published in French as *L'oreille et la vie*, Paris: R. Laffont, 1977, 1980.

– *L'écoute et la vie*. Paris: Laffont, 1980.

– *L'oreille et le langage*. Paris: Seuil, 1978. First published in 1963.

– *Vers l'écoute humaine*. Paris: ESF, 1974.

Torgue, Henry. *La pop-music*. Paris: Presses universitaires de France, 1975.

Torgue, Henry, et al. "L'oreille active: Les relations à l'environnement sonore dans la vie quotidienne." Research report. Grenoble: ESU, CRESSON, 1985.

Touché, Marc. "Connaissance de l'environnement sonore urbain: L'exemple des lieux de répétition: faiseurs de bruit, faiseurs de sons?" Paris: Centre de recherche interdisciplinaire de Vaucresson, CNRS, 1994.

Trân Van Khê. "Musique traditionnelle et évolution culturelle." *Cultures, musique et société*, vol. 1, no. 1, UNESCO / Baconnière, 1973.

Truax, Barry. *Acoustic Communication*. 2nd ed. Norwood: Ablex Publishing, 2000.

Valcic, J. *Le bruit et ses effets nocifs*. Paris: Masson, 1980.

Valéry, Paul. *Poems*. Princeton: Princeton University Press, 1971.

Vernes, Michel. "Paysage de la mémoire." *Traverses*, no. 36: "L'archive" (1986).

Vian, J.-P. "Rapport annuel des travaux du CSTB." Grenoble, 1978.

Viollet-Le-Duc, Eugène Emmanuel. *Discourses on Architecture*. Trans. Benjamin Bucknall. 2 vols. New York: Grove, 1959. First published in French as *Entretiens sur l'architecture*, Paris, 1862–72. p. 266.

Vitruvius Pollio, *De theatri vasis*. In *On Architecture*, trans. Frank Granger. vol. 1. Cambridge: Harvard University Press, 1962.

La voix, l'écoute. Traverses, no. 20. Paris: Centre Pompidou, 1980.

Westerkamp, Hildegard. "Listening and Soundmaking: A Study of Music-as-Environment." Master's thesis, Simon Fraser University, 1988.

Wolton, D. "La prospective de l'audiovisuel est-elle une question technique?" *Prospectives 2005*, sept explorations de l'avenir, report of prospective missions, vol. 1, doc. 5, 1985, 176.

Xenakis, Yannis. *Musique, architecture*. Paris: Casterman, 1971.

Zemp, Hugo. *Les voix du monde*. Includes 3 CDs. Paris: CNRS; Musée de l'homme; Harmonia Mundi, 1996.

Zenatti, Alfred. *Psychologie de la musique*. Paris: Presses universitaires de France, 1994.

Zuckerkandl, Viktor. *Sound and Symbol*. Trans. Willard R. Trask. 2 vols. Princeton: Princeton University Press, 1969–76.

Zwicker, Eberhart, and Paul Feldtkeller. *The Ear as a Communication Receiver*. New York: Acoustical Society of America, 1999.